suddenly pulls out a baseball bat and just holds it there,
smiling' Julie Burchill, *Spectator*

'A bravura study of our working nation ... a subtle, observant,
quiet, devastating book' Yasmin Alibhai-Brown, *Independent*

'Beautifully written, the interviews are sensitively pitched, exploring how work fits into, or overwhelms, life, and interviewees' feelings about their paid work and the value of their labour' Dawn Foster, *Guardian*

'Eloquent ... I liked the quietness of this book, the way its argument emerges organically out of the material rather than in polemic' Joe Moran, *New Statesman*

'It feels like a good time to publish a book about work ... Biggs's quick eye and ease with description make her a lovely observer ... the potent, finely drawn impression it leaves is of workers sweating away in their own separate worlds, some happily, some not, most of them accepting of their lot' Andy Beckett, *Guardian*

'A compelling read and easy to dip into, with pithy vignettes ... The book rewards with some poignant insights ... a thoughtful read ... a neat idea, lucidly written, thoughtfully observed and well executed' David Cohen, *Evening Standard*

'I thought *All Day Long* was a brilliant, varied and humane study of the way we have to live now. There's the great capitalist dream, in which we are fulfilled, rich, successful and (preferably) famous with it. Joanna Biggs shows us the brutal reality: one of youthful keenness, talent and desire to contribute, ill-served by a sometimes unequal and unfair job market in which what you can offer and what you get offered don't always match up. Biggs uses her peerless interviewing skills to draw truth, nuance, humour and subtlety from the people she speaks to. As a result *All Day Long* is beautifully complex and multi-faceted, an anthropological study of hard, as-we-live-it capitalism which is judicious yet never overtly judgemental' Bidisha

'Biggs traces her wider narrative with a light touch, without using her interviews as a soapbox. Instead she lets the sad, funny, inspiring and alarming stories they tell take centre stage' Anthony Cummins, *Metro*

'Joanna Biggs offers an excellent contribution to our knowledge of the world of work in all its variety – not through tedious sociological analysis (thank goodness), but through the stories of real people she has interviewed all over the country. Reading this book reminds me how times have changed dramatically since my generation left school or college in the Sixties with no worries about finding a job. We were lucky' Bel Mooney, *Daily Mail*

'A fascinating read' Chris Mason, BBC Political Correspondent

ALL DAY LONG
JOANNA BIGGS
A PORTRAIT OF BRITAIN AT WORK

First published in this edition in 2016 by Serpent's Tail

First published in Great Britain in 2015 by Serpent's Tail,
an imprint of Profile Books Ltd
3 Holford Yard
Bevin Way
London
WC1X 9HD
www.serpentstail.com

10 9 8 7 6 5 4 3 2 1

Designed by sue@lambledesign.demon.co.uk
Typeset in Photina by MacGuru Ltd
info@macguru.org.uk

Printed and bound by CPI Group (UK) Ltd, Croydon CR0 4YY

The moral right of the author has been asserted.

A CIP record for this book can be obtained from the British Library

ISBN 978 1 78125 188 1
eISBN 978 1 78283 014 6

To Mum

IRINA: A time will come when everyone will know what all this is for, why there is this misery; there will be no mysteries and, meanwhile, we have got to live ... we have got to work, only to work! Tomorrow I'll go alone; I'll teach in the school, and I'll give all my life to those who may need me. Now it's autumn; soon winter will come and cover us with snow, and I will work, I will work.

Anton Chekhov, Three Sisters

CONTENTS

IN DOVER

IN THE COLD BACK ROOM of a charity shop, a group of volunteers are working. Eve steams clothes with an orange hoover-like machine, eating sweets from a bag in her pocket as she goes. Every so often the steamer foghorns and she tops it up with water. It's March 2014, and three times a week she works a morning shift; on the other days she goes to English and maths lessons. 'I've done my ones, twos, threes, fours, fives, sixes – I'm on my seven times tables now.' Eve's 50 and grew up in a children's home; her best job before this one was sorting potatoes on the back of a tractor. She's shocked I have never eaten Kentish gypsy tart, and offers to make me one. Is it like Bakewell tart? 'It's more whipped,' she says.

Eve's paper bag of sweets came from Sarah, who she met at literacy classes. Sarah's 23 and had just done a trial at a supermarket – 'I couldn't read the products' – and one for a cleaning job – 'They say I'm not suitable for doing the paperwork to be a cleaner. That is so ... How do you need paperwork to work, to be a cleaner?'– but she wants to work in a nursery. 'That's why I'm doing my English.' She receives Disability Living Allowance and comes here four times a week, brings sweets, makes cups of tea. Today she arranges an armful of plush cats and dogs on a shelf, after Karin, the shop's manager, has pierced the ears with a price.

If you ask people why they work, most will say for money. Eve and Sarah work without getting paid; Karin gets the minimum wage of £6.50 an hour, but works so much overtime she earns £3.27 an hour. What we do for money seems like the essential but dull part of our lives – in tired phrases such as 'work–life balance', work is set against life, as if it were life's opposite – but it's also where we make friends, exert power, pass the time, fall in love, give back, puff ourselves up, get bored, play, backstab, bully and resist. And as the days slide by, it changes us almost unobserved. Jane Eyre goes to Thornfield Hall as a governess but by the end of the book, she's its mistress. Brontë's novel is on one hand a love story: a plain, far-seeing girl gets beneath the rough surface of her master. On the other it's a *Bildungsroman*: a friendless orphan's work gives her the confidence to brave the rattling attic.

Karin runs a covertly Communist system; from each according to his talents and to each according to his needs. Karin began volunteering in charity shops when her children were small, worked in a dress shop when they were bigger but didn't like it ('pressure selling') and then managed the charity shop in aid of the People's Dispensary for Sick Animals in Ashford for twenty-three years. Now that she runs the Dover branch she takes a sporting pleasure in surpassing Ashford's daily earnings; last week they managed it twice. She chose the PDSA because the family dog got sick once when she was a child: her mother sent her from their council estate in South-East London to the local PDSA. She held the money, her sister held the dog's string and their little brother followed behind. The vet handed over an envelope with white pills inside, 'and the dog got better'. What needs does work meet for Eve, Sarah and Karin? 'I love working here. It's well nice,' Eve says. 'You meet new people,' Sarah says. 'Here, animals suffer if you don't make money,' Karin says. Sorting through bin bags of donations is one of Sarah's friends from school, Kayleigh. 'Are you a journalist?' she asks. 'I can't speak to you then,' she says and listens instead.

The radio plays 'Simply the Best' by Tina Turner. I can see the board game Battleship, a 'Cadbury Collection' 100-piece puzzle, a tiny blue satin Chinese tunic on a hanger, embroidery hoops in different sizes, books by Alan Titchmarsh and Barbara Taylor Bradford, children's plastic sunglasses with coloured frames and a box of 'Ladies' Microwave Slippers'. Katherine untangles costume jewellery. She's wearing a gold 'key volunteer' badge and says we used to go to school together, but at first I don't recognise her. She'd wanted to be a librarian, but when she became one for Kent County Council the dusty life she'd hoped for no longer existed. Being a librarian now meant helping people get on the internet and extinguishing burning loo rolls in the toilets. She left and worked here and there, trained to determine the clarity, cut and quality of diamonds at a jeweller, the reason she's given the necklace tangle to sort out, then had seven months off work. It hits me: her red hair used to be brown in the sixth form at Dover Girls' Grammar School. I can picture her waiting for Latin while I waited for my French lesson. She works a Saturday morning at the PDSA even though she has a new job in planning at a perfume company. 'Anyone can do my job. I do enjoy it and I get on with my colleagues and that, but I do it to pay the rent. If I had a choice ... If I won the lottery, I'd just study, and volunteer here. There's a lot more pride in what I'm doing here. And I feel a lot more loyal to the PDSA than I do to work. Work's just work. I can work in Tesco if I have to! I don't want to,' she laughs, 'but, you know ...'

At five I told my mother I wanted to be an actress, at nine I said a dancer, but later I more wisely said I wanted to go to university (my parents hadn't gone). At 22, just graduated from Oxford, I hoped to do something meaningful, absorbing and perhaps also glamorous, like Esther Greenwood going to work on a women's magazine in Sylvia Plath's *The Bell Jar*. Work I might love. I had babysat, delivered newspapers, helped my mum with Avon orders, washed cars, worked in the office of a translation agency, sat on a till in WHSmith on Saturdays, stuffed envelopes for one miserable half-week, assisted the manager of a Christmas card factory (who used to say 'we're cooking on gas, and we're cooking on gas' which I still hear in my head in his voice), took payment for water bills and logged car crashes in a call centre. I came to London to study for a Master's degree in eighteenth-century literature, still not quite knowing if I wanted to be an academic or not, and moved in with two girls I knew as an undergraduate: one was starting work on a national newspaper, the other at a literary agency. In the evenings, we sat on the floor of the mostly empty two-bedroom Hackney flat we were using as a three-bedroom one, shared a plastic bag of prawn crackers from the Chinese around the corner and talked. I heard about worries, colleagues, expectations; who sat where, what happened at lunch, what everyone wore. It was a way of finding out what we wanted to avoid and who we wanted to be. University had made us employable, but hadn't prepared us for work. The novels we had studied were about love and depravity; they weren't set in offices.

When I started an entry-level job at a literary magazine at the end of the year, I finally got to join them. We were (mostly) conscientious and wanted to do well at work, as we had done at school, but it wasn't just that: before the financial crash in 2008, there was a general sense that the work we were beginning would fulfil us for a long time. Companies talked about themselves as ethical employers, threw parties with fizzy wine at the Groucho Club and gave out silk scarves at Christmas. If we stayed late and worked well, work would return our love. The benevolence of the businesses we worked for muffled our doubts. (In that first year, I spent a lot of time opening envelopes.) And besides, at house parties, leaning against kitchen counters sticky with spilled beer, we were asked: 'What do you do?' and we weren't ashamed to reply.

Karin doesn't stop for lunch. There's a hot dog van outside the shop's open door, and the smell puts her off. There are two shifts of volunteers: one leaves and the other starts at 1 p.m. (The PDSA estimates that it would cost £12.5 million to run their shops for a year if they paid the volunteers.) The charity no longer accepts people on the coalition government's programmes known as workfare, but they used to. They require people who have been unemployed for three months or more to work for free or lose their Jobseeker's Allowance; workfare was judged in the appeal court to be illegal. 'It's not right,' Karin says. She remembers those on workfare 'didn't want to be there quite a lot. Yes. And they would do a lot of sitting about and all the rest of it, so.' The shop does take people on 'Community Payback' who have been ordered by the courts to work unpaid. Karin finds them 'more capable'. I never discover what Ben, tattooed and Reeboked, did wrong. He helps Eve, Sarah and Kayleigh sort out donations and tidies crammed clothes rails. Chelsea is getting beaten by Aston Villa, and he chats to Eve, a Liverpool fan. Sarah finds a dictionary among the donated books: does anyone want it? 'Nah, my phone does everything,' Ben replies. He says he doesn't trust himself talking to me. Before I can persuade him otherwise, someone rings to say his daughter has had a fall and he leaves early.

Work can also be about guilt. In Hardy's *Tess of the D'Urbervilles*, Tess, having confessed her 'not inviolate past' to her husband, leaves the dairy farm's lush fields to work at the 'red tyrant' of the threshing machine. That part of the novel is called 'The Woman Pays'. 'Community Payback' itself suggests a debt – moral as well as financial – to be worked off. Who are we if we don't work? Politicians of all parties talk of 'hardworking families'; the Protestant work ethic persists. The idea that work is a duty and a calling, or even recompense for original sin, is embraced from the church to the charity shop, prison, nursery and gym. In the 1963 film *Billy Liar*, Billy fantasises about leaving his dull job at an undertaker's but when Julie Christie as Liz comes to take him away, he can't leave. Work has a hold over him he didn't realise it had.

Every so often someone will burst into the back room for knitting needles, or children's sunglasses, or to ask: 'Somebody wants to reserve the wedding dress until Wednesday. Do we do things like that? I don't know why Wednesday.' Katie has arrived for the afternoon shift. She's been volunteering for eight years as she doesn't like the thought of people being cruel to animals. Katie, Karin jokes, is her 'project': she's being trained on the till (not everyone can be trusted on the till). In Ashford, Karin had brought a young man with learning difficulties out of his shell; he ended up running the shop on Sundays singlehanded. (Karin has a nice line in teases: 'We get on well, don't we?' Eve says. Karin replies, 'Yeah, and if we don't, I hit them.') Katie sells a pair of lime, turquoise and pink running shoes for £7.49 to a girl who's wearing the grey blazer of Dover College, the private school a few minutes' walk away. 'Everyone loves a bargain,' the girl's mother says. Pauline, a volunteer in her seventies, suddenly feels faint and Ben sits with her in the back room until he's called away and I take over. She would be 'bored stiff' indoors; it's no good to be around your husband all day every day. The shop has fallen quiet an hour before closing time, and Karin has me walk Pauline to the bus stop on my way home.

The average full-time worker in the UK works 39.2 hours a week and earns £27,200 a year according to government statistics, but these numbers, like the rise and fall of GDP, don't get at what work feels like. Katie's work looks like rearranging clothes but it might bring her a sense of ownership. Ben seems to be sorting donated books but it could feel to him like admonishment. Katherine is pairing up cheap earrings but she gets more from it than from what she does for money. Karin's job began as a way to get out of the house but has become a sort of social activism.

I walk back to my parents' house along the High Street. The travel agency where Mum and I arranged a holiday one dull Easter is now an empty glass box with a red and yellow estate agent's sign propped on the floor. The KFC is quiet at this time of day, but in my teens, it was where everyone met to kiss and make bad jokes and fight after the clubs shut. The banks are still here, joined by pawnbrokers; the PDSA competes with the British Heart Foundation, Scope, Barnardo's and the RSPCA. I pass Allen Hughes, the gentleman's outfitters, virtually unchanged since the 1960s. From here you can look up towards the Western Heights, the fortifications first put up in 1804 against Napoleon's armies, now overgrown. The beauty salon that used to be a game shop that used to be a record shop is a few doors away from what was an independent café. I stop to read a handwritten note in faded biro taped to the inside of the door:

Dear Loyal Customers

I can only apologise for this inconvenience.
Have tried to succeed in very hard times but to no avail!
Many thanks for your support over the last 6 years. I am extremly sorry it has come to this.
I will try to open a new outlet for the bakery.
Thank you for your understanding.

J. King and staff

J. King and staff don't have to say there's now a branch of Costa Coffee next door.

Woolworths has gone; Boots is clinging on; M&S is there for a while longer, but there are shops whose names I don't recognise: Shoe Zone, Savers, Store Twenty One, Card Factory, Price Less Furniture. And there are amusement arcades that weren't there when I was younger. The signs say: CA TLE AMUSEMENTS, PALACE AM S MENTS.

The high streets and the market squares of the country can't help but reveal how work has changed since the 2008 debt crisis. The PDSA's Dover branch itself would close in the autumn of 2014, when the lease came up and the shop was sold; Karin held the Christmas party on 29 September. The cost of living has gone up by a quarter while the means of earning one became less stable. Workers have agreed to freeze their wages, to take fewer hours than they'd like, or to set up on their own to avoid being made redundant. Wages are 8 per cent lower than they were before the crash; wealth has accrued to the already rich. The nation of shopkeepers has become a nation of disappointed bakers and momentarily cheerful hot dog men. The idea that good work brings a good life no longer holds.

In 1974, Studs Terkel travelled America talking to workers about what they did all day; while spending the last two years talking to workers from the Isle of Lewis in the Outer Hebrides to the North Wales coast, I've often wondered what Terkel would make of how we think about our work now. Wages were at their highest in the USA in 1973; as the economic historian Robert Brenner has shown, the beginning of the 1970s can now be seen as the start of a long downturn that followed the postwar boom. I've tried to capture what work as a CEO, a below minimum wage care worker, a ballerina or a robot feels like seven years into a financial crisis. When our work is less reliable, less remunerative even, how do we feel about it? I continuously heard that people loved their jobs, and sometimes this worried me: it felt as if work was becoming more insecure on one hand, and the work ethic increasingly revered on the other.

I can't pretend to have covered all the work done, in all its forms, by 30 million Britons. When I told people I was writing this book, they said: what about a window cleaner, someone who works in a betting shop, a shaman, a chimney sweep? Do they still have chimney sweeps? I didn't have a good answer for them – the obvious ones of time and money excepted – and I've called the book 'a portrait' because that's the only thing it can be. But a few ideas guided me. I wanted to think about work not simply as waged labour, but more broadly: isn't being a mother work too? Wages have gone down and work has become more insecure, but how did that show in our daily lives? And, more simply: what does a rabbi, a cleaner, an intern, a fishmonger do all day? And even if I knew I couldn't come close to properly representing all work in the UK, I wanted to include as many different voices as I could. But more often than not, I looked for the job and found who did it.

Workers are harder to reach than they were: the PR companies want to know that the brand will be enhanced; a Premiership footballer might ask for £5,000 for a friendly chat; bankers may suggest a reading list before meeting (or tell you how you ought to write your book); mothers could say it's impossible for anyone who's not a mother to understand them. I abandoned nearly a third of all the interviews I did; some would only talk under cover of anonymity. Nearly everyone told me they were unrepresentative. Maybe all of us are, but we add up to something nonetheless. I'm no anthropologist or sociologist or statistician; what follows is a portrait – fragmentary, personal, fleeting – of the UK at the beginning of the twenty-first century. We may love our work, hate our work, find meaning in our work or none, but it's what we do all day long, and it shapes us.

MAKING

potter
shoemaker
robot

Alan Goldsmith, 65, pot glazing supervisor, Stoke-on-Trent

On the gentle evening of Monday, 22 July 2013, a woman in a white cropped jacket crossed the gravel forecourt of Buckingham Palace with a wooden frame in the crook of her left elbow. Cameras zoomed in on two sentences on a sheet of creamy paper: 'Her Royal Highness the Duchess of Cambridge was safely delivered of a son at 4.24 p.m. today. Her Royal Highness and her child are both doing well.' Of the many articles about the royal birth over the following July days, none specified the maker of the white jacket or of the wooden frame. Britax made the car seat in which the new prince made his first journey, clunked gently into the back seat with a 'Phew!' from his dad: 'We are delighted to confirm that [the car seat] is from the BRITAX BABY-SAFE infant carrier range – a favourite among new parents and winner of a 2012 Mother & Baby Award.' The lacy blanket the baby first appeared in was made by G. H. Hurt and Son in Nottingham. 'It's been quite exciting – rather hectic,' said Gillian Taylor, whose great-grandfather started the firm in 1912, 'but we wouldn't swap it for anything.' (A month later, orders for the merino wool blanket were still subject to a ten-week delay.)

For the potters of the Midlands, the framed announcement was a false alarm. They needed a name. At 6.19 p.m. on Wednesday, Clarence House tweeted: 'The Duke and Duchess of Cambridge are delighted to announce that they have named their son George Alexander Louis.' In Stoke-on-Trent, where you walk out of the redbrick train station to a statue of Josiah Wedgwood with a replica of the Portland Vase in his hand, workers at Emma Bridgewater were called back in to start on the royal baby mug. On a tour of the factory that morning, I'd seen trolleys of creamily naked ware set aside and labelled 'ROYAL BABY'. 'A lot of other potteries in the industry have already gambled what they're going to do: "It's a prince!" Or "It's a princess!"' the head of manufacturing, Mark Thomas, said. But 'we want it to say: "Hooray for Prince ... George!" "Hooray for Prince Albert!" You know, whatever it's going to be. The minute we start we will be able to do the design within an hour.' For the royal wedding in 2011, the company had sold £1 million of commemorative ceramics. Within two hours of the tweet, sponges were cut, colours were mixed, then the ware was hand-printed with the design, dipped into glaze and placed in the kiln. 'The longest part is waiting for the kiln to fire,' Thomas said. 'Sixteen hours and then it's off, ready to see.'

On Friday morning, the TV cameras had gone and left smudged mugs behind them: out of sixty-six mugs inspected that morning, twelve were in best condition (new designs often get smudged, but the cameramen were guilty too.) Bridgewater ware had made the front cover of the *Stoke Sentinel*, the inside pages of the *Daily Mail* and the BBC evening news. There had been some exaggeration in the press – yes, they got in at 6 a.m. yesterday, but they get in at 7 a.m. anyway – but no fuss on the factory floor: 'We did well – we're professionals!' one sponge decorator said. A copy of *OK!* – 'Kate's Post-Baby Weight Loss Programme' – had been left on an empty bench. Julie Davies, a sponge decorator, worked on the royal baby mugs in the deco-rating hall, where Union Jack bunting put up for the Diamond Jubilee still fluttered. Davies was 39 and had worked for Bridge-water for twenty years; there was a poster of Mourinho above her workbench and photos of her family along it. Another sponge decorator, Lynsey Gidman, had described her bench as 'like a little mantelpiece'. Everyone said Bridgewater felt like a family.

Work starts at 7 a.m. with breakfast at 9.30 a.m. for fifteen minutes, lunch at 1p.m. for half an hour, tea at 3 p.m. for ten minutes, and then away before 4 p.m. The 'day goes quick' for Davies on the royal baby pattern. She starts by nicking the rim of the mug three times with pencil and signing each piece with her initials. The first element to go on is a crown, then the words 'Hooray for Prince George!', which appear pink but fire to a baby blue: 'They're pretty before they're fired.' Then hearts, laurels, the date, another crown, more hearts, sixty-eight tiny dots placed by hand all over the mug and a row of thirty-one hearts inside the rim. Her hands weren't tense: either loosely balled inside the mug, drawing figures of eight with her sponge in the paint and squeezing it out; or slowly turning the potter's wheel as she pocked the mug with dots. She worked in even numbers: each element twice and twenty-six mugs at a time. Moments of concentration dissipated and returned easily; she hovered a moment before the first crown went on. Sponge decorators are paid by the number of pieces they finish in an hour, which adds up to a rate slightly above the minimum wage. We 'just try to keep our heads down really,' as Gidman put it, 'because every second counts'. (They're paid for any pieces they complete over their target of around 120 mugs a day.) Opposite Davies a colleague worked with earphones in on a bowl for the Christmas collection, but working on the royal baby mugs is 'just nice, isn't it? Some relation has got a plate or a mug sitting in the dresser or something,' Gidman said. 'And obviously they bring back memories of something else, of what you were doing then.'

Emma Bridgewater began her company when she couldn't find commemorative ware of a certain kind. She was looking for a birthday present for her mother, Charlotte: 'Something personal, and something that showed her that I wanted to be with her, even though I was not there at the time. I decided that a pair of cups and saucers would be just the thing, conjuring up the image of us sitting together talking, drinking coffee, eating toast and, maybe, honey,' Bridgewater wrote in her 2014 memoir, *Toast & Marmalade and Other Stories*. The homely air carries into the factory, with the bunting, the mantelpieces, the cakes for a kiln man's sixtieth birthday. Homely has other sides too: when I asked if the sponge decorators were unionised, I heard they'd had a meeting in 2012, but Matthew Rice, Emma's husband and managing director of the company, 'didn't want us to'. Harry Hockaday, the general secretary of Unity, the potters' union, represented around half of the factory's workers at the time. In 2012 the union sent out a questionnaire and found they would have around 60 to 80 per cent support in the factory, and, as they got on well with the management, asked them to give Unity voluntary recognition. Bridgewater didn't want to give recognition, ACAS was called in, and a ballot was held after the workers met with Unity and Matthew and Emma separately. (Hockaday said Emma and Matthew promised trips to the zoo, among other things.) At the ballot, Unity lost.

Matthew could be seen as the iron fist inside Emma's velvet glove. In an effort to save Stoke-on-Trent's industrial buildings, Matthew has compared Stoke's scarred landscape to Helmand Province – 'there is lots of bare land where things have been demolished. I've no idea what it looks like in Helmand Province but I get a feeling it would look a little like here' – while Emma is photographed smiling in front of heaving dressers, insisting that manufacturing in the UK isn't dead. The company has become a synonym for British entrepreneurship of a boosterish, eponymous type, along with Boden, the clothing company, and Cath Kidston, the homeware retailer. David Cameron took Emma on a trade trip to Mexico in 2012 (she has a house near Cameron in Witney and they have lunched together), though she told the *Financial Times* in 2014 that she votes Green or Lib Dem.

When Emma was 29, her mother fell from a horse while hunting and sustained a serious brain injury. An early nineteenth-century cup, bowl and saucer had always stood on the family dresser; university friends had given it to Emma's mother as a jokey graduation present because the set was inscribed 'To the memory of Charlotte'. The china marked the death of Queen Charlotte in 1818; now that the royal Charlotte is all but forgotten (that is, before George's sister Princess Charlotte was born in May 2015), the ware remains, layering personal memory on top of national memory.

Charlotte is remembered in the Stoke-on-Trent factory too. The week Prince George was born was the week Alan Goldsmith, glazing supervisor, retired. The factory gathered at midday, and Mark Thomas gave a speech – 'Alan has been an inspiration to us all at some stage or other' – while Goldsmith shook his head, eyes on the floor. He spoke, recalling that the company had started because Emma couldn't find the right cup and saucer for her mother. He swallowed. 'She gave me 24 years, and the chance to meet some lovely people.' Applause echoed between the redbrick walls. He laughed when he was presented with the card they'd made: 'That's fantastic, that.' They'd put Goldsmith's head on Bradley Wiggins's body (he planned to complete the Alpe d'Huez stage of the Tour de France in his retirement) under the line: 'Sir Alan, Emma Bridgewater's golden hero – He came, he dipped, he conquered!' He opened a box wrapped in Bridgewater spots and thick orange ribbon. 'Oh my word.' A watch.

Like a golden carriage clock, the gift of a watch on retirement marks the return of the worker's control over their time. One of the ways the Industrial Revolution is remembered in our working lives, even if its industries are in decline, is in time discipline. Before then, you might measure the boiling of an egg in the time it took to say an Ave Maria, or judge the time for reaping by the appearance of the cornfield. Potters in the 1830s would work fourteen to sixteen hour days from Wednesday to Saturday, so that they could extend the weekend to the early part of the week, kept as Saint Monday or Saint Tuesday. (This rhythm relied on women and children going into factories on those days to do preparatory tasks like moulding mug handles.) 'The work pattern was one of alternate bouts of intense labour and of idleness,' E. P. Thompson wrote in 'Time, Work-Discipline, and Industrial Capitalism' (1967), 'wherever men were in control of their working lives.' At Etruria, Josiah Wedgwood's factory, fines were given for lateness – thought to be the first instance of a clocking-in system – and bells were rung when work began and ended. Time became currency, 'not passed but spent'. Time thrift was reinforced in the eighteenth century by the school and the Church; would continue in the nineteenth century through the theories of scientific management of Frederick Taylor; and persists today in Amazon's warehouses, where a time limit for each task is calculated and transmitted to workers' handheld scanners. 'In mature capitalist society,' Thompson wrote, 'all time must be consumed and marketed, put to *use*.' The move from preindustrial or agricultural task-oriented work to urban, industrial timed labour made it possible to think of leisure time as a problem, or as just another sort of work.

'I don't know whether to laugh or cry to tell you the truth,' Alan had said a few days before. 'The beginning of the week you're thinking: "Aahh, five days!" then I think to meself, you know, fifty years' work. It is strange.' He had left school at 15 without qualifications, and went to work first in a chemist's and then down the pit, where the money was better and he didn't have to work Saturdays. He couldn't train to work on the coal face until he was 18, where 'top money' was earned, so went back to the chemist's. When he got bored, he rang Wedgwood to ask if there was any work, 'which was the best thing I ever did. Both my parents come from big families, and you're either in pits or pots. Most of my mother's brothers – father, uncle, brothers were all in the pit; so was my paternal grandfather, he was in the pit; my mother had got five sisters and all the sisters worked on the pot banks. "You must! Go down! Get yerself down there!" And luckily I chose glazing.'

He learned to spray glaze on oven-to-tableware from Ma Cadwalladr, who was far past retirement age. 'Only about that big! Smoked like a chimney, 'cause you could smoke in the factory then, and she used to sit in the office, smoking away, smoking away, keeping an eagle eye on everybody. She used to be picked up and chauffeured to work and chauffeured home again.' There were fifteen men in his department, and everything was glazed by hand (as it is at the Bridgewater factory, though elsewhere glazing is mechanised). Alan lived in a house on the Wedgwood estate with his family and played interdepartmental football after work: glazers v. placers, 'then in the bar after'. His life was there: work, football, darts in the pub, schools for the children. 'You know, it was a good time.' Alan signed each piece of ware he glazed: 'If I see any old Wedgwood anywhere, I look for the letter M.' That was his mark.

In 1982, 'everything went pear-shaped'. Alan was made redundant two weeks before Christmas; his two sons were 5 years and 18 months old. He would work night shifts at Creda, the white goods manufacturer, for the next six years. 'I went from the best days of my life to the worst. Zombie. But there was nothing else. I had to look after my family, I had to look after the kids.' They used the redundancy money to put a deposit on a house in Stone, a market town nine miles from Stoke, 'which in turn, turned out to be the best move we ever made. So you know, it's all peaks and troughs.' Alan came back to pots in 1989 through a friend, who mentioned there was a job going at Sam Spencer, the forerunner of Bridgewater, during a weekend's fishing. There were twenty people, 'if that', at Bridgewater then; twenty-four years later the firm has 170 employees and an annual turnover of £15 million.

He doesn't look back in contentment. The work week is 'so

regimented. Monday it's bleary-eyed, just going through the motions in't it? And then you pick up towards the end. Each day's the same.' What does he think about when he's glazing? 'Everywhere bar here. All sorts of stuff goes through your head. Because it is mind-numbing, really repetitive work. You just go into your own world. Make plans. What you'll do when you win the lottery.' Does he think he's earned enough for what he's done? 'No! Never enough, never enough,' but he's lived 'comfortably. We've never had loads of money. Two kids see to that, don't they? We had holidays and everything.' He sees his biggest achievements at work as the qualifications he's gained: he was the oldest on an electronics evening course, and at the end of the first lesson, he went up to the Glaswegian teacher and said: 'You might as well have been talking Mandarin to me tonight. Do you think it's worth me staying?' His teacher replied: 'Certainly laddie!' He sat the exam on a broken hip, but still got a merit: '"Goldsmith! You've got it! You're not completely dead in the head!"' In two days' time his working life would be over: 'Some people say: "Get yourself finished! Don't do more than you have to!" Some say: "Ah, you're daft finishing, you won't know what to do with yourself after a month." You just don't know.' Janice Whitley, the only other worker left from the 'original lot', thought he would be upset: 'I think I might just stay out the way and go down at two o'clock and say Ta-ra. You spend more time with people at work than you do at home, don't you?'

Alan and Janice's working lives belong to the 'pots, pits, Mich' era of Stoke-on-Trent, where people worked on the pot banks, down the pits, or in the Michelin tyre factory. It's a period that ended in 2008; now ten people apply for every job advertised at the factory, because otherwise work is in call centres or recruitment companies. When Emma Bridgewater first visited Stoke-on-Trent from a life of stylish bohemian chaos in North Oxford and Chelsea, she saw 'rows and rows of down-at-heel terraced houses, battered pubs, sad chapels converted into exhaust workshops'. Today, the red brick of the bulbous bottle kilns is preserved and shiny near the train station, but blackened in a row of houses sold by the council for a pound at the end of 2013. I started to see the Bridgewater works as a commemorative factory to a disappeared industry: two of the kilns came from Spode when it folded in November 2008; the plate maker, like Alan, came from Wedgwood, which went into administration in January 2009. Wedgwood was bought by KPS Capital Partners, a New York private equity company, and so part of the estate Alan lived on is being sold to property developers. Mark Thomas came from Mason Cash, which makes the old-fashioned beige mixing bowls, now moulded and fired in Portugal. 'We're almost like Noah's Ark,' Thomas said. 'We're collecting people from all the businesses that are gone. So there's this sense of pride and of wanting to make it work. We are the chosen ones dealing with it now.'

Daniel, in his 40s, and Taksim, in his 50s, shoemakers, Hackney

'That's the one. That's the first one. My very first shoe.' Daniel nodded at it as he eased the fabric in front of him into pleats. The sole of his first shoe read 'Made in England' and showed a dancer under a curved banner reading F R E E D, the logo of his employer; the number 5½, the shoe's size; an X, the shoe's width, and in the centre, a butterfly. The butterfly is Daniel's mark, the pointe shoe equivalent of a painting's signature. Every pair of pointe shoes made by Freed of London since it was founded in 1929 bears the mark of its maker – a crown, a fish, a wine glass, the letter O – and what began as a way to find out who had made a faulty shoe has become a reminder of the sort of manufacturing thought to have disappeared from Britain. Before work was organised into Etruria-style factories with steady wages and steady discipline, artisans in cities arranged themselves in small workshops and made pots in a way that didn't divide work from life so insistently. (A way that perhaps needs to be relearned in the twenty-first century: as Thompson put it, workers need to rediscover 'how to fill the interstices of their days with enriched, more leisurely personal and social relations'.) At Freed, preindustrial elements remain – each artisan works to his own pace at his own bench, developing his own style – even as each shoemaker works towards the day's target.

In July 2013, sweat dripped down Daniel's temples. He had the unthreatening look of the Pilsbury dough boy until he picked up a hammer. Born into a circus family in Mexico, he spent seventeen years as a wire walker, trapeze artist and clown before marrying an Englishwoman and moving to south-east London. There he worked in retail – 'I was just hanging stuff. Very boring' – before arriving at Freed in March 2013: 'How the hell am I going to do that?' he thought when he first saw the way the shoes were made. 'And he was doing the pleating, my manager, and I thought ... He made it look so easy.' Freed's shoes have been made inside out since 1929. 'I just couldn't do it, I got all my fingers muddled in there. "Too many fingers!" He'd say: "You've got too many fingers! Only two!" Now I look back and think: yeah, I mean, I've come a long way. But now I see what he meant when he said two fingers – look, I don't even think about it.' Learning how to make a shoe is learning to make your mark stand for something. Daniel compared it to becoming a performer: 'You have to be original as a clown as well. You must to be recognised. It's like the butterfly stamp! They know who you are, just by looking at your face.'

Work begins five days a week at 7.30 a.m. with the makers stamping the leather soles with their mark. (If they have a lot of orders, they'll also work on a Saturday until 11 a.m.) Pointe shoes are made of nothing more mysterious than hessian, flour and water, hidden in peach-toned satin (Freed buys up all the seconds of its satin from a Scottish factory so that no other company can use the same colour or weight). The fabric parts are cut out with a sort of biscuit cutter pressed into satin and leather, producing a click inaudible over the artillery whirr of the sewing machines. A half-moon-shape toe is sewn to two long side parts, which are then joined at the heel, reinforced with ribbon and fitted over a resin last ready for stiffening. Tea is at 9.30 a.m., then the twenty-six makers begin adding paste and layers of hessian and cotton to the shoe. The paste is made every morning in a room whose floor is white with spilled flour; paste has dribbled down the sides of the oversized kitchen mixer it is made in and pooled on the floor. The recipe is on the wall – the makers take it in turns – and includes insecticide to discourage weevils. When the American dancer Toni Bentley visited Freed in 1984, the factory director Bernard Kohler got a dusty box down from the top shelf: 'Here's something you might appreciate.' He produced two shiny, hard, size four shoes: an unused pair from Margot Fonteyn's last order. Fonteyn had had three makers in her career and three partners on stage, Kohler explained as he shook out the flour-glutted bugs and handed the shoes to Bentley.

What does Taksim, who has made pointe shoes for Freed for sixteen years, think about all day? 'I'm thinking about I'm going to have another hard day. I'm honest! I'm thinking about I'm going to have another hard day. Because it's a very physical work to be honest. It is very very physical work.' Taksim, whose mark is an anchor, used to be a machinist for Vivienne Westwood before coming to work for Freed. As a child in Cyprus, he had wanted to be a pilot: 'But it's never going to happen. Is never going to happen. The children even now, you go and ask anyone there, they will tell you they want to be a pilot. Right now. It's still the same. All those years.' Did he know anyone who became a pilot? 'No, no. I'm honest, no.' With short grey hair and the black string of his apron curving underneath his belly, he bent over his workbench. He has received letters from ballerinas across the world thanking him – 'It's good feelings, basically' – and sees his work as craft: 'When you're finishing shoes, you should be a little bit more extra care. Because they pay money to buying it, and then you have to make nice shoes to give satisfaction for customers basically. That's the way I think.' He didn't romanticise what he did: 'I don't mind what kind of work it is as long as you're going to get paid, for me that is what is matter at the end of the day, for me.' He'd never seen a ballet. When he finished work at 4.30 p.m., he might watch Liverpool play: 'We're still a long way behind Chelsea, Man United, Arsenal, City, even Tottenham now. I always see football as you never know, still, Liverpool need a couple of good players.' He had been to see England play at Wembley once, the football equivalent of Covent Garden. Daniel makes twenty-six pairs a day, and is working up to the standard of thirty pairs a day. A few benches away, Ray, whose mark is a crown, makes forty pairs a day. Taksim makes thirty-eight pairs. They are paid by the pair (no one will tell me how much) and so Ray will earn nearly double what Daniel earns.

Most makers eat a sandwich brought from home at their bench at midday. They have to work quickly; if the paste dries too soon, the shoe is ruined. After the toe is built up with layers of paste, hessian and cotton, the pleats on the back of the shoe are made, and the pointe shoe begins to take shape. The upper is sent to be sewn to the leather sole with wax thread, and then the shoe turned the right way out with a broom handle and sculpted with a glass hammer with a flat, round head. This is the moment Daniel likes best: 'When you turn them over, that's when you're happy and they come out nice. They're even, they're not lumpy, they're not funny, they stick nicely. That's definitely the best, when you do finish and they come out nice. Good! Well done. I done a good job.' The shoe has to stand on its own on a tablet of resin before it can be sent to the ovens to set for ten hours, unless the dancer has asked the shoe to be off balance, and a ramp is pushed into the toe of the shoe in order for it to tip forwards or backwards unbidden. In the binding room the neck of the shoe is shaped and bound with a drawstring. The binders are mostly women, with headphones tucked in their ears, lozenges of snipped peach ribbon around their feet, and finished shoes, the dancers' surnames in biro on the sole, stacked in curving peach lines at their side. After a few weeks' drying time, the shoes are checked, packed and sent to ballet companies across the world. New York City Ballet orders the most per year, nearly double the number of the Royal in London. A pair costs £38 and lasts a dancer around eight hours in stage time.

What does it feel like to dance in shoes made for your feet? Nathalie Harrison, first artist with the Royal, could only describe what it felt like if her shoes were wrong: 'You know like a really good pair of jeans, or a really good bra? A bad pair is just the most uncomfortable, you just can't do anything.' She had danced in other shoes while training but had returned to Freed, where she joked that 'Gepetto men' made shoes, 'like on a chocolate box'. She visited the Hackney factory in summer 2013 to meet the maker of her shoes, but he had just left the company. 'I've been in complete denial because my Key shoes were so perfect. I keep on thinking maybe he'll come back.' Freed had given one of her old shoes to other makers to see if they could create something similar – 'If you're a size three it's the simplest thing, but I'm a 6¾' – and she was trialling Q maker in Leicester and O maker in Hackney. I watched O maker, who is Polish, turn out his day's shoes with the broom handle, buff the hard toe with a hammer, and check if they balanced. He worked quickly and confidently, but not prettily. When a shoe didn't balance, he looked over and said 'special order' so that we knew he had done it on purpose. But there's nevertheless a frisson: if they hover, a ghost has put its airy foot into the unbaked satin.

When a dancer goes to fetch a fresh pair of shoes from the shoe room, it's to destroy them. Harrison reinforces hers with shellac and pounds them against concrete to bring them to the perfect degree of ruin. Even bespoke shoes hurt: Harrison dresses her feet with plasters and sticky silicon puddles called 'ouch pouches'; others slash into the sides of their shoes to get relief from corns or bathe their feet in surgical spirit to harden the skin. 'Ballet dancers, they're suffering from feet,' Taksim said, 'and we're suffering from hands.' The life of a shoe is brief, bright and not unpainful. 'I go home, my hands are throbbing, they're red and they're swollen,' Daniel said. 'It's not soft, it's not easy. But it does give satisfaction. You do finish it and go home, and you're happy.'

The pointe shoe symbolises ballet's contradictions – light yet strong, delicate yet tough, ephemeral yet lasting – contradictions also true of the way they are made. For the ballerina, each shoe is different and over a career, they will refine their shoe order yearly, as well as adapting it for each role: a harder shoe for ballets with a lot of running on pointe, a softer shoe for ballets with less. But for the maker, each shoe must meet a set of standards. It takes two to three years to master the making of pointe shoes. 'If I'm making twenty-six,' Daniel said, 'and ten of them are lovely, but the rest are a bit wonky, or ... it is no good! They all have to come out like a machine. Obviously it's impossible, but they need to come out as uniform as possible.' Does Daniel feel like a machine? 'No. No, no no. You know you're not a machine, because the shoes *don't* come out perfect. You know that! But they need to be uniform. At least very similar to each other. There isn't a machine that could do this, 'cause I'm sure they would be using a machine. They have to be made by hand.' Perhaps the allure of work is its promise of perfectibility. It's what Irina, the aristocratic and idealistic youngest of Chekhov's *Three Sisters*, hopes for when she takes a job at the Post Office. The crowns, anchors and butterflies on the soles of the shoes are, in the end, forgiving: an admission that aiming for faultlessness might mean accepting all the ways you can't help but fail, and calling it a style.

In 1980, one out of every four people in the UK worked in manufacturing but by 2008 it was one in ten. Despite this, Britain is still the eleventh largest manufacturer in the world, after India, largely because planes, cars and drugs are still made here by high-tech robots in co-operation with precision engineers. Our MPs have jealously looked to Germany's *Mittelstand*, the substantial but unsexy 'middle group' of businesses that accounted for 52 per cent of the country's output in 2011. *Mittelstand* businesses have fewer than 500 employees and a turnover below €50 million; they make unrivalled glass eyes or movie cameras or fish feed and then export them to the world. Freed of London, a family-founded business that makes specialised shoes needed in great quantities, is what a British *Mittelstand* firm would look like. There have been advances in pointe-shoe-making since 1929: US-based Gaynor Minden produces shoes with an 'elastomeric' toe of urethane foam which is supposed to never soften and St Petersburg's Grishko adds silver to their shoes for its antibacterial properties. Both companies emphasise that, despite innovation, they make their shoes by hand. Making pointe shoes isn't yet something robots can do.

Industrial robot arm, 2 years, Swindon

Light comes through the glass panels in the roof of MINI Plant Swindon and bounces off the silvery bonnets the robots are making: we can tell it's morning even if the robots can't. They work twenty-two-hour shifts, with a two-hour pause in the early morning for maintenance, penned inside a high grey fence in groups called cells. A human offers parts to the cell, conveyor belts process them in and then the robots lift them off and begin bending, connecting and welding the metal into shape. Each robot is an oversize orange limb with pincers, suction cups or a small circular welding head where a hand would be. The air smells of oil and vibrates with the swooshing of the arms. Once their work on a part is completed they wait. In a moment another bonnet will arrive and they will do the same thing again, until 4.30 a.m. the following morning.

One of the robots picks up two curved silver bonnets and then swings them up into the air like an orange and silver fist, or an upside down exclamation mark, before letting one bonnet and then the other down. The robots might seem to be twirling unnecessarily – they can't feel weight, after all – but they scoop and swirl in the service of the only beauty they know: optimisation. Dan Hart, an engineer who puts robot cells together, said: 'It's artistic, really, in a way, the way that it's just moving from one thing to another. We want to try and make it as smooth and as quick and reliable as we can, and whatever it takes to do that.' Even elegance. 'They're all doing the same movements, the same noise going on in the background, the same beat all the time in your head,' Declan Kearns, a 20-year-old apprentice in the maintenance department, said of a night shift. 'It's very hypnotic.' The robots hover over the thin skin of the bonnet to avoid damaging it when they pick it up; they delicately brush past each other. Their relentless productivity makes cars cheaper to buy. Their precision makes the factory safer for humans to work in. Their indifference to repetition allows them to work in a way that would drive men out of their minds. They do things people never could: the laser used in closed laser welding, which largely eliminates the air that used to get caught in joints and cause them to rust, would boil a human eye in its socket.

Humans have always wanted to make obedient machines. In Ovid's *Metamorphoses*, Pygmalion sculpted the perfect woman, fell in love and brought her to life. In George Bernard Shaw's version of the myth, and Lerner and Loewe's *My Fair Lady*, the consequences of such magical thinking are made clear when the guttersnipe rebels. The word 'robot' was invented in 1920, when the Czech writer Karel Čapek wrote *Rossum's Universal Robots*. Karel had wanted to call his inventions 'labours' but his brother Josef suggested robots, from the Czech *robota*, meaning servitude. The play, a success from Warsaw to New York and translated into thirty languages, tells the story of a company, Rossum's, which has learned how to manufacture human workers (from primal gunk rather than bolts and steel). Domin, the general manager, argues that robots will liberate people 'from the degradation of labour' by producing corn and cloth in such quantities that it will be virtually free. 'There will be no poverty. All work will be done by living machines ... Everybody will live only to perfect himself.' The Robots see it differently. Their leader announces in Act Two that he won't work for humans any longer: 'You are not as strong as the Robots. You are not as skilful as the Robots. The Robots can do everything. You only give orders. You do nothing but talk.' But when the Robots kill their creators, and have reaped the world's corn and turned the world's cotton into cloth, there's no next generation to appreciate the corn mountains. Čapek's Robots, who want only something to do, reveal that work for work's sake is pointless.

The early twentieth-century robot panic was followed thirty years later by the first industrial robots, modelled on arms. (It has been historically difficult to create walking robots, so they have tended to have either arms or legs, not both.) The first industrial robot, the Unimate, was developed by George Devol and Joseph Engelberger in 1959, and sold at a loss in 1961 to General Motors, where it stacked pieces of hot metal. It could only complete simple tasks because its memory was stored on a magnetic drum, which turned and instructed the arm in a sequence of 200 different steps. To alter a robot's course, you changed the drum. The breakthrough came in the 1960s at Stanford University, when Victor Scheinman, a PhD student, created an arm that could be controlled by a computer. By 1969, robots were welding at Lordstown, GM's plant in Ohio, where it would make the Pontiac Sunbird. Advances were made by Hitachi (the first robot that could undo bolts in 1973) and Kawasaki (the first arc-welding robot in 1974) in Japan; the German firm KUKA (the first robot with six electromagnetically driven axes in 1973); Olivetti in Italy (the first robot with two hands in 1975) and ABB in Sweden (a robot that could pick food from a conveyor belt faster than a human hand in 1998). In 1973, 3,000 industrial robots were at work; by 1983, 66,000 welded, picked and stacked in factories across the globe.

Robot-length days mean that the machines last for ten human years of continuous work. The newest cells at Swindon, which make doors, were installed in 2014: they can be adapted to make any of the doors for the different models, they laser-weld, they change their own welding tips, and they insert the finished doors in pallets. (The first robot to arrive at Swindon picked up a piece of metal from a press and put it in another press; apprentices had to chip solder off the robots every day, a pleasure similar to peeling dried glue from the palms of your hands.) But, the engineers said, even these year-old robots were 'years behind'. Intelligent machines now perform surgery. There is a factory in Japan run entirely by robots, they added.

After lunch, the robots were still working with matinal strength, and four engineers huddled in a group on the factory floor looked at the newest cells. Did they think of the robots as colleagues? Did they give them nicknames? They laughed. 'Thinking of it as a maintenance engineer would,' said Craig Scott, who had an orange robot arm embroidered on his black polo shirt, 'within any cell, there's generally one or two robots that tend to be a bit more of a pain in the backside.' 'But they're normally called things that we probably couldn't repeat on that,' Hart said, pointing to my dictaphone. Robots in movies have cute names like Wall-E or not so cute ones like Terminator; I liked the idea that in real life there might be a robot called Fuckwit. The robot engineers treated the robots as the machines they are: the car parts the robots made, however, did have nicknames. A 'bird bath', named for an indent shallow enough for birds to splash in, was the rear floor of the Mini. There were also 'bull horns' and 'ski slopes'. Stuart Hilliard, a maintenance engineer, admitted that working with robots can get lonely.

Plant Swindon was built by The Pressed Steel Company in 1955 – the first sod was dug in February and the initial pressings came off the line that December. Built as a feeder plant to the Oxford car works in a railway town that understood manufacturing, it was surrounded by workers' housing, and still is. The town of Swindon is unusual in the UK for being heavily dependent on private enterprise – for every person employed in the public sector, there are four employed in the private, and in 2008, that made it the anecdotal 'worst-hit town of the recession'. The car industry was less a bellwether than the government's chosen herald of growth; in 2009, the Labour government introduced a scrappage scheme handing out £1,000 to anyone trading in an old car for a new one. Although the industry was one of the first to suffer in the downturn, it was selling cars at pre-recession levels by 2014. Anecdotally, many buyers were using cheques from banks' misselling of payment protection insurance as a down payment on a car. The £3,000 cheques weren't 'enough to put a deposit on a house,' Mike Hawes, chief executive of the Society of Motor Manufacturers and Traders told Radio 5, but they were 'certainly enough to put a deposit on a new car'.

In 1965, ten years after the pressings plant opened at Swindon, 6,595 people worked there. In 2014, there were 1,000 employees, including contractors. (There are 140,000 people and 44,784 robots employed in the manufacture of cars across the UK.) Lines that used to operate with ninety people now operate with six. The jobs left are in maintaining the robots, moving the finished bonnets and car doors, checking the quality of the robots' work and planning and programming the robot cells. 'People here are certainly more skilled than they were ten years ago,' Hart said. 'But you're standing in the way of progression. It's just the way it's going to go.' Henry Ford doubled his workers pay to $5 a day in 1914, the legend goes, so that his workers could afford what they made (Ford may also have been encouraging them to quit less often); Bob Crow used to ask how robots were going to be able to buy the cars they make. But who owns the robots? A new robot costs between £30,000 and £50,000. Who gets the robots' share of a company's profit?

We might be happy to let robots heave car bonnets, but less so to have them looking after our children. Erik Brynjolfsson and Andrew McAfee argue in *The Second Machine Age* (2014) that while robots can take on routine tasks, even writing simple share price reports successfully, they have trouble with non-routine tasks, both of thinking and doing. They're not good hairdressers, care workers, handymen, poets, financial analysts and cooks. They can't write software, or come up with a scientific hypothesis, or sniff out a story. They can solve a simple problem again and again, but they can't come up with a new question. But artificial intelligence looks likely to surpass us eventually, bringing a fully automated working world. Perhaps that needn't be as bleak as it may seem. Would it be terrible if the four-hour work day predicted by Keynes in 1930 became possible? We could spend our afternoons in a version of the retirement we currently have to wait forty years to know. I noticed a placard at the 2014 student marches: 'FULLY AUTOMATED LUXURY COMMUNISM'. In the comments below the YouTube video by Aaron Bastani for Novara Media, where the phrase first appeared, utopias were imagined: we could all sleep more, learn more languages, study more, protest more, have more sex. 'I'd actually finish *Das Kapital*,' one commenter said.

We can't think about robots without comparing them

to humans. The engineers called the central computer 'the brain', talked about panels being 'fed' to the cell and the robots themselves as being like 'limbs'. In the eighteenth century, the mechanical Turk seemed to be a chess-playing robot, when in fact it was a disguised man. Are the robot cells in Swindon like that? 'The human element of the robot comes from the guy programming it,' Scott explained. 'I could go and programme that robot, and Dan could programme the one next to it, and the two of them might do the same job, but how they get there might be slightly different. Even though we have standards, all the simulations in the world, there are still going to be elements where you need to have that bit of: "Yeah, I could do it like that" "I could do it like that."' Brynjolfsson and McAfee show that while computers can beat human chess players, a human and a computer working together can't be beaten. 'The better the programmer, the smoother the movements, the more it looks human,' as Hart put it. I looked at the bonnet cell, swooping, waiting, welding. Any politeness I saw could only come from our idea of what work ought to look like. But even Hart 'wouldn't want to get in the way of one, to be honest.'

SELLING

fishmonger
creative director
councillor
homesteader
legal aid lawyer

Alan Coffey, 64, fishmonger, Belfast

'Can I help you chum?' Alan Coffey sets down his paper cup of coffee for the first customer of the Sunday market at St George's in Belfast. The customer, in a leather jacket, asks for whiting and Coffey picks up a few fillets with a plastic sheet and holds them out, pale and lolling. The man with the leather jacket nods then hesitates while Coffey turns the fillets into a bag. 'And some potted herrings,' he says. He walks to the other side of the stall. 'And three of those oysters.'

Coffey's corner of the market – three tabletops of fish, smoked and unsmoked, shellfish and a chiller cabinet with cooked scampi and crab – sits between a fruit and veg stall and a table selling mobile phone covers. The stall is called 'Something Fishy' in the 1980s punning style and its name is embroidered on the breast pocket of Coffey's white coat. Underneath grey hair, he has a ginger moustache. Every weekend for fourteen years Coffey has run a stall at St George's. 'I won't sell a lot of that orange fish today,' he says, 'but it makes the fish stand out a wee bit.' At the centre of the iced white, coral and yellow flesh is a silver hake with a yellow eye and an open maw. As people come into the market, they stop. 'A good attraction.' Gawping 6-year-olds are small enough for the hake's eye to meet theirs. 'That looks delicious,' a man with an American accent says on his way past. It's a sales trick: when someone stops to notice the hake, they also see pound bags of dulse, burgundy ribbons of dried seaweed. I've never come across dulse before, and Coffey tears some off and lets me taste it. Iodine and sunshine. 'The Belfast people love it,' he says, but tourists are baffled. 'You just eat it?'

A twentyish blonde in a striped blazer stops to make an order. Could Coffey slice some salmon into thin slices as he did last week? She'll come and pick it up once she's been round the market. 'Oh it was beautiful,' she says of last week's sashimi. 'It lasted until Wednesday.' Coffey lays two fillets on the cutting board next to his black-handled knife, almost narrow enough for a fencing sword, then goes out for a cigarette, picking up a whiting fillet on the way. A seagull is standing on the top of the van – he knew it would be – and he tosses the fish up, the yellow-beaked bird gulps and it's gone. He's a Protestant but he's met politicians of a different religion to him on the stall and even ended up voting for them. Coffey lights up. 'Benefits,' he says, 'are too easy to come by.'

Coffey's alarm goes off at 3.30 a.m. on Friday in Portavogie, the fishing village he lives in on the east coast of Northern Ireland: he'll pick up his son-in-law and his son-in-law's father to drive to Belfast. Just before 5 a.m. Coffey goes over to the all-night petrol station opposite St George's to pick up five cups of coffee. On Friday, there are five fish men – 'we're all friends and everybody specialises in different types of things, so we don't tramp on each other's toes' – and for that first half hour they drink coffee and smoke together. 'We talk a lot of nonsense. The price of fish. Things like that.' At 6 a.m. they're ready for business, and the first to arrive, Coffey says, very often come from the city's Chinese restaurants.

Coffey notices the dulse isn't selling, and moves it to the top of the chiller cabinet: three bags are bought immediately. 'It's not the market it was.' When he started, he had six girls working for him, serving people on their way to work. He sighs. 'The traffic wardens used to wear yellow coats and they turned them to red. And they were like Nazis. They were just giving everybody tickets left, right and centre. That done us a lot of harm for about two years. And a lot of people just never come back.' Now cars are parked along the edge of the market, and I don't spot a red coat.

The cast iron pillars of St George's rose in 1890, when the Catholic area of Belfast near the Ormeau Road was home to several markets: May's for butter, eggs, potatoes and vegetables; Smithfield for cattle, hides and pedlar's goods. When Belfast was blitzed in 1941, St George's survived and became a mortuary for 255 bodies no one could identify. Twenty years later you could still go to Smithfield and buy vinyl, saws, brooches, boarding-school-style leather-edge trunks, plastic moustaches, type-writers and statues of Buddha, but it was destroyed by firebombs in 1974. St George's is the last market standing. During the Troubles, Coffey remembers the market being evacuated every so often for bomb scares at the courthouse 300 yards away (he would lose a day's trading) but the market didn't close: 'Everybody came here. This would be a Catholic area. But people came from all areas.' There used to be a wholesale fish market across the road. 'Fish was so cheap in those days. So so cheap. Fish used to be the cheap alternative to meat. And now fish is so expensive. It's crazy.' Coffey began work when overfishing was just fishing and has lived through the moratorium on herring of 1977–80, the introduction of EU quotas in 1983, and the alarming depletion of fish such as haddock, cod and salmon. And as fish stocks have shrunk, so has his business.

The racing green paint on the pillars came from a lottery grant in 1997. 'Here today now they're nearly all craft people. Us real market traders, we don't class them as market traders. Most people have jobs during the week and trade for a wee bit extra money.' He stops. 'But they're a great bunch of people.' Opposite him are three stalls: Ginger Rosie Crafts sell candles in jars, Yes Darling, It's Vintage is strung with bunting and Bineve-nagh Ceramics displays brown glazed dishes. 'They'll set their stall up lovely but the next thing you'll see they'll get a chair, a cup of coffee and a book, and they'll sit all day. It makes me angry. I'll go over to them and say: "If you want to sell something, you'd better get in front of the stall."' Coffey resigned from the market committee when a cupcake seller suggested they needed to attract a different sort of customer to the Saturday market: 'What class of people do you want in on a Saturday that donae come in on a Friday? Do you think we're down here selling to the riff-raff of the community? Here on a Friday we have the top judges, top businessmen, top doctors, plus the ordinary run-of-the-mill housewife. You know what's wrong with this Saturday market? Your cupcakes at one bloody fifty each. If you bring your prices down to a realistic pricing you'll sell them.'

Coffey's son Matthew, with red hair and yellow rubber boots, is helping him run the stall today. He's 22, at university in Dundee, and while stroking his smartphone with his thumb he says: 'There's nothing like the smell of fish when you're hungover.' Coffey, drinking his fourth cup of coffee, doesn't want lunch – he has a longstanding deal with the coffee stall: he pays 50p a cup and they get some fish – but Matthew and I go to get boxes of butter chicken and rice, and sit down away from the stall to eat. Matthew doesn't know what he wants to do as a job; he shows me pictures on his phone of a trip to Australia he made last year. He started work on the stall when he was 15 and 'quite shy', but he learned to talk to people; and now he unfussily covers the stall while his father goes for another coffee or to see what he can trade six oysters for today. Matthew doesn't like oysters.

On Fridays, oysters are sold closed but on Sunday, Coffey shucks and arranges them on ice with cut lemons. Three people stop for competitive oyster-swallowing selfies; a man buys one oyster with his pregnant wife, who teases: 'We don't need any more aphrodisiacs: one's on the way!' A woman tries her first oyster, tipping it down her throat swiftly. Her hand says OK!

but her eyes are tightly shut. 'Am I going to get horny now?' she asks as she leaves. 'Here's a girl who loves oysters,' Coffey says as a middle-aged woman comes over to the stall. She tips away the juice, tilts her head back with the shell to her mouth, then purses her lips in satisfaction. She visits the stall every weekend with her husband: she runs a nursing home for sixty-four patients with dementia; he assesses fire safety for pubs. Someone else asks: 'I've never tried them: is it worth it?' 'If you try one,' Coffey replies, 'you'll want a second.' Matthew and I have finished eating; Coffey asks Matthew to give the fish 'a wee gush' and Matthew arcs crushed ice over the fish with the silver pan of a scale. It sounds like hail.

Over by the coffee stall, a woman collapses and Coffey rushes over. 'She just missed her seat,' he says as he comes back. 'She's more embarrassed than anything else.' He catches her eye and waves. 'When somebody's in distress, you like to think you can go and help.' Coffey used to be part of the Portavogie lifeboat crew; he was the 'bow man', who had to jump to the distressed boat first. He was born in 1950 and started work in a prawn factory at the age of 8, packing prawns from 6 a.m. to 10 a.m. Sometimes he would take a bag of fish to school instead of his homework. He earned 2 shillings for a morning's work, and when he gave his brown enveloped salary to his mother, she sent him away with sixpence. 'I would say Matthew has been down to Portavogie harbour six times in his life,' Coffey says, 'whereas when we were youngsters we were never clear of the harbour. Because really all we wanted to do the whole way through school was go to the fishing.' When he left school, he wanted to join the merchant navy, but his family wouldn't let him leave. Then he wanted to be a printer in Fleet Street, but still they wouldn't let him leave. He worked as a butcher and in a fish factory until they gave in and let him go to sea in his uncle's trawler in 1966.

He was at sea for nearly fifteen years: 'Loved every minute.' In the summer, he would get up at 2 a.m., sail for two hours, trawl for three and then spend until 9 a.m. on deck tailing prawns and fish. If there was 'a gale of wind', you didn't go out. One winter they couldn't go out for ten weeks: 'In those days you got the brew as we called it. Benefits.' (Perhaps that's the reason he thinks benefits are easy to come by.) He came ashore when he married: 'In the 1980s, we were maybe going away for a fortnight, fishing, you know. And you're maybe only home two days every fourteen. That was all right when you were young and single, you didn't mind, you'd land in different ports and there were good pubs, a good time. But it's not a life for a married man.' He had three fish shops in 1980s Belfast, and 'although they were quite successful, with the rent and rates, we were struggling to make a living. So we wrote to Belfast City Council and said although my shops were all right, I thought seeing I was a commercial rate payer here in Belfast, I was seeing whether they might let me into the market. It would save me maybe putting three girls out of work. So they let me in. We've been here ever since.' Some of his pals from fishing bought trawlers and made half a million when the quotas and licences came in. 'I'm here for ever and ever. But I love every minute of it. Very very lucky that way. You know, I really really enjoy my work.'

On Saturday he'll make £900 on the stall and on a Sunday he'll make £300 to £400. 'You never get a bumper day in here now. Those days are gone.' He earns less than £26,000 a year. 'There's not a lot of profit. Which is a pity. We sell fish as dear as we can to the public, you know, I don't think we would get any more for it.' He doesn't think he'll retire: 'If somebody was to come up to me and say are you going to the pub? Are you going for a game of golf? I'd say: "No I'm going to the beach to gather dulse." I would get honestly more enjoyment doing that than going for a beer.' He smiles. 'Stupid, but.' Coffey spends the days he's not at the market on the beach: 'First thing I do is leave my mobile phone in the van. Pack of cigarettes in my pocket. Can of coke, or a bottle of coke. Away I go. I fill two, maybe three bags of dulse. And I sit down, smoke a cigarette, sit on a rock and look at the scenery. Just brilliant. And then I get up. To me, that's heaven.'

At 3.30 p.m. the crafters are packing away their bunting, brown dishes and candles in jars. Coffey sighs. 'I would say there's another £20 or £30 in the day yet.' The market foreman buys some smoked cod; there are no more tiger prawns, but there are fillets of hake, mussels and oysters. The tannoy announces that 'St George's Belfast is officially closed' while Coffey is opening oysters for a small woman in a running top with a smooth afro. She's his 'best customer – a top children's doctor'. Coffey hands half-shells to us both and we spritz the wincing oysters with lemon and swallow. She comes here from the village of Keenagh every week. Doing her shopping at the market, she says, means she's 'less likely to get horse meat'.

When she leaves with her fish, Coffey counts the day's sales. The salmon and the hake went well: 'a good average day'. Coffey and Matthew pack the fish into white plastic boxes and squeegee down the tables. There is a thumbmark in the yellow-eyed hake – the Saturday girl must have picked it up by its neck instead of its tail, Coffey thinks – and he decapitates it and smoothly cuts it into fillets. His wife Lynn will cook it for their tea.

Caroline Pay, 39, creative director, West End of London

Between 1971 and 1974, Studs Terkel travelled America talking to people about their work. He spoke to baseball players and baby nurses, piano tuners and factory owners, stone cutters and spot-welders. In Beverly Hills, he met Barbara Herrick, a 30-year-old producer at a big advertising agency, in her book-lined, painting-filled apartment. Her secretary saw her as the epitome of second-wave feminism – 'When I think of Women's Lib, I don't think of Germaine Greer or Kate Millett, I think of you' – but Barbara wanted to talk about the male colleagues who'd asked to come to her hotel room and whom she'd had to fob off without hurting their feelings. She laughed at her industry. Yes, she bought eight-dollar pots of face cream, but didn't that just mean she was fooled too? 'You're saying to a lady, "Because this oil comes from algae at the bottom of the sea, you're going to have a timeless face." It's a crock of shit! I know it's part of my job, I do it,' but it felt to her like 'whoring'. Terkel notes that shortly after the interview she was 'battling an ulcer', as if the argument she was having with herself had to be expressed in some way.

Even now, people think advertising 'is the enemy. They think it's a big, bad industry. They think that it's all lies and fake and all about ... ' Caroline Pay, with bright red lipstick and a plait curling around her hairline, has been thinking up advertising campaigns for sixteen years. I glimpse a black bra underneath her sheer pink shirt as she sighs and draws her knees up onto a sofa in a glass-walled meeting room at Bartle Bogle Hegarty (BBH), one of the biggest advertising agencies in the UK, in February 2014. 'I think there's a big preconception that it's very jazzy and glamorous, and it isn't any more ... And then the picture is painted that it's all men. *Mad Men*, and laddy northern stand-up comedian fat blokes with beards.' The walls are covered with ideas for her next campaign for Bailey's Irish Cream. She laughs. 'I think advertising people are seen as estate agents. Quite slick men in black suits selling you stuff. Talking you into buying something.' She pauses. 'I don't subscribe to that way of working.'

But did she have doubts about it, like Barbara Herrick and the algae face cream? 'No, I'm not that deep or intellectual! I'm just not. I just think I've never been a bra-burning, table-thumping, chest-thumping ... my project now is Bailey's and

I could definitely take against selling alcohol, but actually my bigger mission is to get women to feel brilliant about doing stuff together, and I'm happy with that.' I looked at the pictures on the wall, which seemed to be early ideas for the Bailey's campaign. They were photos of nights out, slightly more artful than the ones you see on Facebook: 'Florence and Friends', the captions ran, or 'Alexa and Friends'. The idea of two pop stars singing together had been abandoned by the time the campaign came out in December 2014: the new idea was to make something that would be understood all over the globe, and that moved Bailey's on from the drink you had on the sofa at Christmas to the one that 'millennial women' might begin a night out with. (In 2014 sales of Bailey's were down 8.3 per cent year on year.)

The sixty-second TV ad was shot in four locations but suggested twenty-four. Stockholm was created along the canal in Hackney with fake snow in October. It showed 'a global girls' night out': young women in sequins and skinny jeans getting ready, hailing a taxi then meeting at a bar to begin their night with a shot of Bailey's. The endline was 'Here's to us' over a shot of glasses of the hazelnut-coloured liqueur being clinked together: the line 'has the product and the cheers at the heart of it so it's like a dream for the client,' Pay said. Beside the fact that adverts for alcohol aren't allowed to show anyone drinking it, making an ad that will be shown all over the world has specific difficulties: while the idea of drinking Bailey's as a shot might be novel in the UK and USA, in Russia everything is drunk as shots and in Germany shots are seen as unladylike. (You are not allowed to show anyone holding alcohol in Russian adverts, so a handless 'Cheers!' was shot.) Pay was at first 'repelled' by the idea of an all-female creative team to make the ad: 'I'm against putting women on women's brands: it's not thoughtful.' But Pay's agency happens to be 51 per cent female and an all-female creative team came up with the best ideas. And although the virtual gynocracy was an accident (the directors of the ad were male) it was 'much easier' to 'capture the spirit' of a girls' night out that way. 'You know the way you feel when you're with your girlfriends is a very very deepset emotion,' Pay said. 'It's like a buzz ... a chemical charge in your body.'

The worst sort of advert, Pay thought, used shock tactics – 'I actually fundamentally disagree with shocking people into doing something' – or the all-singing, all-dancing characters who are supposed to help us remember where to buy car insurance. 'Nowadays, I think, in 2014, a joke with a product stuck at the end isn't enough. I think that's just a very lazy way of doing stuff.' The result of an ideal ad is the product selling out (Pay told me of an advert for Super Noodles that was so successful Batchelors had to build another factory): 'Advertising's not about art or telling jokes. Advertising is about selling stuff to somebody because they've got a problem that they want you to solve. So I'm very very interested in multi-award-winning work that sells out of product. That's got to be the goal. If your work wins a lot of awards but doesn't sell anything it's failed. If your work sells a lot of stuff but doesn't win any awards it's succeeded. But the ideal is both.'

Pay wanted to be an artist when she was little – 'getting my artist brownie badge, that kind of level of artist' – but after graduating from Bournemouth, she was accepted on to Tony Cullingham's postgraduate diploma course at Watford, the Oxbridge of advertising. 'Everybody was shitting themselves and competing at the same time,' she says of the interview in 1997, 'and Tony was just setting you tasks like: half an hour, ten ideas, fifty ideas, dance on the table, sing a song, sum yourself up in five words, team up with that person, you've got an hour to do this. He was basically quickfiring impossible tasks at you, so confirming that you didn't know what you were doing and you weren't very good, and then seeing how you coped with that. Because that's basically the job. The job is constant rejection until you have the right answer.' On graduating, newly made creative teams – one copywriter, one art director – take their book round the London agencies, hoping to get a placement: a few weeks paid between £150 and £300 a week that might become a job. (Many don't: you hear of copywriters on placement for two years, getting rolled over week by week and never knowing if they're going to make it.)

After graduation, Pay was on placement at an Amsterdam agency for seven months before being taken on by the Shoreditch-based Mother, where she stayed for nearly seven years making ads for Boots, Coca-Cola, Amnesty International, Cup a Soup and the drugs service FRANK. At first, she'd wanted to work with an older man she could learn from, and was disappointed to get a woman her own age, Kim Gehrig, but one of their ideas for an ad wasn't chosen and they decided they would never be beaten again. (The layers of competition in advertising agencies – an idea is to attract the attention of your colleagues, other agencies, and the jaded public – are partly mitigated by working with a partner: you know you have at least one person on your side.) Pay and Gehrig weren't ever beaten after that day: 'Every idea we ever sold was made.' She moved to BBH to run the Levi's account, then worked freelance and 'permalance' (freelancing for one company full-time) for several agencies before she found out she was pregnant. She had met ad creative Al MacCuish in the early 2000s and their son, Buddy, was born ten weeks early in May 2009. 'The day Al went back to work I was just like: "Oh my God. He's got our old life, and I've got someone else's life, and I really don't like it very much." Because being at home ... I hate being on my own. I'm not very good at being friends with people just because they've got babies, so I didn't really do that NCT thing, blah, blah, blah.' She went back to Mother because she wanted to remind Al 'who I was when he fell in love with me rather than this real miseryguts at home who wasn't very good at washing up.' After a few years back at Mother she returned to BBH, where she is now Deputy Executive Creative Director. 'Your job is to go: "And that's it, there." Throw enough shit at me and I will find a tiny diamond and make it all right.'

On the Victoria line to work in the morning, she'll write emails that will ping off as soon as she is above ground. 'And from the moment I get in, I talk, until the moment I go home.' She tries to avoid long meetings, even though 'my job is meetings: if it's not a creative review, it's a briefing, and if it's not a briefing it's something like this interview. I would never ever sit in front of my computer and open a document and write something.' At lunch, she might ask one of the teams to take her to eat somewhere she hasn't been before, or meet up with a friend, or just let off steam on a walk. 'Lunch is like a reward!' She tries to get home before 7 p.m. to send the nanny home (London nannies earn around £32,000 a year): 'It's just a weird working mum thing: you tend to give yourself these deadlines.' She must earn somewhere in the region of £250,000 a year, though she says 'money's not really ever been a driver for me. It's about impact.' She pauses. 'Money's weird. I know people who are worse at their job than me and get paid three times as much.'

There is a moment in *Mad Men*'s fourth season when Don Draper's elderly secretary, Ida Blankenship, catches the young copywriter Peggy Olson on the way out of Draper's office; Draper has told Olson she can fire one of her colleagues. Blankenship looks up and deadpans: 'It's a business of sadists and masochists, and you know which one you are.' Women make up only 3 per cent of creative directors in advertising; of the women Pay knows who have made it to the top, 'one is me, one is a lesbian with no children, one is a lesbian with two children and one had her children twenty years ago'. They may not have to discreetly avoid sexual advances as Barbara Herrick did, but women in advertising still have to navigate how gentle and how hard to be. Pay has taken charge of her younger colleagues: 'I am really maternal and very very open with being loving and supportive. I'm very protective of the creatives.' But she also likes leaving being an actual mother behind when she comes to work: 'I love my mornings where I'm a mum until nine o'clock then I'm me until seven o'clock. So the whole doing your hair and putting some lipstick on, putting high heels on and leaving the house and when I get on the tube, nobody knows that I'm a mum, or married or whatever my whole life is, they just see me as an independent working person.' (I couldn't help thinking of the moment in the Bailey's ad when a girl locking up an apartment that could be in Brooklyn dashes back inside to pick up some velvet loafers.) Work is where Pay 'shows off': 'It never really feels like work work. Like grown-ups' proper work.'

Ann O'Byrne, 48, councillor, and Jayalal Madde, 50, homesteader, in Granby, Liverpool

Two weeks before Christmas 2014, Jayalal Madde moved into the redbrick terrace house he had bought from Liverpool City Council for a pound in May. In the spring it was two houses, with pink wallpaper, no gas meter, no water, no heating: a 'nutshell', he said. A joiner was still fitting skirting boards but the bedrooms were already fitted with wardrobes, mirrored dressing tables and soft pale carpet. The van parked outside – 'Piano Removal Specialists: Fully Insured' – had just arrived to carry a walnut upright piano with carved claw feet into the front room: Madde's two daughters were learning the piano as well as the violin and the trumpet. The family had come to the UK from Sri Lanka for the daughters' education: 'This is the best country for children's education. If they are British educated, anywhere in the world they go, they'll be better off.' He was happy that discipline was good at the girls' school.

Madde rented a house nearby for five years and often walked up Cairns Street with his wife while it was a tinned-up terrace, wondering: 'Why are they keeping these houses closed when they could be refurbishing?' He had arrived in the UK on a migrant's visa in 2005; now, approaching 50, he went to the bank to see if his taxi driver's salary of £15,000 or so a year would qualify him for a mortgage. The bank rejected him: even though he'd always paid his rent on time, they needed three years of accounts before they could lend. So the day Liverpool City Council let him know he could have a derelict house for refurbishment 'was the best day in our life'. 'Every man likes to have their own house as opposed to living their whole life in rented property,' Madde said. 'If I can have a freehold property before I retire, then I can give it to my children who might one day admire that I made a freehold house for them. We, anyway, Asian people, most of our friends, want to have their own house.'

Cairns Street is in an area the council calls Granby Four Streets, but which used to be known to locals as Liverpool Eight and to the rest of the UK as Toxteth. On 3 July 1981, police attempted to arrest a young black motorcyclist at the corner of Granby and Selbourne Street, eight streets down from Cairns, triggering six weeks of anti-police rioting: 150 buildings were burned; 470 police were injured; 500 were arrested, many without being subsequently charged; one protestor was killed and many more injured (though no one counted them as carefully). It was the summer The Specials' 'Ghost Town' – with its reminder that young people in the UK were jobless and angry – was released and there were also riots in Bristol, Southall and Brixton. After 1981, Liverpool Eight felt targeted: 'We were condemned,' Hazel Tilley, who still lives in Granby, said. 'It was punishment for the riots.' The feeling wasn't unfounded: government papers released in 2011 showed that Thatcher's cabinet discussed the 'managed decline' of the city after the summer unrest. In 2002, John Prescott designated Liverpool a 'Pathfinder' of his Housing Market Renewal Initiative, which aimed to 'renew failing housing markets ... to improve neighbourhoods'.

This was to be done along the old model of the 1960s slum clearances: Liverpool got £152 million to buy up redbrick terraces which then would be demolished and replaced with fewer, newer houses. The artificially created scarcity and desirability would push prices up; the solution to a failing market was more market. Was Prescott's scheme social cleansing, barely disguised? And why demolish houses that had lasted more than a hundred years, and that could be inhabited again?

Ann O'Byrne, Liverpool City Council's member for housing, grew up in Toxteth. Her mother gave birth to four children before the age of 21 (but she trained as a lawyer in her thirties and went on to lecture in law); her father was a councillor before her. She was born in 1966, just before the family was moved out in the clearances: 'Because of the housing conditions in the area – two-up, two-down – there was a mass demolition taking place in the 1960s, so we were shipped out to Kirkby, which is in Knowsley. Actually if you live in Kirkby you don't think of it as anything other than Liverpool because everybody that was in Kirkby was from Liverpool. It was a natural thing!' She remembers joining the Labour Party following the miners' strike – 'I was a young teenager and it just seemed utterly wrong and immoral' – and took her nan's shopping trolley around the neighbours to collect tins of food for the hungry miners. She became a social worker in a children's home and set up credit unions before being elected a councillor in 2007, and in 2012, two years after Labour took Liverpool council from the Lib Dems, she took on the housing brief, with a target of building 5,000 new homes and bringing 1,000 empty homes into use.

When Liverpool City Council announced it would be selling houses for a pound, they received enquiries from as far away as Russia. And when they published the criteria – you had to be a first-time buyer, have a job and live or work in Liverpool – 1,000 people applied for twenty homes. Liverpool took the idea from Stoke-on-Trent, which in April 2013 said it would sell thirty-five derelict houses for a pound and lend successful applicants the money to refurbish. As Liverpool narrowed the applicants further, based on whether they had children, savings and earnings between £20,000 and £30,000, their scheme acquired its own character. It would help people 'who are caught in not – quite – having the finances to go for a full-on mortgage but have enough,' O'Byrne said.

Successful applicants included a lecturer at the University of Liverpool, a trainee teacher and a young solicitor; many were Muslim, as not being able to take on an interest-bearing mortgage due to Sharia finance rules meant they hadn't been able to take out a conventional home loan. 'What can we do for those people sort of trapped in this middle bit? Obviously the pound was symbolic because we were saying you need at least £40,000 to invest in these properties, but we know at the end of it you're going to have a stunningly beautiful home. And the whole point was that it was genuine homesteading.'

I thought of something Madde said when I asked him if he had ever watched TV programmes about building, refurbishing, rescuing and making money out of houses: 'My wife used to watch every morning on telly that *Homes under the Hammer*,' he said. 'I have been watching them, and we learn a lot from them.' As Madde showed me his house, he pointed out where he'd knocked down walls and replastered others: 'I made it bigger,' he said. 'I extended that.' The house had been replumbed and rewired: 'A total 100 per cent refurbishment project.' He'd stripped wallpaper and painted the house himself; friends who run off-licences and newsagents offered their vans for moving. Madde had worked eighty to ninety hours a week taxi-driving – 'I sacrificed one year and I can enjoy it for the rest of my life' – and hit problems with utilities companies and insurers, but his was the first £1 house to be completed. The conversion had cost £40,000 (he had got some money from his local credit union, the rest came from savings) but an estate agent had just told him the house was now worth £120,000. A few houses down, Ibrahim, his friend, was spending £60,000 on converting his £1 house, including the cellar and the loft. Madde had seen it: 'Ground floor, totally open-plan, very beautiful.'

Just as the Pathfinder scheme was characteristic of New Labour bombast, so the bootstrap nature of the £1 houses scheme tells of our Poundland coalition austerity. Central government decided to cut 58 per cent from its funding to Liverpool City Council in 2011. 'We are one of the poorest cities in the country yet we are the hardest hit,' O'Byrne said. 'In the House of Commons David Cameron gave this bland statement about how actually his constituency had taken a similar level of cuts. Which was utterly disingenuous. Our council tax base is predominantly council tax band A, the lowest council tax band, so the ability for us to generate revenue is very low. Council tax band A, I think, is just over £1,000 a year coming in. David Cameron's constituency, his council tax band is between D and H, so the level of income that he's got coming in to that constituency! It's really unfair to try and say that the cuts are even, given your starting point. It's such an unfair comparison.' Figures calculated for the Shadow Communities Secretary, Hilary Benn, have shown that Liverpool District B will lose £807 a household, while Hart District Council in Hampshire is losing £28 per household. 'How does that not make you want to tear someone's throat out?' says a character in Jack Thorne's 2014 play *Hope*, about a fictional local council trying to decide where its cuts should fall. In the end they decide – as the real Liverpool City Council did in 1985 – to refuse to set a budget, in the hope that this would reveal to the public who really decided where the cuts should fall.

Building houses is a way of increasing the council's revenue: 'The problem is that we have an oversupply of pre-1919 terraced properties and we haven't got the mix that people want, so if you get a really good well-paid job in this city, the likelihood is that you will live on the Wirral, or in Sefton, or even in Manchester or Chester – you know, you will spread out. Liverpool was built in Victorian pillars and porticoes; only London and Bristol have more listed buildings in the UK. 'The only way we're going to increase our revenue base is if we have really good quality homes of a higher council tax base, that's why it's a priority. We're capital rich but revenue poor.' As we talked over instant coffee in O'Byrne's dockside corner office in the old Cunard building, I noticed she often finished discussing a problem with the pragmatic question 'What can we do?' We both had colds; she interrupted herself to fetch a tissue. 'If you live somewhere that's warm, and safe and where you feel secure, the whole of your life chances dramatically improve. Somebody who lives in Kensington, Liverpool, and somebody who lives in Kensington, London: they die thirty years younger in Liverpool than in London. That is just disgraceful. As a country, we should be ashamed of ourselves that that's still allowed to happen.' A side door opened and a man in a suit reminded her of her next meeting (she is Assistant Mayor as well as Merseyside's Deputy Police and Crime Commissioner) and she stopped talking, blew her nose and asked me: 'How was that? Was that all right?'

There are 635,000 empty properties across the UK, from the decaying mansions on Bishops Avenue in London to the tinned-up terraces on Cairns Street. Many people in Liverpool told me that the £1 houses represented 'a failure of the market': a phrase that seemed to hide everything from the post-Toxteth 'managed decline' to low wages, avaricious London buyers, the closure of the Albert Docks in 1972 and the halving of Liverpool's population. But the failure of the market also opened a gap for non-market solutions: further up Cairns Street the volunteer-led Granby Community Land Trust was planning to renovate ten buildings; the Plus Dane Group, a social housing provider, has renovated a row of terraces parallel to Cairns.

Perhaps the meaning of market failure is literal: of the thousand applicants for the £1 houses, many fell away when they saw the scale of the project, as private developers before them had. For private developers, a £1 house is an expensive way to secure a low rental income; for O'Byrne, a £1 house sells the idea of her town regenerating, even in a downturn; for Madde, a £1 house is a working life's prize.

Greg Foxsmith, 47, legal aid lawyer, Southwark Crown Court

Barristers don't have to wear wigs but Greg Foxsmith is the only one today in Southwark Crown Court without grey horsehair curls. He's wearing court dress though: the white strips of fabric hanging down the front of his shirt are supposedly mourning bands for Queen Anne: 'I don't miss her,' Foxsmith says, 'so I don't know why I should wear bloody mourning bands.' The robes themselves are peacocking: 'There's all grades of gowns, and you wear a different gown if you're a judge and you get three stripes of orange here and a dash of claret and purple there and three extra curls on your wig if you're a QC – I mean what a load of rubbish!' Foxsmith's naked head makes him look tougher than his wigged opponents: 'I just want to get into a fight,' Foxsmith said, outside Court Two. 'I want to go to the police station and have an argument. I want to stand up in court and present a case.'

Today, in late July 2014, he is in court waiting for the jury to agree on a verdict of an eight-week trial that has outlasted the World Cup, Tulisa's battle against the Fake Sheikh and Rolf Harris's trial for indecent assault (Foxsmith met Harris in the lift after the verdict: 'Going down?' he asked as he went to press the button). His client, a Premiership footballer who gambled his money away, became addicted to drugs, but got clean, is on trial with eight others for conspiracy to import drugs. The jury had already been out for several days. Southwark Crown Court is a huge brown brick cube on the south bank of the Thames, punched with small brown square windows: inside, there is lino, glass reinforced by wire mesh and dark wood. In Court Two the judge sits below a coat of arms with barristers in front of him and a jury to his left. The accused sit behind the lawyers, in a glass box guarded by G4S contractors. You can hear them before they arrive, as doors slam and keys clink.

The clerk is flipping between his court list and a crossword. Last to enter is the jury: one member has faux daisies pinned into her hair; another turns and looks at the defendants for the entire time she's in court. The judge asks the foreman to stand up and give us his verdict. The barristers put their pink-ribboned bundles of paper and their iPads aside. The defendants raise their eyes. There is a pause as the foreman stands, and then a sigh when we see his face. He looks exasperated: the jury can't agree on a verdict. The defendants lower their eyes. The judge speaks: the jury is now permitted to reach a majority verdict (if ten members agree and two disagree, the verdict will stand). The jury files out, the defendants go back down to their cells. We have been in court for perhaps five minutes in all. Foxsmith will have to wait another ten days before the jury finds his client not guilty.

Are lawyers no more than slick salesmen who can persuade someone that black is white? How do they defend someone they think is guilty? 'You're a mouthpiece for people for whom there is a presumption of innocence,' Foxsmith says. 'The reality is that many people tell me they're guilty. And then you say: "Well, then let's plead guilty." Then your job is to mitigate. There are always reasons why people do crime, and let's not forget, over half of the cases in criminal courts are guilty pleas. So it's not that there's always lawyers saying "let's plead not guilty" and "we'll find a defence for you" and "let's worm out" – most people plead guilty and the job of a lawyer is to try and put exculpatory factors in and get the appropriate sentence.' Lawyers keep the 'taxi rank' rule: they speak for whoever waves them down. Foxsmith has never refused a case: 'When I start becoming judgemental, choosing my cases, it's the thin end of the wedge because somebody might be wrongly accused of horrific things and if they're then abandoned by every competent lawyer on the grounds that it's too bloody horrible – that happened with the Birmingham Six.' Beyond these rules, a lawyer develops his own way to persuade: rhetorical tricks, intellectual nimbleness, all the charm we've seen so often on screen. 'There's a great art to doing a great speech, and I try to do a great speech. You modulate your voice, softly spoken and then loud booming declarations and pauses and, you know, all the rhetorical flourishes, the advocacy tricks of public speaking, of course you do. I like to inject a bit of humour. I'm always disappointed if I haven't had one laugh out of the jury, no matter how unfunny the case is.' He finds it hard to sleep the night before a jury speech. 'I hate to see poor quality advocacy in courts, poorly prepared. I find it risible.'

For Foxsmith, being prepared means work days that end at midnight. (He isn't unhappy about regularly doing sixty hours a week, but 'I do resent it when I can't sleep.') He is a solicitor-advocate, a new type of lawyer created in 1994 who can act in all UK courts (solicitors act in magistrates' courts but have to hand the case over to a barrister if it goes to crown court). There are around 15,000 barristers in the UK, but only 6,500 solicitor-advocates. Foxsmith is the first lawyer to have represented a defendant at every stage of a case: from advice in the police station to the Court of Appeal. Unless he's spent the previous night at the police station giving advice, he gets up around 7 a.m. with his two young children at home in North London and once they're off to school, he'll work at home preparing cases.

For his current case, he had to listen to hundreds of hours of covert recordings. Two defendants are eating bacon sandwiches in the bugged van: 'Why have they fried the bread? Why can't they just toast the fucking bread?' The other replies: 'Yeah, it's swimming in oil! They may as well have put it in the fucking deep fat fryer,' in an embarrassingly British version of the Royale with Cheese scene from *Pulp Fiction*.

At home, Foxsmith reads through documents and drafts arguments. If he's in court his day starts differently: he'll commute while thinking about or reading through his cases, and spend the morning presenting the case or cross-examining. At 1 p.m. court breaks for lunch and he'll eat a homemade tuna sandwich before heading down to the cells for 'conference time', often the only moment in the day he can talk to his client about how the case is going. Court sits until 6 p.m. when he might go to meet another client or drop off some papers, before getting home for about 7.30 p.m. He'll read a story to his children, eat with his wife and then work again, going over tomorrow's case, until midnight. Foxsmith is self-employed and earns under £50,000 a year, and his income goes up and down according to the cases he gets. His morning coffee comes from Sainsbury's; his holidays are in Cornwall. 'Even if it goes well I'm not really going to make significant amounts of money.' He'll read a novel before bed. When we met, he'd just finished Hilary Mantel's *Wolf Hall*: Thomas Cromwell, he reminds me, was a lawyer.

If Foxsmith doesn't like wigs, are there legal traditions he does like? He smiles: 'The presumption of innocence? Or being properly remunerated for a case? Or the Magna Carta?' In 1215 the Magna Carta set a principle that has defined Foxsmith's career until now: 'To no one will we sell, to no one deny, or delay right of justice.' He works as a legal aid lawyer, getting fixed fees from the state to represent people who otherwise couldn't afford a lawyer. The coalition government have arbitrarily cut

Legal Aid fees by 30 per cent, allowed whole areas of civil law to fall out of scope and allowed 'legal advisers' to give advice in police stations over the telephone: measures that have put hundreds of small firms out of business. Increasingly, lawyers have to defend their profession, and sell what they do for the public good in a country hardening against those who get into trouble. 'Everyone thinks about the Health Service because most of us use it at some point, but most – touch wood – don't need to use a criminal legal aid lawyer and therefore they're, I suppose, indifferent. I don't say they're anti it, I just say they're indifferent or unaware. And I think politicians cotton on to that and think: "Oh, we can make the cuts there and get away with it. The only people they're going to upset is the criminal defence lawyers." And there ain't very many of us. We're not like the white van man of whatever election that was, or the Mondeo man, or the Essex man – there's always a swing vote that people are trying to target. Well, it's never going to be us. So I'm a bit despondent.' In January 2014, the Criminal Bar Association held a half-day strike over the Ministry of Justice's plans and Foxsmith spoke in front of the Houses of Parliament. With the London Criminal Courts Solicitors' Association, he has begun a judicial review of the changes to legal aid. They have funded the action themselves, which doesn't help him sleep. 'I like the tradition of jurisprudence that dictates a level playing field, equality of arms and fairness,' Foxsmith says. 'And I'm a big fan of the European Convention on Human Rights. You know, what's not to like? When people say: "Oh, bloody Europe! Interfering!" I always say: "Well, read the ten articles and tell me which one you don't approve of – what is it you don't want? Right to a fair trial or right to freedom of expression? Which one do you want to lose?" Because people haven't read it. They don't even know what their rights are. They feel critical of it because they think it's their big bogeyman. Absolute nonsense.'

Legal rights don't seem so disposable to anyone who's

been on the wrong side of the law. 'I had a few brushes myself growing up,' Foxsmith says. 'I was expelled from school and was in trouble with the police.' His father was in the Merchant Navy before marrying his mother and settling in Plymouth, where he framed pictures from a small shop. Foxsmith didn't know what he wanted to do after school and he worked in door-to-door sales, fruit picking, manual labour, telesales, factory work, security and gardening. 'I don't think people are good barristers who go to public school, university, bar school and then swan around in their stupid gowns and wigs: what do they know about life?' His friends told him he ought to be a lawyer because he was argumentative; the idea appealed to him and he went to law college in his twenties in London before beginning in an East End criminal legal aid practice. He earned £18,000 in 1995 as a new solicitor going every day to the magistrates' court, acting in perhaps twenty cases a day. He went on to develop an interest in civil liberties and protest cases when he moved to Hodge Jones and Allen, a big London firm; he became a partner at Shearman Bowen and then went freelance when he was elected a Labour councillor.

Foxsmith sat on the sticky, torn and intermittently stuffingless pleather seats of the Southwark Crown Court waiting room. Between tannoy messages, he talked about the cases that had stayed with him. A man who stabbed someone when drunk was sent down for murder, though he couldn't remember the stabbing. Another man killed a family in a car accident, became addicted to heroin in prison, got clean but died after a relapse at the age of 24. A 13-year-old turned on the school bully with a butter knife and got a criminal record for ABH. A man who beheaded another man with an axe; he was discovered to have been fostered at 13 to someone who eventually hung himself while on bail for child sex offences. 'The criminal justice system is a very blunt instrument for dealing with these issues. And it's adversarial: there are two sides and you're fighting over guilt or innocence. Some of these cases should be brought out of the criminal justice system altogether. It doesn't need an adversarial guilty or not guilty, it needs a 'you are ill and you need help' kind of diagnosis.'

When he was a young lawyer acting for the accused in police interviews, he used to ask to go to the loo when he didn't need to go. There he would look at his law books. 'I didn't want to show my lack of experience by getting the books out. But I very quickly realised that actually the contrary was true. Police officers are far more intimidated by law books, and clients are more impressed by them than by somebody who seems to know it all. So I soon learned that when I get to the police station, I should take as many law books as I can and thump them on the desk. And then give a big smile.' Foxsmith paused and I thought of the silver hake in Belfast, the artful Facebook photos on the walls of an advertising agency in the West End, O'Byrne's talk of homesteading in Liverpool – was this his equivalent of a sales trick? 'I realised that actually law is the only asset that we have as lawyers in the police station. The police have every other advantage, they have home territory, they control the clock, they control the disclosure, they choose what to tell you and what not to tell you, they have the decision on bail, they have the decision on charging, but I'm the fucking lawyer! Yeah, that's all I've got. So why should I be shy of it? Here's my bloody law book: now what are you going to do about it? In fact, sometimes, for the fun of it, if I've got a boring interview, I might let a worried look cross my brow, open the law book, flip through and then run my finger down and go and put a little bookmark in, close the book and look smug – and they don't half look worried!'

SERVING

sex worker
baristas
call centre adviser
special adviser

Ina, 22, sex worker, Central London

The sign on the wall of the flat where Ina works reads 'Beautiful Young Lady'. 'That's it,' Ina says, 'it doesn't say nothing more. It doesn't say name, it doesn't say colour, it doesn't say nothing. And who wants to come up, comes up.' Then Ina waits. 'It's a gamble. You flip the coin. The same as working in an office. You might have somebody calling who pisses you off with a million questions and asking something ridiculous which doesn't exist in your type of job. It does piss you off. For example, they come to me and they say, "Oh, I would like blow job without a condom!" *Crrr!* Who do you think you are! "No." They are like: "Why not?" And I'm like: "Because I don't want to." "Why?" "I don't do! So that's it!" Same as in an office: we don't provide this paper, we don't do this.'

Ina had worked until 2 a.m. last night and woke up at 7 a.m. The Crossroads Women's Centre is in a mews behind Kentish Town Road: she arrived early with a sandwich, and napped on the sofa as she waited. She wore a black top edged with black and silver plastic jewels, and her wavy blonde hair was pulled into a ponytail. The English Collective of Prostitutes, formed in 1975 with the aim of decriminalising sex work, has shared the centre with fifteen other women's groups, such as Women against Rape and Global Women's Strike, since the late 1990s. There is a pink babygro with the slogan 'I'm a full-time job' on sale in the entrance hall and Selma James, the feminist writer and activist who helped found the ECP, is being trailed around the building by an old white sheepdog and a young black labrador.

Mary Barton, Elizabeth Gaskell's 1848 novel about industrial Manchester, began with the disappearance of Mary's aunt Esther, who has fallen in love with an army officer and become pregnant by him. When the officer disappears and their daughter falls ill, Esther stops working to care for her, but needs to buy medicine. 'Oh, her moans, her moans, which money could give the means of relieving!' Esther remembers. 'So I went out into the street one January night – do you think God will punish me for that?' Sex workers are no longer primarily presented as fallen women to be pitied and rescued; more recent depictions such as the Cinderella story *Pretty Woman* and the glamorous memoir *Secret Diary of a Call Girl* are more likely to talk about the pleasures than the difficulties of sex work or about the conditions that led them there.

Ina grew up in Bulgaria. (Up to 81 per cent of off-street sex workers in London come from elsewhere, and a quarter are from Eastern Europe.) She wanted to become a model but her father thought she should do 'something serious and realistic, not a fairy-tale dream world like a ballerina or a model or whatever, or celebrity and stuff like that – he didn't want that. He wanted us as serious as possible, hard-working people, serious job, you know?' Only her mother knew when she started working as a model. The day before a shoot she had done was to be published, her mother told her father and 'he snapped'. She came to England at 17 with a boyfriend, knowing that she would be going into sex work, almost in a rebellious spirit. 'First time I started the job, I could say it was revenge. That I'm beautiful and I can make it without anybody stopping me – even if I need to lie, I'm going to lie and prove that I can make it. I don't need to be that terrifying, hard-working woman and proving to people that yes, I've got an important job and I'm highly qualified and smart. No, I don't want that. I want just to be me, to be free. And that's it.'

On her first day, as she spoke no English, she was talked through what was on the menu card and she memorised it. 'And the customer only needed to point a finger. And each time they were trying to do something else, thinking I was stupid. I used to *pting!*' Ina mimed a comic-book bop to the nose: 'Go between their eyes! I was like "No!" I wasn't speaking English so I was speaking my own language. And if they were trying again I was like *schting!* And I was pressing the button for the maid!' She punched at least two customers on her first day, but she made money: 'My first day at work, it was the best day ever! I made a thousand pounds, my first day. I was new. This is what they usually say, the maids, "Oh, if you're new you make lots of money and then it slowly goes down."' She paid the rent and part of the deposit on the flat she lived in, sent some money to her mum, bought clothes for herself, topped up her mobile and called all her friends. A Scottish colleague at the flat she worked in taught Ina English by pointing at things, getting her to repeat the word and then testing her on it later. The boyfriend who brought her to England became a drunk and an addict; they fought and he hid her passport. She got a pickpocket to steal it back, dumped him and never looked back. The maids were right about the money. After four years of sex work, Ina earns £400 a day, and rates have fallen after the financial crash of 2008. On average, Ina earns around £65 a visit.

Most of the week Ina studies English, Maths and IT as she hopes to move into care work, but when she has a shift, she'll wake up around midday, have a coffee and two cigarettes and take the train for thirty-five minutes to Central London. She likes to watch other commuters: 'I try to read every person on the train: the way they behave, the way ... their body language. What they tell you. This is what I try to do because it makes me understand the customer, the way they behave if they are angry or they're pissed off and stuff like that. So I'm trying to read as many people as possible to make it as safe as possible for me.' She might pick up a toothbrush or some mouthwash from Boots, and then get ready by undressing, washing her hands, using the bidet and putting on work clothes. 'I could be a police officer, I could be a schoolgirl, I could be a dominatrix, I could be in sexy lingerie. It always depends on the day and how you feel like.' She puts on make-up and then arranges condoms and lubricant in a basket and the maid – who acts as her receptionist as well as intervening for safety; she is paid from customers' tips – helps her lay out tissues, baby wipes, hot water, soap, mouthwash and a toothbrush, plastic cups so that she can have a clean cup each time she needs to rinse her mouth, as well as clean towels and bedsheets. The room has four lights, two orange and two red, for atmosphere. She switches them on, and she's ready to work.

She sleeps while she waits, or she goes shopping (the maid will ring her if a client arrives). She aims for the day to unfold undramatically; she pushes customers away 'if they're bad in language'. 'Most of the time I try to make it as comfortable as possible, as relaxing as possible and to forget that it's a job. But obviously with some rules. Always use a condom, never French kissing, no anal, no this, no that. Make sure these things are all cleared out from the beginning. So yeah. And then it just rolls on. It comes easily.' She'll have around six clients a day who stay for around half an hour, and prefers a day with 'less money, nicer people. Better than too much money and arseholes.' She knows she's good at her job – 'I am a very confident person at work. I'm not outside. But at my job I'm very confident in myself because I know what I'm doing and I know I'm going to get it right' – but that she's not good at giving marital advice. 'I'm terrible! I'm not married! I've got a relationship but I didn't get to the point where I wanted to marry that person, so I don't know how to ... They always ask me: "How do you keep so well? How come you can make me happy any time I come, and smile all the time?" I don't know what to answer to them.' Other clients ask: '"What can I do better in my relationship?" How would I know how you behave at home? They expect you as a sex worker to give advice on their personal relationship but you don't get to know them so well because some of them they don't want to open so much. You can't give them an advice or even if you try to give them an advice, you're sort of pushing back and trying to … Am I doing the right thing? I don't want to ruin his relationship.'

Many clients think they're buying loving attention rather than unadorned sex. On PunterNet, clients write reviews of the sex workers they've visited: they'll give a rating for the room, whether the sex worker matched her photo, what positions she did and where she let him come. PunterNet is its own world with its own language: a 'punt' is the half-hour or so they spend with a sex worker, 'OWO' is oral without a condom, 'mish' is missionary. (Sex workers have a parallel version of PunterNet: the Ugly Mugs Project collects sex workers' accounts of clients who rape, or are violent, to be circulated among other sex workers and shown anonymously to police.) The majority of reviews on PunterNet are positive – the website says it 'aims to promote better under-standing between customers and ladies' – but negative reviews are most reliably earned for lack of enthusiasm. 'She made no attempt at conversation let alone seduction,' Peachmuncha says of a visit to Sabrina in November 2014, 'and was looking off into the middle distance whilst she prodded my back with her fingers. I don't know about other guys but when a lady just asks "you want blow job with condom or without?" the passion of the moment is kinda out the door and into the Thames for a dampener.' The punters don't want to think of it as a transac-tion, but as a service. In summer 2014, *The Economist* argued that the arrival of websites such as PunterNet were changing the sex industry: 'The shift makes it look more and more like a normal service industry.'

Ina and the maid will prepare dinner in the flat from food bought at the supermarket downstairs and eat together, feet up in front of the TV. Her shift ends at 2 a.m. unless she's had a good day when she'll leave at 10 p.m. She'll clear the room up, change the bins, take her make-up off, brush her teeth, shower, put her clothes on and leave. 'When I go home I want my peace and quiet. After twelve hours of work, you don't want to hear anything, or you don't want to see anything. I'm just too tired sometimes.' When she gets home, she'll take her shoes off, put the TV on, and at 3 or 4 a.m. she'll go to sleep.

Her family, most of her friends and her boyfriend don't yet know she is a sex worker: 'When the right moment will come, yes, I will tell them. But I don't think they are ready yet to listen.' She sees colleagues outside of work, but 'obviously we don't talk about the job. We talk about different things. I tend not to take home my work. I always ... That is my main thing. Don't ever take your job home. Like even if you work in an office or in a restaurant, don't take it home with you, don't take the stress with you at home. Try to enjoy it as much as you can. I advise everybody don't take your job with you home. Just leave it at the desk and that's it. It's the best thing. Otherwise it drives you crazy. You can't sleep if you worry "What am I going to do tomorrow? What am I going to do? I need to do this paper, I need to do this." No: relax, chill out. You have time. You have time to do it all.'

In 2012, the flat Ina works out of was raided by twenty police officers, looking for drugs and women who were being forced to work. Sex workers' flats are periodically raided by the police, in the name of combatting trafficking and other crime. The laws around prostitution are complex but broadly speaking the act of paying for sex is legal, but the promotion and coercion of sex workers – pimping, brothel-keeping, soliciting, advertising – is not. 'They came in and started accusing me of pickpocketing, robbing, begging, many ugly stuff,' Ina says. 'They called me a gypsy, they called me rotten and stuff like that. They talked to the customer at the same time and asked him if I use drugs or if

I drink, which I didn't. The customer said, "Not what I know of. I knew this girl for a long time so I only saw her sober and she's really nice, she's really polite."'

The police wanted to know her employment status: did she have a National Insurance number? Did she have proof she was self-employed, a student or on benefits? 'I never claimed benefits: how can you ask me for benefits? I never claimed for benefits. I work! Can't you see I'm working!' She had to bring a letter with proof of her status to the police station within two weeks; in the meantime they reported her to the immigration authorities. She knew that police often took money on a raid without giving a receipt as proof of its existence, so she put her takings in her pocket, and told them they would have to beat her up for them. The police found no drugs, underage or trafficked women or evidence of coercion at her workplace.

Ina rang several lawyers afterwards to help her but none wanted to get involved. On her monthly sexual health check-up a woman she'd known for years gave her a leaflet about the ECP. The ECP found her a lawyer and helped her prepare a letter confirming her student status. 'Being an Bulgarian, don't forget, you are allowed to stay in this country, because we are in the European Union. What they actually done, it wasn't right. They thought I don't know, they thought, oh, she's young – I was only 21 – they said: "Oh, she's only young, she doesn't know nothing about it." I proved them wrong. They let me go. They were so lovely when I went there. They treated me so nicely because I was the only one with a lawyer. The lawyer talked very properly and she handed the letter and you don't have a right to do this, you don't have a right to do that.'

Since then she's been working with the ECP, visiting sex workers to talk to them about their problems and handing out rights sheets in English, Spanish, Italian, Chinese, Thai and Bulgarian. In December 2013, 200 police officers (trailed by photographers from the *Daily Mail*) raided twenty flats in Soho on suspicion of trafficking and trading in stolen goods linked to the crack cocaine trade. Sex workers were evicted and given cautions; thirty were arrested. Others were body-searched by male officers, and one woman was thrown on to the street in her underwear. Officers confiscated earnings and threatened to tell sex workers' families what they did. In response, the ECP organised a protest through the streets of Soho. Their slogans were drawn on pink cardboard hearts: 'Bulgarian Women Say No Evictions, Safety First', 'Benefit Cuts Drive Women into Prostitution' and 'No Bad Women Just Bad Laws!' They also fought the evictions in the courts: two flats in Brewer Street closed down for coercion were reopened in February 2014 when Judge Kingston at Isleworth Crown Court was persuaded that the sex workers organised themselves co-operatively and freely.

When the ECP was founded in 1975, they argued that housewives should stand with sex workers: 'All women benefit from prostitutes' successful attempts to receive cash for sexual work, because the cash makes it clear that women are working when we are fucking, dressing up, being nice, putting make-up on, whenever we relate to men.' Apart from a Premiership footballer I approached, Ina was the only person who asked to be paid for the work of answering my questions. She suggested a rate of £50 for half an hour, and I agreed: sex workers let us see that just because something is performed for free, or understood as a service that is often given for free in different circumstances, doesn't mean it's not work.

In the last few years, there have been more downs than ups. 'It's a lovely job to be in but when the raids are coming in, it's just outrageous what is going on.' Ina wants 'to be treated as any other job. I want to be treated as an equal. So if I have a problem to be entitled to call the police without me being prosecuted. This is what I want.' The most recent parliamentary inquiry in March 2014 recommended the Swedish model, which criminalises the clients. Sex workers themselves point to New Zealand, which has decriminalised sex work, making it safer for women and men: when a man pulled off his condom in a brothel, he was fined NZ$400 and his name was printed in the local newspaper covering the case. He was the bad guy. Ina voted in the 2015 election 'no matter what they think of my job', but without much conviction: 'Talking about election it just drives me mad. Everybody says I'm going to do this, I'm going to do that, but when it comes to actually doing it, they don't.' Politicians might not campaign with sex workers in mind, but that doesn't mean sex workers don't contribute. In 2014, sex work was included in GDP figures, in order to harmonise with the rest of the EU's financial reporting. (Counting the grey economy into GDP in dark times is an old trick: Italy recognised sex work as economic activity in 1987 and raised its GDP by 18 per cent overnight.) With no reliable figures on prostitution, the Office of National Statistics guessed, using a 2004 Poppy Project report about London's sex industry, that it added £5.3 billion a year to the economy. The British economy grew at 0.7 per cent in the third quarter of 2014; a good proportion of this growth is down to the kind of work many people would like to pretend doesn't exist.

Sex has been linked to servitude for a long time: Samuel Richardson's 1740 novel of seduction, *Pamela*, showed how serving a master in the dining room might slide into serving him in the bed chamber; in the mid-nineteenth century a Salvation Army register showed that 88 per cent of prostitutes they helped had once been domestic servants. The service industry employed 44 per cent of the British workforce in 1948, and employs 85 per cent of it today. All kinds of workers in all kinds of jobs are now encouraged to create an experience out of an ordinary transaction – the smiling and fucking that the Wages for Housework campaign identified as worthy of payment – and we are only just beginning to understand what sort of experience of work the service economy allows. The way emotions are used at work is something sex workers understand better than most of us. Ina is used to changing how others feel: judging the emotional state of the customer, calming him down, relaxing him. She does this part of the work by taking another name, putting on a costume and acting a role: 'I can be a man: so I have a strap-on and wear leather, you know, trying to be rough and stuff like that. I could be a little angel sometimes. Sometimes you need to pretend you are a schoolgirl. I'm good at uniforms, you know, playing a role.' It may have become central to our economy, but the invisible demands of service work, and how to defend ourselves against the effects of those demands, are rarely talked about. You can legislate for a safer working environment and a shorter working day, but how do workers organise against emotional labour?

Esther considers herself lost to society at the end of *Mary Barton*: 'She had longed to open her wretched, wretched heart,' Gaskell says when Esther meets her niece Mary again at the end of the novel, 'so hopeless, so abandoned by all living things, to one who had loved her once; and yet she refrained, from dread of the averted eye, the altered voice, the internal loathing, which she feared such disclosure might create'. When Dickens founded Urania Cottage in Shepherd's Bush in 1847, it was because he thought he could rescue prostitutes from themselves. But do modern Esthers need saving? Ina chooses sex work over other more menial service work; she organises her hours, defends herself against the state, and works uncoerced. *The Economist* noted that sex workers behave like freelancers in other labour markets; there is even a graduate premium. (The situation is different for the women who have been trafficked to the UK to work in the sex industry against their wishes.) Esther may not have been able to turn people away and Pamela couldn't escape from Mr B, but Ina can follow the mood she wakes up in: 'If I'm at work and I don't fancy sex I will be like, no, I will wait for the next customer and probably he will want dominations and he won't touch me.' She finds enjoyment in her work: 'You could have good times at work, you know, like having a pleasure moment.' Did she mean orgasms? 'Yeah, yeah, yeah. You still can have it. But it's like having sex with your partners: one time you might come and one time you might not come. Sometimes it can be too quick and you are like *Crrh!* "Oh come on! Not now!"'

B and R, 28 and 33, baristas at Pret A Manger, Central London

From outside, the plate glass almost seems to glow. Inside, I pass a photo of Stonehenge made of butter and walk over faux wood to reach the rows of cut sandwiches. It's lunchtime and I pick a tuna salad – the tuna in its beige, flaky diagonal, egg discs alongside it, as always – and a man in a TEAM PRET shirt refilling the fridge with water bottles turns to me and smiles. I queue for the till: 'Can I help?' 'Would you like a tray?' 'Are you sure?' 'Many thanks, madam.' 'Thank you very much.' The server smiles and scrunches up the receipt I don't want, and I leave the shop feeling different from the way I felt when I came in.

Pret A Manger, which runs 300 shops worldwide and made £61 million in profit in 2013, has precision-tuned customer mood. 'The first thing I look at,' said Clive Schee, Pret CEO, taking a journalist on a tour of his cafés in 2012, 'is whether staff are touching each other: are they smiling, reacting to each other, happy, engaged? Look, she's just touched her colleague – squeezed her arm. If I see hands going up in the air, that's a good sign. I can almost predict sales on body language alone.' Schee's almost flirtatious 'good signs', however, aren't spontaneous. Each employee is given a book detailing 'Pret Behaviours' which has three columns on each page: 'Want to see', 'Don't want to see' and 'Pret Perfect!' For a chain in which even the serviettes speak to the customer – 'if Pret staff get all serviette-ish and hand you huge bunches of napkins (which you don't need or want) please given them the evil eye' – it is not enough to make someone a decent cup of coffee, to keep the tables clean, to turn up every day because you need the money. The first core 'Pret Behaviour' is passion.

B, who wanted to be an astronaut when he was little, arrived in London from the Czech Republic in 2009 to study finance, and worked at Pret throughout his degree, from 2010 to 2013. He stayed mostly in the kitchens but was also trained on the till: 'There are two things. First thing is the transaction: when the customer comes to you, he gives you a baguette, he wants a coffee, he makes an order and you will charge him. But there's another part which is really big in Pret A Manger and it's the smile, and also the conversation you should have with the customer. You are encouraged to have a little chat with the customer while his coffee is being prepared. This was extremely challenging for me because I come from a nation where strangers normally don't talk to each other. And when someone was telling me: "Just ask the customer how he is, how was his weekend, stuff like that." I was like: "I don't know what to ask him, you know! I don't even care!"' B, tall and muscular with a shaved head, laughed as he described a colleague who arrived bouncily at 4 a.m. every morning, and charmed the customers despite her imperfect English. 'She was always asking customers: "How was your weekend?" And I thought: that's a good question. I can ask them how was your weekend. So I was always asking: "How are you? How was your weekend?" But the problem was that I was still doing it on Thursday!'

His manager gave him an exemption from smiling. After a year he knew how to make most of the sandwiches by heart, laying the slippery avocado from corner to corner of the bread, and he began to feel he understood English ways a bit better. B's shifts began at 4 a.m. and finished at 12 p.m. – the managers would always ask him to stay longer but he needed to sleep before getting up again to go to lectures. He was paid £6.22 an hour, just over the minimum wage (which was £6.19 an hour in 2012), but there was a big party each year, free lunch and the weekly bonus. Over a year, he would earn something approaching £13,000. Friends in the Czech Republic envied him: 'I would love this job, it's so perfect.'

Unlike other restaurants where customers can reward service by tipping, at Pret the tip was automatically part of the salary, and employees could only lose it. 'At first I didn't believe the mystery shopper existed,' B's friend R, who worked at Pret a few years before B did, said. 'I thought it was like Santa Claus: something to keep you in line.' If the mystery shopper employed by Pret to spy on itself didn't observe 'passion' the whole shop would lose that week's bonus. Eighty per cent of mystery shoppers are satisfied on their visits, which is just as well as the weekly basic salary of £200 went up to £245 with the bonus. 'It's a pressure on you,' R said. 'From Monday to Monday every single customer that you serve you have to give your absolute 100 per cent.' If you lost the shop its bonus, everyone knew about it. R described Pret as 'like a church, or congregation': 'I've had quite a few jobs and I don't know if I worked physically the hardest there, but it was definitely the most stressful because you felt responsible at any point in the chain. There wasn't really anywhere to hide.'

In his first year, B had four 'file notes', or informal warnings. One was given because he was sick more than three times, another because his uniform was dirty, but each time he went to see the manager, the file notes turned out to be about something else. Did he have to play nu metal while he worked? The Euro crisis had worsened that May and graduates worked in Pret for lack of other jobs. B stayed on. After a year's employment, he knew he could claim for unfair dismissal, and so 'lost the fear': when

he saw a manager breaking rules he pointed it out. The management staged an investigation of him; B defended himself by filing
a grievance. Pret struck a compromise and transferred both him
and the manager to different branches across London. 'They
were just waiting for me to slip,' B said.

At the new shop, every sarcastic comment B made became
a disciplinary matter; each time he received a warning he filed
a grievance in his defence. Then in 2012 he made a £10,000
claim to the Employment Tribunal for whistleblowing. Pret
suddenly gave him a fixed schedule (whereas shifts were determined as late as the night before), increased his pay to £7.80
an hour (including bonus), and sent his payslips to him by post
when colleagues often didn't even receive theirs at work. He said
to his fellow team members: 'Do you think this is right? Look at
me, I'm getting my payslips by post!' And they began to come
to him with their problems. One was being threatened with
dismissal, another on a full-time contract wasn't being given
the contracted hours. B helped them write grievances of their
own. 'It was really easy. People didn't know that there were
any procedures. Or that they are protected by the law in this
country.' (Ninety-one per cent of Pret's workers in London are
immigrants: Pret admit they prefer their employees 'flexible'.)
B noticed an odd thing in the first draft of their grievances:
they didn't include their manager's name. 'The biggest part is
the fear: nobody wants to write a letter saying the manager did
something.'

It wasn't B's idea to start the Pret A Manger Staff Union
(Pamsu); he was more interested in a campaign demanding
the London Living Wage (£9.15 an hour, without bonus). A
Colombian colleague, B and four others sat down to write 'a list
of demands': they sent them to Pret HQ on 1 September 2012,
with a request that their union be recognised. Pamsu emailed
every branch of Pret, and many people joined. B remembers that
the Italians signed up with most alacrity. But the company chose

not to recognise Pamsu: it proposed dealing with each union member individually, undermining the collective action they wished to take. B was called to a disciplinary meeting with less than twenty-four hours' notice and fired for a silly comment he'd made ten months before, that his branch of Pret was the 'gay' branch. The timing didn't feel to him like a coincidence. Other Pamsu members were scared and fell away, but B protested his dismissal outside his old shop with a few supporters from the Solidarity Federation, a section of the International Workers Association; the police let them wave a banner for half an hour before bundling them away. Articles about his dismissal appeared in the *Daily Mail*, the *London Evening Standard*, *The Independent*: each focused on the way Pret controls its employees by withdrawing bonuses on one hand and encouraging smiling on the other.

In the meantime, B graduated with a First Class degree in July 2013 and flew to Bangkok, hoping to teach English. He came back to London that winter and worked in NCP car parks before finding work that used his degree as a research analyst in Central London. He plans to return to the Czech Republic one day and go into politics. 'I'm proud,' B said. 'I know the other people just take the beating without doing anything. I might have a problem in the future to find a job, but I know that Pret couldn't humiliate me in any way. I know that I caused a lot of damage to their reputation. They damaged my reputation too. I'm an individual, you know, and they are a fucking corporation. And I stood up against them.' He receives at least an email a week into the Pamsu email account though the union is effectively defunct: 'You can always do something, you know. You can always give them some basic advice. In most cases, you can avoid the disciplinary very easily. They're just so scared because they have no clue about the procedures.' Last time B tried to go back to see colleagues at his old Pret, the manager refused to serve him. A few weeks later, HR wrote to him to apologise: as a customer he would always be welcome. Even someone Pret had fired would still be permitted the warm glow of the 'Pret Behaviours' when he was paying.

After leaving Pret, B has begun volunteering at an informal refugee centre, where he met R. Twice a week, they spend four hours cooking and serving food that would otherwise be wasted for people under threat of deportation; they couldn't tell me where it was because the Home Office would 'love' to know the location. 'Customer service in the shelter is personal. You know who you're serving,' B said. 'There are no name badges or anything like that,' R added. B laughed. 'You can lose your bonus for not using your name badge! Where's your name badge?' He said he almost felt selfish when he worked at the shelter 'because when I cook food and serve it to the people, I feel good about myself'. Pret was a simulacrum of service; this was the real thing. 'I'm not from a religious background, but the whole process of serving somebody ... it's good for everyone,' R said. 'You're giving them service but at the same time, they're feeling welcomed.'

T, 32, call centre adviser, Lincoln

Behind a branch of a fast-food chain in Lincoln, there is a featureless yellow brick building. It's a call centre, open from 7 a.m. to 11 p.m. every day. From the level of noise as the advisers walk in, they can often guess what's happening across the country. Bad weather causes a surge in the number of calls: a dense, chattering sound. A terrorist attack is loud. But less dramatic worries are quieter and more frequent: anger at a lost connection, sorrow for a family member passed away, simple loneliness.

T has spent eleven years solving problems with people's phone and broadband connections through his headset. When we meet on his lunchbreak in a side room of the call centre too small for the many office chairs in it, he's already eaten the pasta he brought from home at his desk. Tucked behind his ear is a rollie with a neat twist at the tip, and he takes it down to turn it over in his hands as he talks; normally he'd smoke through his lunch hour. He's wearing long jean shorts and a Homer Simpson T-shirt; above a wedge of beard on his chin, his eyes are ringed with yellow-blue shadows. 'To be honest, this place takes so much out of me,' he says. 'It's hard to pull away when I get home. I certainly swear at home more because I'm allowed to, but other than that really, unless I've got a couple of days off together, I do feel I've lost a large part of myself working here. I just had two weeks off through sick and holiday, and it was painful coming back. I really, really had to make myself come in. Because I just didn't want to. I know it has a detrimental effect on home life for me. I can't talk for definite about everyone else. I know there's quite a few people who drink a lot more since they started working here, but ... '

When T was 4 or 5, he wanted to be a bin man: 'You get to make a hell of a mess.' His mother was a lab technician at a secondary school and his father a civil engineer but he had 'never been able to apply myself in an academic situation. So it took me three years to do half-decent at my A levels, whereas my sisters both cracked on, knuckled down and got excellent grades.' He dropped out of university after four months and worked in kitchens and bars (he would work in bars if he won the lottery; 'You're chatting to people who actually want to talk to you not because something's gone wrong and they have to talk to you'). He came to the call centre through an agency as a 'stop-gap and eleven and a half years later I'm still here. So I fell into the trap.' He thought it would be a good job for a year or so, but 'the money just keeps you here'. T is married with children, and though it's September, he reminds me Christmas is coming. 'That's what's difficult to get away from because part of me wants to try different career paths, try something that's not answering the phones, but there's nothing with the same money for this level of qualifications.'

He gets up at 6 a.m. most days and walks the two and a half miles to work listening to music: 'The music is to stop me thinking about the fact that I'm heading here.' (His MP3 player is broken, so he has been borrowing his wife's; he cannot skip quickly enough when it gets to 'Bailamos' by Enrique Iglesias.) When he gets to work the first thing he'll do is have a cigarette outside: 'You find out what's going on here two months before the management do.' He must be logged in and ready to take calls at 8 a.m. Somewhere between 9.15 and 10.45 a.m. he'll have a break for fifteen minutes: a coffee in the canteen is 90p, but T brings milk from home and makes his own. He used to have a coffee every hour 'because it was an excuse to get away from my desk'; now he has cut down to three or four a day. As he works, sitting in an ergonomic mesh chair in his headset, he'll be reminded by large electronic screens on the wall striped green, amber or red how well he and his colleagues are doing in responding and handling calls. The standards change but they create both time and emotional pressure: T is supposed to answer and deal with whatever arises after a call is finished in a certain time, he has to direct the problem to the person who can solve it on the first call; he must collect details like mobile numbers, email addresses and assent to a text message customer satisfaction survey. 'You have customers who don't want to listen but you've got managers breathing down your neck, saying you've got to let them speak to you like crap basically.' A noticeboard at the entrance divides ordinary phrases into two columns: 'I'm not sure', 'usually', 'obviously' and 'maybe' are 'below the line' and ought to be avoided. 'Above the line' terms include: 'lovely', 'excellent' and 'what can I do?' The emotional labour of a call centre isn't just learning to withstand a customer's impatience but also learning to speak in a voice other than your own.

At lunch he'll smoke or he'll call his wife, his kids or his grandparents: there's 'someone to ring every day'. Everyone who works there gets free broadband and there are landlines provided in the atrium, under nursery-bright murals of slogans like 'Let's Pull Together – We're One Big Team' and 'We Don't Shift the Blame' and 'Do Something Brilliant'. In the yellow-walled staff canteen, most sit alone, eating in front of a propped-up tablet computer, or hunched over a smartphone. The next break is around 2 p.m. If there's a particularly nasty call, he'll go out and smoke, hoping someone will be out there: 'That's really the only way to survive it when you're getting calls like that. You need to vent about them.' If you get stuck on a call at 4 p.m. you can't tell the customer, and managers don't always notice the ends of shifts. T doesn't feel satisfied at close of day: 'You've got no vision of what will happen to a call once you put the phone down. It goes off somewhere else, someone else deals with it and whether they get things right, get things wrong, get it fixed, you don't know.' At the end of the day, T will walk home again, or maybe stop for a drink with a colleague. 'I couldn't tell you the amount of people I've been friends with, gone out drinking with and whatever and I never see now because they don't work here.' Thirty years ago and seventy miles west of here, the pottery glazer Alan Goldsmith's work and life were happily interwoven on the Wedgwood estate; here work actively diminishes T's life. The next morning as T gets ready for work again, his young son might tell him: 'No Daddy – no work. Work's closed. No. Work's closed.'

T earns £10.90 an hour, which brings him a salary of £20,423 a year without overtime, a figure above the UK living wage of close to £16,000 but below the median wage of £30,000 a year. He's still employed via the agency that got him the job when he was 20. (Young people increasingly use an agency to find their first job, as companies make permanent contracts rarer.) Sometimes, as for T, the permanent contract doesn't come; perhaps it will never come. He can't count on his hours or claim sick pay and doesn't have access to all the services more secure employees do; he sits alongside colleagues on permanent contracts who are paid £3, £4 and £5 an hour more than him. A campaign led by his union, the Communication Workers' Union, led to him being put on the same accelerating pay scale as permanent employees three years ago, following EU legislation on temporary workers. He was lucky to get in before agencies developed 'Pay Between Assignments' contracts, which keep workers on less money because of the way they got the job. These new zero-hours arrangements use a legal loophole to stop workers claiming equal pay with their colleagues after the three-month trial period; several agency workers on PBA contracts I approached felt too vulnerable to talk to me. A contract is seen as a 'golden ticket' by workers and a 'carrot' by managers, according to Jonathan Bellshaw, the CWU representative for T's call centre. It seems that for each new generation coming into the workplace, the conditions get worse.

On 5 January 2015, the first working day after Christmas, adverts appeared on underground trains. In black type on canary yellow, there was a sentence – 'It's as if someone were out there making up pointless jobs just for the sake of keeping us all working' – which came from an article by David Graeber for *Strike!* magazine about 'bullshit jobs'. Productive jobs, he argues, have been automated away and replaced by administrative ones which masquerade as service: HR, PR, financial services, ancillary industries like dog-washing and all-night pizza delivery. These are the bullshit jobs that are, you could add, very like T's. It's work that looks like work – it fills up a forty-hour week – but that feels pointless to the people doing it and which no one would miss if it disappeared. 'The moral and spiritual damage that comes from this situation is profound,' Graeber writes. 'It is a scar across our collective soul. Yet virtually no one talks about it.''When the stress of it all gets to you, it doesn't matter what you do to separate work from home,' T said. 'I've been on antidepressants twice at least here. You can't separate home from work, and because I'm agency there's no sick pay for it. So when I've had that, I've just had to put up and shut up. It's not like I can take off a month to pull my head together, because there's just no financial way to be able to do it. I had a rough spell of it recently with an interaction with my manager but I'm hopefully getting beyond that because that really did have a negative effect on me, to the point where I was contemplating not coming back in. I was really close to saying: "Sod it. It's not worth it. I'd rather have something minimum wage and not deal with that." But I came back and I'm still here.' Unqualified or low-skilled workers used to be valued for the things they did – work that may have exacted a physical toll, but might leave them enough mental space for the life they wanted to live outside of it. Now they are valued for emotional resilience, and the shortfall is left to Seroxat and Heineken. Would T be happy to think that his identity came from what he does all day? 'I really hope not. I could not say enough how I hope not. I used to like who I was, and if this place is now my identity, then I don't like myself. Literally, apart from the few people that I can sit and have a chat with and a gas with, the money is only just passable as the reason I come here. So, if the money changed, or certain people didn't work here any more, I can safely say I would probably be at the Job Centre looking.'

Phil Reilly, 32, special adviser, Downing Street

At the Liberal Democrat autumn 2013 party conference in Glasgow, I watched the side aisles of the main auditorium of the Scottish Exhibition and Conference Centre. They were mostly empty, but during the conference set-pieces – Nick Clegg's rally speech at the beginning, Vince Cable's on the economy a few days later – they filled up with young men in blue or grey suits with security passes around their necks. I'd read about special advisers, or spads, advising that 11 September 2001 would be a 'good day' to bury bad news, watched fictional ones on *The Thick of It*, even seen them in the background of photos in the newspaper; here, in the flesh, they leaned against the walls of the auditorium and crossed their shined brogues over one another. They must have been listening to the speeches but I saw them stroking their smartphones, glancing down at the day's paper, rocking their heels, checking their watches and yawning (three hours a night during conference season, I'd heard, was a decent night's sleep).

Spads – who many see as more important than democratically elected junior ministers – have grown in number since they arrived with Harold Wilson in 1964, and most ministers in the coalition government have at least two: one for policy and one for press strategy. (Spad numbers declined under Thatcher, who 'discouraged' them, but doubled under New Labour. Gordon Brown had nineteen – the most of any minister so far – at the Treasury.) Their job is to make sure their minister's political will is being felt in their department; they're not public servants in the way civil servants are, but they are servants, and ones often suspected – think of Alastair Campbell, Andy Coulson, Damian McBride – to be working to their own agenda. A recent survey of spads found that they are most likely to be 33, male and to have studied politics at Oxford or Cambridge; after four or so years as a spad they frequently move into the business world. They exist at the edges of power, operating via briefings and bollockings, influencing what happens in the centre. 'Politics is all about proximity to power,' Phil Reilly, a spad to Nick Clegg, said in Portcullis House over coffee in March 2013. His preferred aisle in conference week is the dark back balcony one; a paceable strip outside becomes his Glasgow office, where he talks with soft conviction on his mobile phone. In July 2014, a year into the job, Reilly moved to 10 Downing Street to a desk in the office that used to belong to Alastair Campbell.

A handful of tourists in anoraks huddle by the black gates protecting Downing Street on a drizzly morning in August 2014. Reilly has invited me for coffee during the parliamentary recess; the press pens opposite the glossy black door are empty. I am told to leave my phone in the entrance hall (I choose pigeon-hole 10) and the geometric carpet along the corridors and the burgundy leather armchairs in the waiting room make me think of the glimpsed uncool living quarters of a National Trust home. We walk via the yellow staircase lined with prime ministerial portraits, and he pauses by the black and white stare of Lloyd George; when we reach the top he points up to a Tracey Emin neon – installed by Cameron in 2011– which demands 'More Passion'. (If you look down the staircase you see a huge carved globe on top of a Persian-style rug at the bottom of the stairwell, as if nothing's been altered since it was first furnished in the 1680s.) We camp in Lord Young's office, pouring the coffee that has been laid out for us into white porcelain cups. There are tasteful government art collection photos of blue and white icescapes on the walls; I spot a Yo! Sushi executive's business card lying on the desk.

I first met Reilly in June 2004 when we worked together in the Saga motor insurance call centre in Folkestone. He had just finished a degree in Film Studies at the University of Kent. We learned to log prangs and crashes, to enunciate, explain and navigate computer systems. Reilly took it all just seriously enough; he and his friend Nick made me laugh a lot more than I expected to in a minimum wage job. I left at the end of the summer to study for a master's in English Literature; Reilly stayed. He had wanted to write novels when he was little; at

13 he wanted be a journalist at the *New Musical Express*. After a year in the call centre he took four weeks' leave to do work experience at the local paper. At the end of that month, he was offered a job at the *Dover Express* on a salary of £12,600 a year.

As a reporter Reilly covered David Cameron's visit to a walk-in clinic in Medway: 'I remember I spent the whole time trying to photograph him underneath this poster that they had on the wall that said: "How do you know if you've got gonorrhoea?" I did get it but it was a bit blurry and it wasn't useable,' Reilly laughs. 'It just went on my Facebook instead.' (Reilly's father stood unsuccessfully for the Lib Dems in Newham when Reilly was less than a year old, but at least beat the Conservative candidate: 'I reckon the cute baby in the pram at the time was probably good for a few of those votes – I take that as the first time I ever beat a Tory!') Reilly wasn't actively political when I knew him, but as we drink our coffee he says that seeing hospitals shut ward by ward when he was working on the *Dover Express* affected him. He covered a crack den raid, which turned out to be two doors down from where a 16-year-old mother of two lived, behind the hospital that was closing, and across the road from a school that was being condemned. He stood on the pavement for hours while police combed the house and neighbours peeked around their net curtains, long enough for a group of 8-year-olds to start kicking a worn-out tennis ball around in front of a 'No Ball Games' sign. 'I wouldn't say it was like an epiphany moment or anything, because I didn't exactly walk away from it going: "Oh God, I'm going to get involved in politics," but it was, if you like, one of those moments that highlights to you how many different problems politics can create and politics can solve. In the general negative tone in which politics is discussed,' Reilly said, 'I think it's mostly overlooked that it is about public service.'

Does he reach for his phone as soon as he wakes up? 'Yes.'

Because he's wondering what's happened? 'Wonder ... is a very positive word to use for it. It's more a ... It's long past the point that I do it out of natural curiosity, now I do it out of my work routine. At that stage, first check of phone, it's checking that nothing major has happened.' He's up at 6 a.m. and commutes by bus from the flat in North London he shares with his fiancée, a political campaigns consultant, listening to the *Today* programme and reading the press briefing he receives by email every morning. Before he gets to work he'll buy a coffee from Caffè Nero by Westminster tube or from the No. 10 café: 'Coffee is a big part of my working existence,' Reilly deadpans. 'If I could inject it I probably would.' He has a meeting in No. 10 at 8.15 a.m. with the Tory spads and the civil service press team to run through that day's news and what's coming up; a meeting at 8.45 a.m. to catch up with the Lib Dem communication team at HQ; then a meeting at 10.30 a.m. in Clegg's office.

The day unfolds from there: he'll field calls from journalists wanting to speak to Clegg, and brief him for any interviews that are scheduled. He'll weigh up whether the issue of the day is something the party should be involved in: 'Say, for example, the Conservatives have said something awful about benefits claimants, which we fundamentally disagree with. We have to decide if we want to weigh in on the story by disagreeing publicly. Now, welfare reform is one of the key reforms the government's doing. Actually for very good reasons: we've got a benefits system that basically discourages people going into work. There are large parts of the country where you have generations of people not in work – I saw that in parts of Dover. So there's a problem that needs to be solved and you need to do it by reforming welfare so that you incentivise work even at the lowest pay. So I think there's a progressive argument for it. But the Tories know that publicly, and with their supporter base in particular, the progressive argument is not the one that's most powerful. It's the punitive one: scroungers and ... So they use that language a lot to describe something that we would want to describe in a different way. But when they're using that language, that's what the story's about. So we have to decide if we want to argue back and in doing so risk a row with them on their terms. You might think you can make a different argument for the same reforms, that you could make this case for the progressive need for benefit reform while defending people who have fallen on hard times, but that's not always how it comes across. The way it can be framed by the media – especially in the right wing press – can mean people don't hear the substance of the argument. They hear a row with all the nuance lost and your message is gone with it. So it's all about being aware of how any intervention you might make is likely to be reported. I'm not saying we duck rows on benefit reform, obviously we don't, but it's an example of what you have to consider when you decide whether to respond to something in the news and how you do so.'

At lunch he'll get a sandwich and some apple juice from the stacked-high Westminster Tesco, or bask briefly in the Pret Behaviours at the other end of Whitehall. In the afternoon there will be speeches to vet, press releases to examine in detail, formal and informal briefings with journalists, media strategy to work on as well as reacting to whatever is happening on the news that day. Another of Reilly's roles has been to accompany Clegg on country-wide visits. 'Some local reporters – and I did this myself when I was one – see a visit from a well-known politician as a chance for a "Gotcha!" moment. So we might be there to talk about childcare policies, or school funding, or apprenticeships, and the reporter will politely ask a question or two about that and then attempt to hit Nick with a zinger about tuition fees, or our poll ratings, or something negative designed to get a rise out of him. That happened a lot in the first year of government, after the controversy of forming the coalition with the Tories and the tuition fees policy. There's not a lot you can do about that beyond making sure Nick is prepared for it and ensuring that the story you are there to talk about is strong enough to be newsworthy for them in its own right.' His exasperation with the local press is that of the poacher turned gamekeeper. 'The bolshiest journalists in the country,' he says, 'are regional TV political correspondents. They always try to ask extra questions. And so I have to quietly threaten them with not speaking to them next time we come into the area, and that sort of bollocks.' (Reilly told me that real-life spads swear a lot less than their fictional counterparts in *The Thick of It*, but I'm not sure I believe him.)

When Parliament is in recess, he sometimes leaves at 5 p.m., but he can be at work until 10 p.m. He's used to giving tickets for football games away at the last minute because he can't use them. At weekends, he sleeps. 'I basically have no life. This is my life! One day when all of this is over I'll find time to remember the things I used to be interested in.' He knows his job can only last as long as the government does: 'I've got no complaints about the work. It's long hours and perhaps the work–life balance isn't all that, but you know, it's a privilege to be doing this sort of work and I enjoy it. I don't think I'd be here if I didn't. I've done some ... less enjoyable jobs in the past, so I think it would be a bit precious to complain about it.' He earns around £50,000 a year, less than the £64,000 threshold at which a spad's salary must be made public. Both David Cameron and Ed Miliband were spads before they led their parties, and although Reilly thinks about going into politics proper, he disagrees with parachuting candidates into safe seats: 'My big problem is that the places I care most about are not ones that are likely to have a Lib Dem MP any time soon.' And besides, he likes being a spad: 'It's nice to be doing something important, that feels important,' Reilly says. 'When decisions are made, they're important decisions and you're able in some way to influence them.' Proximity and influence and flattery are all part of a spad's armoury: 'I'm not going to say Nick would ask my advice on forming benefits policy.' But he might end up talking to him about it? 'We might well talk about it.'

Machiavelli argued that a prince's choice of his servants was of 'no little importance' because faithful, capable servants suggest a wise prince; Clegg's choices reflect on Reilly: 'He's a really nice guy. He's genuinely a really nice guy. Especially since he's come under attack in that post-election period. I'd known him for a couple of years before then, and obviously we all got very excited during Cleggmania. We all thought, you know ... You try not to get carried away but a little part of you thinks, you know, we've always been the underdogs and we're in the spotlight, and this guy I really respect, he's now getting all this adulation. And then when it turns, you're kind of like: "No!" Because it's your team, you know, your guy.' They are each other's guys: Nick 'might recommend something and I'll go and read that. That's how I ended up reading the David Mitchell book, *The Thousand Autumns of Jacob de Zoet*, because Nick recommended it. He reads a lot of books. He's very literate guy. And I think there's quite a bit of crossover between what I read and what he reads anyway.' Was he happy to mould himself to his boss's tastes, valet-like? 'But, I hadn't ... I don't know, maybe it is subconsciously trying to please him, I don't know. I never really thought of it like that.' Reilly's job is to judge the political mood of the nation as well as that of his boss; I thought of Ina working out the mood of a client who came up to her central London flat, and working out the best way to soothe him.

LEADING

company director
stay-at-home mum
hereditary lord

Susan Rice, 68, company director, Edinburgh and London

Most women today work, but they rarely lead. When the Conservatives and the Liberal Democrats signed a coalition agreement in the spring of 2010, they included a wish to 'promote gender equality on the boards of listed companies'. At the beginning of the twentieth century, women made up 29 per cent of workers – formally entering the workplace when their husbands, sons, friends and fathers were away fighting the First World War – and by 2000, they made up 45 per cent of workers. Now the majority of women work outside the home. The Fawcett Society have shown that they are more likely to have zero-hours contracts, to work part time and in the lower-paid public sector.

The Europeans legislate against the inequality. In 2003, Norway set a quota: at least 40 per cent of board members would have to be women by 2006. Spain, France and Germany followed. The former EU Justice Commissioner, Viviane Reding, has proposed an EU-wide quota of 40 per cent by 2020, but legislation has stalled following opposition from the UK, among others. The British way is more informal. Why can't change be voluntary? It stands to reason that in a globalised business world, companies can't afford to ignore half of the population. To nudge foot-dragging firms along, organisations like the 30 Per Cent Club create mentoring programmes and target investors in companies with few women on their boards. (There are two boards in the FTSE 100 with no women members: Antofagasta and Glencore Xstrata, both mining companies.) In the USA, women are encouraged to look to themselves. Sheryl Sandberg, the COO of Facebook, said in her book, *Lean In: Women, Work, and the Will to Lead*, that women haven't positioned themselves well in the marketplace: they still don't speak up, let their partner hold the baby or lean into a career that's heading for maternity leave. What women can do in the world is determined by what they think is possible, she says, as well as by what the world allows them to do.

Susan Rice, 68, became the first woman to run a clearing bank in the UK – clearing banks are the foundational banks in the system – when she was appointed Chief Executive of Lloyds TSB Scotland in 2000. With a handful of women running FTSE 100 companies and a couple of hundred sitting on their boards, she is rare. 'I didn't grow up aspiring to do these things, but somehow I am.'

She never used to think about her gender much. She was often the only woman in the room, but 'that was how the world was, and you just got on with it'. But when she got the top job at Lloyds TSB Scotland she started to get letters: women would say how wonderful it was to see her on the twenty-seven-strong top table at the annual bankers' dinner, but could she wear a brighter dress next year so that she would *really* stand out? (Rice, who has neat bobbed power hair and wears modest skirt suits, added a green one to her collection.) Since becoming a female role model, she's taken on a new obligation to speak about women, not exactly as a feminist – she's 'not sure' she would call herself one – but as someone who believes that companies which reflect the diversity of the population do better. She 'absolutely believes that women have a huge amount to give, in equal measure to men'. Rice wants to be known for her abilities: 'I don't know any woman who sits on a board who wants to be there to meet a quota, because they want to feel that they've worked hard and merit the role.'

Rice was born in 1946 and grew up in Rhode Island. As a young child, she wanted to drive a train: 'In the middle of the night, if I ever woke up, I could hear the hoot of a train in the distance, and I used to just love that sound.' She thought of being an architect, as her father had once been, or flying planes, or of being an actress, but when she started at Wellesley, a year 'above or below, I can't remember which,' Hillary Rodham soon-to-be Clinton, she majored in philosophy and biology. With no previous science at all, in her first-year science course Rice found herself looking through a microscope the wrong way round 'and that made me want to stay with science, which was the last thing I ever thought I would do. Just to prove to myself I could do it, and that I could understand it, that I could get it.' She went on to study philosophy of science at Aberdeen University (having met her British husband, Duncan Rice, who was on a fellowship at Harvard, at a party) and then worked as part of a research team in a lab back in the US at Yale Medical School.

Having proved herself as a scientist, she changed tack and became a dean at Yale College, helping administer the under-graduate side of Yale University. This was in 1973, four years after women had first been admitted, and was followed by a stint in upstate New York, still in academia, at Colgate University. And then her husband was offered a job in New York City. She got in touch with people in financial services and in publishing there, 'I didn't know what networking was, but that was what I was doing,' and chose banking: 'I might have thought: publishing, well, that would have been closer to where I started out in life, but actually I turned to banking because that was the harder thing for me to do. There was this thing of learning, of proving to myself I could do it.' Like the microscope? 'Exactly the same thing. Exactly the same thing. Just to prove that I could do it. And I said to myself, if I failed at it, I would do it for a year, it would help get us settled in Manhattan and then I could look around and figure out what to do.'

She worked in several senior roles for NatWest Bancorp, often heading projects no one else wanted to do because they weren't on the standard career track. 'But I wound up with a broad knowledge of banking and a profile I would never otherwise have had.' Her husband was offered the vice chancellorship at Aberdeen University in 1996; she took a post at the Bank of Scotland. She was then headhunted to be Chief Executive and later Chairman of Lloyds TSB Scotland. She went into the interview with a few calculations made on the margins of the annual report. They phoned to offer her the job before she'd even made it home. Did she really want the challenge, her husband asked? 'And I thought about it and said "Yes – because I haven't done this type of role before."'

Christine Lagarde, the head of the IMF, has said that the banking crisis wouldn't have reached the same scale if Lehman Brothers had been Lehman Sisters. Although Rice disagrees – she'd rather see a mix – she's proud of her results at Lloyds TSB Scotland: 'The bank doubled in size on a four-year rolling basis for a number of years. Customers thought far more highly of us at the end of my stint than at the beginning. Staff engagement scores were much higher. And during the financial crisis, the loan portfolio that we built didn't suffer much at all because we'd been prudent – maybe not all that exciting – and we still made a profit. So I feel very good about that. We were what a bank should be – a growing successful business providing a real service that people needed.' Rice was tempted to leave Lloyds and to concentrate on her board and company director roles in 2009 when so much change was happening, but the bank persuaded her to remain. She stayed for two reasons: a sense of obligation to her staff at a difficult time, and because 'everyone in society was blaming someone else, it was a time when some bankers figuratively hid behind dark glasses. I felt that there have to be some of us who are willing to stand up and say: actually, society needs banks, most bankers are good people, and we need to see that there's a way ahead, we need to see our way out of this.' Rice was asked to become chairman of a new initiative to create professional standards for bankers in the UK for the first time.

Good bankers are rare in books and films, and even the good ones were once boring. The children's father in *Mary Poppins* is a bowler-hatted figure who heads to the Bank of England every day until he's sacked and lightens up; Jarvis Lorry in Dickens's *Tale of Two Cities* saves the heroine from ruin, battling his love of the accounting ledger to do so. Augustus Melmotte from Trollope's *The Way We Live Now* portrays the downfall of a banker who believed he could buy his way up in society. (Rice loves Trollope – 'I read every one of Trollope's novels years and years ago. And then I read them all over again about ten years ago' – but she has no interest in Melmotte.)

Rice's style is unusual by any standards. When she worked at Lloyds, she started her day at 6 a.m., getting to her Edinburgh office at 6.30 a.m., where she would have a bowl of cornflakes and a cup of green tea while reading her emails on her iPad. The day would be spent in meetings and she usually skipped lunch unless it was put directly in front of her. Away from home during the week, she worked most evenings, either writing speeches or representing Lloyds at an event; she only drank on the weekends. (Tonight we eat lightly at a bistro opposite the Bank of England: burrata, sea trout and a decaffeinated americano.) On weekdays, she lived in her flat in Edinburgh, or came on business trips to London. But the family home is in Aberdeen and holidays are spent on the Isle of Harris in the Outer Hebrides (the sister island to the Isle of Lewis).

Across the corporate world, CEOs boast of 5 a.m. workouts; confess to Steve Jobs-style perfectionism and saving decision power by owning only blue or grey suits. Gone are long liquid lunches, making a call to a pal from school and knocking off early to go to the golf course. CEOs are now more frugal, sensible, you might even say feminine. Could the world of work be gently leaning towards women? Rice took only a few weeks' maternity leave (as is usual in the USA where her career began) and worked as she raised two sons and a daughter: 'I always had the view that I would go nuts without having grown-up conversation. I just knew that about myself.' She had childcare and support from parents of her children's friends and she kept the week for work and the weekend for family. Along with the early starts and streamlined wardrobe, perhaps another aspect of modern leadership is the ability to be a parent at work and a CEO at home. Caroline Pay, the advertising creative director, described the pleasure of leaving the domestic world behind her when she puts on her lipstick to go to work; Rice separates her work and home lives geographically.

Rice says she surrounds herself with colleagues who can do certain things better than she can; she's good at listening, then drawing out the relevant facts; and synthesising different points of view. She asks lots of questions. 'When I first went into banking I had to get genuinely comfortable with saying "I'm ignorant, I don't know, so help me understand,"' she says of her style of leadership. At 1960s Wellesley, she remembers having long conversations about the war in Vietnam, the civil rights movement, what government was for and what a citizen's duties were. These big questions have stayed with her, perhaps influencing her intensive engagement in financial inclusion and economic development. Now her life fits into the British corporate world: her official title is Lady, as her husband has been knighted; she served on the board, or Court, of the Bank of England (she had tripped on a visit to the Bullion Yard the week we had dinner and wore a square of white gauze above her left eye) and she advises the Scottish government as well as one of Britain's biggest supermarkets and an energy company. Rice became chairman of Scotland's first Fiscal Commission last year and, since leaving Lloyds at the end of 2014, she is taking on several new roles on boards. Her career has been about weaving her own path through her work and her home lives, her American and her British sides, her 1960s beginnings and the eventual establishment trappings, between what a bank is and what it might become.

Rakhshanda Hussain, 41, stay-at-home mum, Finchley

Just before Christmas 1982, Margaret Thatcher gave an interview to a children's TV programme, where she answered questions on her clothes (she was sad not to go to the shops any longer), on women's lib ('I'm not very keen on it') and on those who impersonate her ('great fun'). Then a boy asked her who was the dominant person in her household: 'I don't think we have a dominant,' she said. 'To some extent I think ... don't you think a mother is a very dominant person in the sense that she runs the home? It's quite a management job, you know. I think we girls do a lot more management in a way than some of the men do, because running the home – I get very upset when I hear people say, "I'm only a housewife." I say: "Only a housewife? My goodness me, you're manager of a home, you make all the decisions. You know, you don't just go out and do a job in which you're part of a great big factory, you're actually in charge of running a home."' Running a home as well as being a research chemist and then a barrister was the ideal apprenticeship for her eleven years as prime minister. She explained herself to the electorate during the 1979 campaign that would bring her to Downing Street by saying that 'any woman who understands the problems of running a home will be nearer to understanding the problems of running a country'. Inside her trapezoidal handbag, you imagined a can of Elnett hairspray, government papers and a shopping list.

Running a home takes the sort of leadership that qualifies you for everything and nothing. It's both the pinnacle of womanhood and its lowest common denominator; the work nearly everyone has witnessed and the work that is least understood. Rakhshanda Hussain, 41, took me to the park near her flat in East Finchley, while her 4-year-old son (the younger of her two children) scooted in front of us: 'I find it a little bit difficult talking to you,' she said, 'because you're not a mum, and I didn't get it before I became a mum.' 'The way Maggie ran the country, yes, a lot of people didn't like it, but every drop makes an ocean,' Hussain said. 'I don't believe in living on credit.' Her family isn't 'stretched for money', but they are frugal nevertheless: 'I kind of see things in terms of opportunity cost. I just don't want to be one of those mums who gets twenty years down the line and thinks: "Why didn't I spend that time with my babies? What was I thinking?" Because that time is not recoverable.' Hussain's son wants to be pushed on the swing, so we continue talking as he seesaws his 4-year-old legs into the late morning sunshine. 'Higher!' She pushes him. 'Higher!' She pushes him again. 'HIGHER!'

Hussain went to university, did a summer in Montpellier, worked as a journalist and then moved into HR in the City. She gave birth to her first child while she and her husband were working in Singapore, and went back to work when she had used up her maternity leave. She would get up at 4 a.m. to nurse and get her daughter ready before leaving the house at 7.30 a.m. She quit her job six months later: 'I was so happy. It was just a joy to be able to take her to playdates, just hang out with her really. Each mother has to find their own way. It took me going back to work to realise how important that early bonding time is.'

We'd met at an event run by Mumsnet called Workfest, a day of talks and workshops encouraging mothers back to work at BAFTA in Central London. Mothers sipped coffee in carpeted rooms normally populated by movie stars; from the stage, the stories were of triumph but when the floor was opened to questions, the mums asked things like: 'But how do I get my husband to help?' Hussain's husband had suggested she come to Workfest: her youngest would go to school in September, and she was thinking about what work she might like to do next. One woman told the Mumsnetters how she had started a business in her attic room handsewing quilts. Hussain was inspired. 'It gives her the pleasure, or the satisfaction, of having finished something. Or produced something. I think a lot of mums don't have that. They're just: "What are we doing? Running around after kids."' She called herself a 'massive feminist who recognises we live in a man's world. We live in a patriarchal society. Men are expected to go out and earn the bread. The women, yeah, we've got the opportunity to go back to work but let's face it, it's at the cost of doing everything outside and inside.' Men 'just go to work and just expect meals to be cooked and kids to be fed, washed and watered. They think magic fairies exist! Because they don't put a value on housework, they're like what did you do with your day? So you have to find that worth yourself. I strongly believe in gender definition. It's like the Six Sigma system of running a company in the sense that men and women have their own roles and contributions to make to the tranquility and efficiency of the home.'

In *The Second Sex*, Simone de Beauvoir saw cleaning the house as a way to hold away death but refuse life; Ann Oakley called housework 'work directly opposed to the possibility of human self-actualisation'. In 1963, Betty Friedan documented the suffering of the seemingly perfect housewife in *The Feminine Mystique*. 'Is this all?' she asked, as she slept all day, cried for no reason, felt as if she had no personality, took her tranquillisers or poured another Martini. One woman described her morning's work washing, getting the children to school, gardening, reading the paper, making a phone call for the committee and added: 'By noon, I'm ready for a padded cell. Very little of what I've done has been really necessary or important.' Friedan advises women not to make running a home into a production – there's no need to bake your own bread – and to find some sort of fulfilling work outside the home that allows 'just a housewife' to think of herself as a person. Eleven years later, Silvia Federici, a writer and activist informed by the Italian Autonomist tradition, came up with a more radical answer to the same problem. She agreed that housework turned women into something less than servants: 'We are seen as nagging bitches, not workers in struggle,' she wrote in the 1974 pamphlet *Wages for Housework*. 'We are housemaids, prostitutes, nurses, shrinks; this is the essence of the "heroic" spouse who is celebrated on "Mother's Day". We say: stop celebrating our exploitation, our supposed heroism. From now on we want money for each moment of it, so that we can refuse some of it and eventually all of it.' For too long women had campaigned for inching practical measures – 'day care, equal pay, free laundromats' as Federici puts it – when what was needed was an attack on 'our female role at the roots' by making women's work visible to capital by asking for money for it. With the British writer Selma James, who I'd seen trailed by a sheepdog and a labrador at the ECP's offices when I went to interview Ina, Federici set up the Wages for Housework Campaign, which continues to this day. Instead of agitating for more waged labour, to put another crack in the glass ceiling and occupy another board seat, women would redefine what work is: Why is writing an email work and feeding a baby not work? Friedan and Wages for Housework came up with two different solutions to the problem, but they agreed on its nature. It wasn't the cooking and cleaning; it was the 'smiling and fucking' – the emotional labour service work also calls for – as well as the pretence that it was offered happily that made the work unbearable. 'Just how natural it is to be a housewife,' Federici wrote in her 1974 pamphlet, 'is shown by the fact that it takes at least twenty years of socialisation – day-to-day training, performed by an unwaged mother – to prepare a woman for this role.'

Hussain's son howls as he gets caught in a spinning merry-go-round and his knee drags along the bouncy tarmac. 'It's not bleeding, silly banana,' she says and pulls a flapjack from her bag – 'That's another thing mums do: they always carry food with them' – and breaks it up for him into smaller pieces. Hussain looks back at how she grew up: 'Now that I've become a mum I realise it's my responsibility to educate and inspire my own children and to be the best role model that I can be for them. Being a mum, emotionally, takes a lot out of you. I went back to mosque because I just felt my soul needed feeding. I've gone back to it in a big way.' She grew up in a practising household (though she didn't, and doesn't, wear the veil), and goes to her local mosque every Wednesday and Saturday. She has signed her daughter up to Saturday school. 'A lot of people see Islam as a religion that oppresses women. It doesn't oppress, Islam empowers women to take ownership of their familial respon-sibilities. I don't feel bad about not working: it's my job to keep the family together and provide a place of tranquility for my spouse. I'm happy I have that clarity. A woman's role is equally if not more important than a man's. But it's different roles. It's a woman's responsibility to educate the children spiritually – to feed the soul, and the body, and the mind. That's a big job, right, on top of their physical needs, looking after the husband and obviously in our culture, when you get married, you're respon-sible for sustaining the family bond for your extended family. As a parent, I have a new appreciation of everything my mother did for me. That security is so important.'

Islam has given Hussain the confidence to be a stay-at-home mum. 'I personally think the government has a lot to answer for,' Hussain said. 'The mindset in the UK is: "What do you do? What do you earn? Who do you work for?" Work defines us:

who you are and what you do. But I think it's about how you're contributing to society in the long term.' Hussain has battled with herself about not working, but had come to her own peace. 'Why is it not OK to be a stay-at-home mum?'

Hugh Crossley, 42, hereditary lord, Suffolk

When Hugh Crossley was 18, he inherited a 5,000-acre estate in Suffolk, an Anglo-Italian mansion with a bell tower, two stuffed polar bears, gardens with a maze and the businesses – arable and livestock farming, a lake, a pub and a hotel – that go with them. On a wet May day, our tour group in blue overshoes is being shown the old entrance hall, with its dark wood panelling and green, cobalt and terracotta patterned tiles. I'm the youngest person here. We steam in our rain jackets as we are told the four white tiger skins were brought back from India; the jockey scales were stood by the door as a test of Victorian hospitality (you were supposed to put on weight during an evening here); the doll's house replica of the hall had been made by the estate staff for the fifth birthday of Lord Somerleyton's aunt Mary in 1931; the shiny animal hoof reworked into a doorstop once belonged – can you guess? – to a water buffalo. When the narrator of W. G. Sebald's *Rings of Saturn* came to Somerleyton, he was charmed by 'the sheer number of things, possessions accumulated by generations and now waiting, as it were, for the day when they would be sold off'. Standing upright in the fierce two-armed pose animals take on heraldic shields, the yellowing polar bears – caught by the first Lord Somerleyton on a trip to the Arctic in 1897 – showed their pointed teeth. A couple in fleece pullovers stood in front of the frozen animals: 'They're horrible really, ain't they?'

The current Lord Somerleyton, Hugh Crossley – his portrait, disconcertingly Hugh Grant-like, hangs above the 1953 coronation chairs – took over the pleasure palace bought by his great-great-grandfather in 1862, when his father at 75 learned he had Alzheimer's and decided to retire to a smaller house on the estate. The Crossleys' fortune was made in nineteenth-century Halifax when they developed and patented steam looms for carpet-weaving: 'Let each carpet produced by John Crossley be its own traveller,' the slogan went. The Crossley family bought the house from Samuel Morton Peto, who built the Houses of Parliament and Nelson's Column before going bankrupt from his investments in the railways: he had to give up the house he'd extended, created a model village for and built a railway to. Crossleys have now lived at Somerleyton for 151 years: Savile, made a Baron in 1916 for his public service as a government minister, was the first to grow up here, go to Eton and then serve in the Ninth Lancers; Francis, the second lord, went to Eton then served in the Ninth Lancers in the Great War; Savile, the third lord, went to Eton, served in the Ninth Lancers and became Master of the Horse; Hugh, the fourth lord, went to Eton, but dodged the Ninth Lancers; his 4-year-old son John, who will be the fifth lord, drives a tricycle with what looks like a gazelle hoof doorstop in its trailer through the house. I wonder if he'll go to Eton too.

To visitors, the house is charmingly faded, or an unthinkable burden, but to the current Lord Somerleyton, its 'nooks and crannies' are where he played as a child, picking up where the 'leaks, stopcocks and odd things' are, without noticing. He can walk through the estate in his head: 'Your mind can just go round like a drone and pretty much see every fencepost.' It is at once home, the family business, part of Britain's cultural and industrial history and the carrier of his family's reputation: 'There's a big big thing, a kind of genetic drive about continuing your name, your name to be continued through time, in a way that probably isn't necessarily the same with just sort of Joe Bloggs' – or Jo Biggs, I think – 'in the street, because of what you've come from. You don't want to be the one to screw it up. And you want it to be here, going on.'

The entrance to the part of the hall Lord Somerleyton lives in – the old servants' quarters – is strewn with bikes and tricycles and scooters. Larta, the housekeeper, opens the door. 'Sir! She's here!' Dogs run ahead of him to where I am trying to work out the best place to leave my wet raincoat. In jeans with rips at the knee, red and black running trainers and a caramel jumper, he has brown-grey swept-up hair and tanned skin with a few wrinkles. He takes me to a corner sitting room with a lit fire; a small clock on the mantelpiece, flanked by two candlesticks with pink candles, will chime the hours. Larta brings me a cup of tea in a mug printed with blue flowers.

Hugh Crossley didn't enjoy Eton. 'It's obviously a great school but I floundered and they didn't particularly look after flounderers very well.' He grew up believing that going into the army was what men did, but 'swerved away' at the last minute, studied history at university and began looking back to the first Crossleys instead: 'I was welded to this thing that there's an entrepreneurial gene that's died and it needs to come back to life. And it's my job.' From the moment he made a will at 18, and knew for certain that the estate was going to be passed to him, he understood that the house had to earn its keep. 'Dad kept going on, you've got to make money, Somerleyton needs money. And I ... I thought ... Either I've got to go into the City or I've got to start something myself.' The idea of the City brought 'out the socialist in me slightly' and so instead he opened a restaurant in London called Dish Dash: 'It was on everyone's lips as kind of the cool Middle Eastern place,' he remembers, 'and that was absolutely what I wanted to achieve.' His father's decision to stop running the estate in 2003 brought him back to Somerleyton, with a pang of regret: 'One's always a bit embarrassed about it. The bones of it are here already. I haven't created anything. I'm just doing what everyone else did: plant trees, you know, replant gardens. And it's a wonderful process of renewal and change and it's wonderful working with the experts involved, but you're kind of doing the same thing that everyone's done. It's a kind of glorified landowner role.'

Jane Austen wrote her eighteenth-century comedies of manners from the point of view of the heroines trying to find love and self-knowledge, but from the perspective of the estate-owning heroes, they're stories about men establishing them-selves against the previous generation. Darcy, with his £10,000 a year, struggles with his love for Elizabeth Bennet because his father's generation had chosen a dynastic marriage for him. Edward Ferrars in *Sense and Sensibility* is disinherited and left with £100 a year when he marries for love; Willoughby marries an heiress he doesn't much like for £50,000. (A happy resolu-tion to the problem is shown in the late novel *Persuasion*, when Wentworth, who is rejected by Anne Elliot's family for lack of money, makes £25,000 in the Napoleonic wars.) There is a parricidal aspect to inheriting an estate. The Halifax carpet factory finally closed in 1982, but money had been draining away from the business since the 1920s. The house was first opened to paying visitors in 1958 by Hugh's father. 'I was a pretty naive rural boy,' Hugh says, 'and Dad was lord-in-waiting to the queen and it just seemed set so. It was only quite late into early adulthood, you realise that what was so wasn't that rock-solid.' His father made the house into an attraction in an era when the tearoom was run by ladies in the village, without pay, simply because they liked baking. Somerleyton has always been run by the family that lives there, without the help of English Heritage or the National Trust, and the professionalisation of the 'heritage day out' – when Hugh goes to a rival NT property, he notices the borders: 'Christ! There's just no weeds!' – has meant Somerleyton's 'faded grandeur' wasn't 'anywhere near good enough'. The estate was run by Hugh's father and two trustees, who were enjoined not to profit from the estate but also had a duty to invest wisely. Hugh met opposition when he tried to modernise the estate: 'It wasn't well managed by the trustees, by Dad, albeit he was scared himself. Everyone understands now they played a part in a really catastrophic handover. And in a sense I'm not the innocent party because I was a guy crashing around telling people what to do in a probably unsophisticated management way.'

The estate wasn't profitable when it came to Crossley – he had to sell assets to make it viable – and now he leads the estate it makes money in a sedate way, thanks to the holiday resort he's created. 'Forget what you see around here,' he jokes, the resort's 'the king. It's the king. It absolutely does what it says on the tin every single year.' In June 2013, Crossley opened a new venture with a business partner in Norwich: Hot Chip, a British version of a Belgian chip bar. ('Chips and Fish' is a portion of chips fried in rapeseed oil with 'crispy goujons of North Sea fish, tartare sauce with lemon' for £5.) He had a 'friendly spat' on Twitter with the band that shares the chip bar's name, and he invited them to the restaurant next time they play Latitude Festival, held nearby on the estate of his friend Hector. He hopes his Hot Chip will go nationwide: 'I don't want to be talked about for log cabins. I want to be rung up by Radio 4 programmes about entrepreneurial something, and food industry something, because of Hot Chip, not because of anything I'm doing here.'

The arrival of John – named after the first Crossley – has changed the way he thinks about the businesses. 'I don't want to be hiding worry from him in the way I'm sure Dad was from me.' He wants his tenure as the head of the estate to ensure John's freedom. 'We want to have done enough to say to John, here's a seriously profitable set of businesses and actually although we didn't have that – you don't want to sound too pious about it – you really have got a choice. Which is you really could stop opening to the public. You might even be able to stop doing weddings, or you might just cherrypick a few that are high value and not do the rest. Rather than be beholden to the beast, everyone is but no one wants to be, you want to feel like you're in control. But I need a few years to get to that point I think.' And leading the estate the way he wants to has brought him a sort of peace with his duty to the 5,000 acres. Hugh told the local paper when his father died in January 2012: 'At heart Dad was an estate man, a county man and, most of all, a great Englishman.' Hugh used to avoid the gardens when they were open to the public but now he'll 'stride about like Dad used to and just go and talk to people in the garden'.

Crossley doesn't 'have a career in a formal sense. Maybe I should have, but basically I'm ungoverned.' He gets up most days at 6 a.m. with his children, 4-year-old John, 2-year-old Christabel and baby Margot (born a few weeks after I visited Somerleyton), then takes a turn around the gardens at around 7.30 a.m., either on foot or on horseback with his wife, Lara, who helps him run the estate. The dogs run and he'll talk to the gardener. In the mornings, he might make a trip to Norwich to check on Hot Chip, but in the afternoon, after a toasted sandwich, he'll work in the estate barn that has been converted into an office, answering emails and talking with staff. 'Every now and again I'll say something to an employee that [Ben Davenport, joint CEO of Somerleyton] just cannot believe! "You just cannot do that kind of thing." And I say, "Hang on a minute, it's a family business!"'

His father used to chair local branches of the RNLI, NSPCC, St John Ambulance; Crossley has sat on the board of the Lowestoft Economic Development Framework, whose aim is to revive the town with transport and green energy infrastructure. Wartime bombing, the decline of the fishing industry and of tourism affected the town; now employment is 6 per cent lower than average; obesity and teen pregnancy rates are high and school results at 16 are 20 per cent below the rest of the UK. Crossley's 'not caught up in what one can and can't say': 'Using the dirty word class – you can talk about classless Britain as much as you like, it's nothing to do with that, a village needs layers,' which means the high as well as the low. 'I don't at all believe that you should be allowed to live in society and not work. It's fantastic that the dire state of our condition economically in the crash has allowed it to become politically acceptable to talk about this, because it's been a real problem. It has been literally untalkable about. Apparently it's totally fine to have three generations of benefit junkies who just don't work. And of course there needs to be room, and there needs to be the compassion in society to look after those who need to be looked after but it doesn't mean ... the altruistic mission for welfare for all is a really high-minded one but it's been very hard to manage and it's been very abused, and people have lost their way. Particularly since the 1980s. Thatcher made people greedy and dispassionate and frankly nasty and it's been pretty bad in society in lots of ways, but very good for the wealth of the nation. The next thing was a massive tilt the other way, with this massive state intervention and allowing people to think it's totally OK to do nothing and that's been kind of going on for a while and it's really cancerous and corrosive and bad.' Farming and rents have held up in the recession, despite a few more bad debtors, but he hasn't sold any holiday lodges since 2009. He didn't necessarily want to see the government, which is 'stuffed for money like everyone else', change in the 2015 election: 'To be fair, Tony Blair might have bankrupted us but he was certainly no enemy of people like me in the way that Miliband might be.'

Almost exactly three years after the run on Northern Rock, *Downton Abbey*, a TV series about an English country estate in the early twentieth century, aired on ITV in September 2010. The soothing Sunday evening soap opera made the country estate into a metaphor for the nation: the indebted Earl of Grantham must modernise; the kitchen maid must upskill; the daughter who loves across class lines must die of puerperal fever. For Lord Somerleyton, with his belief in the traditional class structures with layers high and low, the get-stuck-in values of his parents' time have 'been washed away, pretty much', but for the TUC, the Bullingdon Club elite is bringing a *Downton Abbey*-style society back to twenty-first-century Britain. If the nation is a family, and the family a nation, where does that leave women? Lord Somerleyton didn't know until he was 18 that his father would endow the estate according to primogeniture. Why would he? He has four older sisters.

ENTERTAINING

dancer
footballer
giggle doctor

Nathalie Harrison, 29, dancer, Covent Garden

In the £13 seats of the Royal Opera House in Covent Garden, rules no longer apply. A Russian balletomane with a white crocheted collar poses for an illegal photograph, the young men in the standing seats loudly rib each other, and as the lights go down for the overture to the first ballet in tonight's triple bill, Frederick Ashton's adaptation of *A Midsummer Night's Dream*, the woman next to me pulls out a banned punnet of strawberries and begins eating in time to burp at the entrance of Titania's fairies. I can't see from this angle what's happening in the orchestra stalls, where seats are £64. The boisterous summer audience bursts into laughter when Hermia convinces the ardent Lysander not to sleep beside her in the forest but to be content with a kiss, pointing unambiguously to her cheekbone. A dam is broken. There is giggling throughout the short hour in which the lovers are crossed and uncrossed; the fairies gasp at their queen's infatuation with a donkey who is wibbly on his pointe shoes; Titania and Oberon manipulate and humiliate and are reconciled to each other. At the end, Hermia and Lysander walk towards us arm in arm to Mendelssohn's wedding march, Titania and Oberon arabesque together and the curtain falls to applause. Flowers are handed to Laura Morera, who danced Titania, Olivia Cowley, who danced Helena, and there are two bouquets, one long and blue and another round and red, for Nathalie Harrison, who danced Hermia. It is the first time Harrison, who has been with the Royal Ballet since she was 18, has danced the role.

Two weeks before, at the first dress rehearsal for *The Dream*, the donkey had torn his head off with the complaint 'I can't see!'; Oberon couldn't get through the difficult scherzo section because of unexpectedly bright lights in the wings; the fairies had struggled to get on stage in time and Hermia had abandoned a slow arabesque halfway through and had slid unexpectedly down a tree she was supposed to be sleeping against. In rehearsal, you can see the work the dancers conceal in performance. On stage too, the glamour of even a debut dissipates quickly: the curtain call lasts a few minutes, flowers fill the bath for a couple of days. When the show is over, Harrison doesn't step out of the opera house into a limousine. She pulls up her hoodie against the rain and walks home, stopping for a pint of milk on the way. At home, she might take a salt bath, potter around, make a phone call, have a bowl of broth and a sandwich before bed. 'People sometimes think dancers are a bit precious, but we have to be careful. We do occasionally go out for one drink or no drinks. Otherwise you make it more difficult for yourself.'

Dancing is a 'complete lifestyle'. Harrison's days (every day apart from Sunday) begin with porridge and berries, before arriving at the Royal Opera House for 9.30 a.m. to do Pilates or prepare shoes. At 10.30 a.m. it's morning class, the dancing equivalent of 'waking up and brushing your teeth', where the whole company from the stars to those who have just joined work on technique. After a fifteen-minute break to change clothes, rehearsals begin at 12 p.m. – they learn up to five ballets at a time – continue for two hours, break again for fifteen minutes, often for a cup of tea, continue for two hours more and finish at 5.30 p.m. on a show day. When there's no show, they rehearse for another hour.

Before curtain up, Harrison might take a quick shower, dash to M&S for some food if she doesn't fancy the canteen that day, and try to catch her mum or sister on the phone. This is also the time to take ibuprofen and ice aching feet; or stop for a biscuit and a chat; or to nap, curling up on the window seat or on the fold-out mattress kept under the dressing room sinks. Each dancer has a dressing stall, studded with lightbulbs. Harrison's is part desk, part medicine cabinet, part wardrobe, part kitchen counter and part dressing table with chic Aesop deodorant. Newly shellacked shoes dry on a metal shelf and exhausted ones pile up in a cardboard box under the sink: dirty-pink, softened, sweat-soaked, or as Harrison puts it, 'ripe'.

It doesn't bother Harrison that the makers of her shoes have mostly never been to the ballet: 'If they were ballet fans I think I'd find it quite odd. They're doing their job and we're doing ours. It's the working world, I suppose.' Since Harrison's favoured maker retired she's been trying out O Maker, who I watched balance his day's shoes in the Well Street factory. She begins getting into make-up and costume at 6.15 p.m. before curtain up around 7 p.m. 'I'm either a fairy, a court lady or a whore any day of the week,' Harrison jokes. 'You'd be amazed how many courtesans there are in the repertoire.' Each show is different – she might not be on until two-thirds through, or she might be on constantly, changing costumes twice an act – but Christmas is the busiest time, when Harrison can sometimes hear young children gasp from the stage. At 11.30 p.m., once the show is over and the make-up's off, she might take a turn for nine minutes in the blue wheelie bin that doubles as an ice bath, her top half wrapped in a scarf, singing along to the songs on the radio, but otherwise it's on with the hoodie and out into the rain.

Harrison is tall – the tallest member of the corps – with enormous feet for a dancer: a body like that of Darcey Bussell, or back further, of Vergie Derman. She has a fine grand jeté – the bigger version of a leap over a puddle where dancers seem to do the splits in the air – but she doesn't turn as well as she thinks she should. In the 2013–14 season, she danced Dulcinea in *Don Quixote*, Lady Capulet in *Romeo and Juliet*, a Parent, a Snowflake and a Flower in *The Nutcracker* but was disappointed not to dance the Queen of the Wilis in *Giselle*, a role she'd understudied for six years. 'I've got the wealth of experience to launch and do things, just at the moment where heads turn to young, fresh talent.' Physical careers, such as dancing and playing football, are cruelly short. 'Of course it's cruel, it has to be cruel. What goes on that stage has to be absolutely what that director wants at that time. And he's not going to do something out of obligation or sympathy.' Knowing that she's approaching the end of her performing career, Harrison has done a diploma in dance education, getting up at 7 a.m. on Sundays to write her essays, and has got involved in raising the profile of the Royal Ballet and encouraging donors. (Donors contribute £20 million of the £114.6 million it costs to run the ballet and opera companies there every year. But the public grant to the opera house is falling: in 2015, they will receive £24.77 million, a reduction of £0.8 million on 2014; the Arts Council – whose budget the coalition government has cut by 30 per cent – added that both companies were paying a 'premium' on salaries and asked management to 'consider' the issue.) She doesn't yet know what she will do once her first career is over. 'I do have ambition beyond dancing. Some of my colleagues don't. I think it can be hard for any dancer to contemplate.'

Harrison doesn't always tell people she's a professional dancer, but when she does, they have interestingly wrong ideas. 'People say: "I was going to do that, but I became a lawyer." What? You don't understand what it is to be a ballerina! "Is that a full-time job? What do you do all day?" I rehearse for seven hours and then do a show. "Do they give you accommodation?" It's a job, not a school! I get PAYE, I have a mortgage!' Harrison represents the corps de ballet for Equity, the performers' union. It's not 'very powerful because everyone will dance anyway because they love it', but they're necessary. Apprentices start on a salary of £12,000; all dancers work fourteen-hour days Monday to Saturday with five weeks off in the summer, a week off in February, and a few days at Christmas. (Freelancers have it worse: they're paid £9.14 an hour during rehearsals, less than the box office staff's £10.70 an hour.) At Harrison's grade you earn around £35,000 a year. She knows 'everyone would happily pay us more, but no one's making money out of this. It's art! A few people make millions and millions but the rest of us won't. No one's doing it for the money.' 'There's people a lot poorer than us in London,' Harrison reasons. 'We're fine. But when you see what footballers earn it makes you want to cry! Because we're like, hang on a minute, we're kind of the equivalent in our field.' Principal dancers, the top of the profession, earn £50,000 a year. The lighter schedule of a principal make it possible to dance into one's fifties, as Fonteyn did, or to have a baby and come back to work, as Bussell did. The corps has less pressure and is less isolated, but is on every night. 'You can't strive for promotion just to use maternity leave!'

Harrison was a tomboy as a child in Weybridge in Surrey: painting, climbing trees, horse-riding. She started dancing at school and her teacher said she should continue out of school: 'It was only skipping in a circle but I liked it.' At 8, she was spotted by a scout at a class at the Royal Academy of Dance and invited to audition to become an associate at the Royal Ballet School, attending Saturday classes at the main boarding school at White Lodge, a Georgian royal hunting residence in Richmond Park. When she auditioned for the main school at the age of 11, she got in.

Her father (who was a sound technician for rock bands like The Who) promised her that she need only try out boarding for a few weeks. She was terrified. Other girls in her intake announced they'd been dreaming of this life since they were 2. But 'within the first year, I completely fell in love with how impossible it all felt'. She suspected she was just about making the grade, but as she progressed through the school, friends fell away. She'd started with a group of twenty-four 11-year-olds and only nine remained by the time they were 16. (Harrison shares a dressing room bay with Leanne Cope, whom she met at the school when 12; they were each other's bridesmaids when they both got married in summer 2014.) At school, Harrison says she was a 'geek': 'I loved history, I loved art, I loved working.' At 16, 'I was more like a 13-year-old really.' Life was held back for ballet, just as now, she can't ask for a day off to go to a birthday party or a baby shower. 'You're either in or out and that's it. That's quite hard for people to grasp. They're like: "She could have taken time off work," but you can't. Time off means missing a show. It's just not how it works. And that's where it's hard to find family and loved ones who get it, because if they don't, they get offended by that. But it's just the job.'

Harrison's training was about approaching perfection: 'we're all way over the line into obsession, but we're all the same so we think it's OK.' Her teachers told her she would be happy with only three performances in her entire career (the odds Fonteyn gave Roy Plomley on *Desert Island Discs* in 1965 were better: she was happy with one in twenty of her performances). It's an exigent way of life that she worries is being lost: 'I just despair at the whole X Factor generation. It really concerns me.' In an email, Harrison added: 'A lesson that my profession taught me early on and is imprinted upon me is that the most rewarding moments, and the achievements that feel spectacular, are those which you have worked so incredibly hard for. The harder you've worked, the greater the reward, and that is something I am not sure a lot of young people grasp. I think it fuels my dislike of fashionable TV talent shows: wanting to be famous, and crying and demanding it. There is a sense of people feeling they are owed something, but we have to earn success. Anything simply handed to someone doesn't produce the satisfaction that hard graft delivers.'

Harrison won the silver medal in the Genée International

Ballet Competition for young dancers in Sydney in 2002; later that summer she found out she was going to be offered a contract with the Royal Ballet, receiving the call while on the treadmill at the gym. She wasn't on every night of her first season: she first performed as a Shade in *La Bayadère* on 17 October 2003, arabesquing down a slope twenty-second in a line of twenty-four dancers. One of the most memorable weeks of her career was dancing Bussell's role in Christopher Wheeldon's *DGV (Danse à Grande Vitesse)* on the opening night of its revival on 31 January 2009. 'It was one of the best weekends of my life. Because I ... Loads of principals were off and I was the understudy. I'd done quite a bit considering I'd only been in the company five minutes, but I was still a kid. I was 25, 24, 25. I think they didn't want to say I was doing an opening night, but I was *doing an opening night*. I think it's one of the best I've ever danced.' Would it make her top three? 'Definitely, definitely. The next day was my birthday and all my family were up and watched it, and we went for drinks after the show and I just remember feeling ... happiness. It didn't feel like it was all about me, it felt like just a really happy time and I had tea at the British Museum the next afternoon. It was the first snow. The first snow of the year came that afternoon.' She was promoted from the entry-level rank of Artist to First Artist that summer, a reflection of that season's work. 'I never dreamed of that level of performance.'

The Royal Ballet itself was forged in an intense period of work. Ninette de Valois had assembled a company and a school at Sadler's Wells in 1926, but it was when the company danced on during the war, as part of the Entertainments National Service Association (nicknamed 'Every Night Something Awful'), that it came to reflect the nation's mood. Fonteyn, who had started out as Margaret Hookham in the corps, danced three *Swan Lakes* a week, and became the mascot of HMS *Aurora*. When the company reopened the Royal Opera House in 1946 with a performance of *Sleeping Beauty* in the presence of Attlee's Cabinet, it was seen as an 'awakening' for the country.

Fonteyn said morning class was 'therapeutic in times of stress'. Harrison danced the 2013–14 season knowing her father was very ill, and she was often called away at short notice. He had told her as a girl that even if she was 'holding a spear at the back' she should do it the best she could; when I asked her what she was most proud of – meaning in her career – she answered, without hesitation: 'My dad.' In November 2013, she danced the 'huge, angry, breathing' part of Lady Capulet, not a role 'that's thrown around and everyone gets a bash at'. Lady Capulet has to deal with her daughter defying her choice of suitor, the death of her nephew (whom she may have been in love with) at her own ball, and finally her daughter's death. 'I think with everything I had going on in my life, it was the perfect challenge,' Harrison said. 'Because had I had a technical challenge, it would probably have been more complicated for me to process, but this came at a good time. As I say, cathartic in some ways.' Harrison joked that the flesh-coloured swimming cap she wore in preparation for Lady Capulet's severe wig made her look like her dad; she showed me an iPhone picture from her last night as Lady Capulet. She stood on the opera house stage with her arms full of flowers, standing next to him.

In February 2014, he died. The company was working on Wheeldon's adaptation of Shakespeare's *The Winter's Tale*, in which death and loss are changed into life and love. Wheeldon's father had died the week before the opening of the show. The Bohemia scene in *The Winter's Tale*, where Harrison described herself as dancing 'with all her friends', seemed precious. When I met Harrison between her father's death and his funeral, she seemed to think about her profession differently: 'Ballet just demands hard work – there's no option. It really hurts. And the pain some days is like any pain, uncomfortable and not enjoyable, and other days it's riddled with the enjoyment. Hand in hand with how much you love it is how much it hurts. Which is really weird! I've just realised how much I've given to it now, actually, with everything that's happened, I've realised how much I've poured into it and I don't regret a drop of it, because of what you get back. It's everything. So. It's a complicated job, and it takes over everything and I've never resented it. But I have felt slightly: what am I doing? And then with the crisis I've had in the last few months, I've realised it's something I have to do. It's a little bit scary when you realise that. And that you're sort of addicted to how impossible, how hard, how painful it is.' Her work seemed to her 'a microcosm of the lessons of life, actually, because there's disappointment and at random times complete ecstatic loveliness'.

Harrison says she wouldn't overly encourage any daughters she had to become a ballet dancer: 'If it was a boy, yes, but if it was a girl, I would have a bit more of a hesitation. It's really intense and I feel like, not through any cleverness or plan, I've kind of got through it and I'm all right. But I've seen so many people fall off.' (There is both less competition among male dancers and less cultural expectation weighing on them.) Society holds up ballerinas as the perfection of a certain type of womanhood: seen but not heard, slender and strong, dedicated to their work above all things, like the noblest sort of nun. If ballet is therapy for the dancers, it is also therapy for the audience, packed into the balconies for a chance to think about something other than the mortgage, the ill relative, the bad weather, the dirt and the chaos and the imperfection of life. In an age where the mythical red shoes that don't let a dancer stop dancing have become the shoes we are supposed to wear every day, we need ballerinas to preserve a dream.

Ashley Westwood, 25, footballer, Birmingham

'Football,' the philosopher Simon Critchley said, 'is the working-class ballet.' The metaphor highlights the game's beauty – the arc of the ball, the elegant passing and swift runs of a good game – but also hints at the way the Saturday game marks the end of the working week. Football began as an elite pursuit – its rules were written in 1848 by seven public schools – but the polite values of the early game turned demotic when the 1850 Factory Act stopped work at 2 p.m. on Saturdays, freeing the workers, and spectators, for a 3 p.m. kick-off. If you made furniture in Wycombe at the end of the nineteenth century, you might go to see the Chairboys, or Wycombe Wanderers, play the Potters, or Stoke City, on being released by the factory bell. The reward for keeping time in the week is to have it loosened at the weekend: ninety minutes dragging horribly by or disappearing in a moment.

Ashley Westwood, who is 25 and plays midfield in the Premiership for Aston Villa, put the feeling more simply: 'You look forward to the weekends.' The fields around Aston Villa's Bodymoor Heath training ground in the early August pre-season are damp brown and freshly ploughed; the wrought iron gates are claret and blue. There are a few parents and children inside the gates, watching the youth teams training, and they turn to look into my taxi as the security guard waves us through. I notice their faces fall. The training centre is at the back, past green grass marked into pitches and a row of white-netted goals on wheels. The players' car park – the cars are either glossy, sleek and low-down or high, shiny and big-tyred – is dotted with claret-leaved young trees. (Even the foliage is in club colours.) There is a loud hum from an air-conditioning unit throwing warm air into the car park. I rush in to ask for the loo. There isn't a ladies toilet. 'It's a man's world,' the receptionist sighs, and shows me to the disabled loo. On the white plastic soap dispenser, there is an Aston Villa crest. 'PREPARED', it says, underneath a gold lion prancing on a sky-blue shield.

The whole building smells like sweat hastily covered with Lynx spray deodorant, a scent I remember from walking past the boys' changing rooms at school. Westwood was born in Nantwich, Cheshire, in 1990 to an electrician father and a housewife mother, and, like many, wanted to be a footballer when he grew up. Unlike many, he made it. At school 'the teachers used to drill it into me, you need a back-up plan, but I never ... I just never thought I'd do anything else. I wasn't very good at school. I could have been clever but I never tried and that was me one regret when I left school.' He left without any GCSEs and at 16 won one of twenty or so places as a scholar at the academy at Crewe Alexandra (the Railwaymen), an academy known for producing players like David Platt, Robbie Savage and Danny Murphy. There is no guarantee of a professional career even on reaching an academy; just as at the Royal Ballet School, the majority of boys – more than 90 per cent – won't make it into their club's first team. Ryan Mason, a promising player at Tottenham Hotspur's academy, recalled that he'd seen 100 players leave over nine years. The academies are adept at suggesting back-up plans for disappointed parents: their sons are encouraged to play in a lower or foreign league, to study sports science at university, or apply for an apprenticeship.

Westwood got his GCSEs at the Crewe academy and was offered a professional contract when he turned 18, when he began earning between £15,000 and £30,000 a year. He was spotted during Crewe's 2011–12 season – which included a run of sixteen unbeaten matches and finished in the team's promotion to League One – and on the day before the transfer window closed, after Swansea dilly-dallied, he signed a four-year deal with Aston Villa for £2 million. His debut game for Villa was against Manchester United, the club he grew up supporting (Paul Scholes is still his favourite player), and he remembers glancing round in the tunnel and catching sight of Wayne Rooney and Scholes. 'You dream it, yeah, and you're watching them on telly obviously, you think: "Well, I want to play in that," but I never thought I was good enough. Never had that belief until I got the move, and the gaffer's been brilliant with me to be fair. He's thrown me in at the deep end. And then it's either sink or swim.'

Westwood's days (every day apart from Wednesday and Sunday) begin with a cup of tea, 'one sugar, not too many sugars, a bit of milk', having been woken by his 3-year-old son knocking on the wall. He arrives at Bodymoor Heath for training at 9.20 a.m., has a slice of toast in the café with the other players, and more tea: 'I've got to have a cup of tea in the morning.' At 10.30 a.m. the whole squad begins training: a warm-up with the coaches before the manager comes to watch them play. Then, the coaches might 'drag you in the gym doing all your core and everything', before lunch with the squad: 'They have a good spread on ... the single lads if they don't like cooking, the chef sends you some food home.' After changing out of the light blue training kit into street clothes, he finishes around 1 p.m. to 'get me rest in', walking out of the ground with a washbag printed with a photo of his son, Frankie. The players' car park is nearly empty at 1.20 p.m. At home in the afternoons, he'll help his wife Rebecca with Frankie (being a stay at home mum is 'the hardest job of all, actually'), changing nappies and getting him ready for bed, 'and that's it really'. He might play golf; he used to play on his PlayStation before he had children (other players admit to addictions to Football Manager or FIFA). He doesn't drink during the season; he's careful not to get exhausted. It is a gentle, mild life. Conservative, even.

On a match day, 'I'm terrible.' Things must be done in a specific order: 'A lot of footballers are like that, they like to keep the same routine.' The players stay together in a hotel the night before whether the game is at home or away, meeting for 'pre-match' ('all your chicken and pasta') at 11.30 a.m. On the way to the stadium 'the lads play all the upbeat house music and hip hop' in the coach; the set pieces, 'how the gaffer wants you to play', are laid out in the changing room. He gets dressed for the warm-up: 'I do me right shoe lace first. Then me left. Right shin pad, and then left. So it's always the right one. Done that ever since I've turned professional, yeah. I've got the same shin pads from when I was about 18 as well. It's just habit. I check, I know exactly what ... because the right shin pad's got more kicks on it so I know that's the right one.' (He has Frankie embroidered on his boots.) And then he's focused on the game. Xavi, the Barcelona midfielder, once described looking for the next space to play the ball into during a game as 'like being on the PlayStation'. Westwood feels like a different person when he's playing: 'I'm so laid back, and then you step out on the pitch, it's like ... it's like you're possessed and someone takes over yer and it's like, not you. You're shouting all the time. I'm quite quiet, but on the pitch you're constantly shouting. It just takes over yer and you get lost in the game. You're fully focused, adrenaline. You don't know what's going on around you, you just get back to seeing the ball and playing football.' It's not a demonic possession but a pleasurable, or, as Harrison said of dancing, a therapeutic one: Westwood gets lost in the game and the fans get lost with him, both together and alone.

Westwood, whose brown forearms flicker with muscle definition, says his life is 'quite boring'. 'Your friends are turning 15, out in the park drinking,' he remembers, 'and I'm there, stuck in the house, watching *Emmerdale*, while they're out drinking with girls. It is hard. You've got to give up a lot, but it's well worth it in the end.' On a Saturday night all he needs is '*X Factor* and I'm happy!' Stan Collymore estimated he worked for ten and a half hours a week when he was at Aston Villa in the 1990s. 'It's the best job in the world,' Westwood said. It's also one of the best-paid; a Premier League player will earn between £25,000 and £35,000 a week, when the average UK salary is £26,500 a year. Until 1961, when the Professional Footballers' Association threatened to strike, footballers' wages were held at a maximum of £20 a week, with a £4 bonus for a win and £2 for a draw. (The average worker earned £17 a week in 1961.) When the rule was abolished, Fulham announced it would pay its top player £100 a week. Further loosening of the rules took place during the 1980s, as clubs began to court sponsorship and float on the stock market. The high wages in the modern game date from the formation of the Premier League in 1992, when twenty League One clubs broke away and negotiated £305 million from Sky for TV rights; the deal for 2016–19 is worth £4 billion. But as club revenues went up, so did expenditure. The Premier League as a whole has hardly made a profit, partly because 70 per cent of club expenditure goes on wages. In 1992, a Premiership player would earn £75,000 a year; in 2010, a player earned £1.4 million a year on average. Bonuses each season the team reaches the Champions League range from £300,000 to £800,000.

Westwood said he would keep playing if he won the lottery 'without a shadow of a doubt'. He laughs gently, perhaps nervously, when I ask what he thinks of what footballers are paid. 'At the top level it gets ridiculous. And like I said, but ... it's always on telly, that's why it is so big ... it's our game, people watch it. Like Christmas. It's worldwide. It's part and parcel of life. It is a comfortable living but like I said, people don't see the hard bits that come with it. It can be mentally tough. People have committed suicide, tried to commit suicide through football. Ex-players and that, so it's not nice, it does take its toll. But like I said, the money side of it is ... there is a lot of money in the game now, but for us ... you're not going to turn down money, like if you were in a normal job and someone offers you double the money you're not going to ...'

Sitting next to Westwood was Aston Villa's Head of Press, who had vetted my questions. He was nervous of my asking about money, and didn't want me to ask Westwood one of the questions I'd asked all my interviewees: 'Do you think you earn enough?' When I had first approached footballers for interview through a friend who worked on the sports desk of a national newspaper, he was told that Premiership footballers 'don't do favours for friends of friends' and that a friendly chat would cost £5,000. I approached twenty clubs before getting an answer from Aston Villa; in the end the half-hour interview took five months to set up, and was arranged with a day's notice. The Head of Press intervened at this point in the conversation, perhaps judging that Westwood was stumbling: 'But it wouldn't necessarily be your motivation.' 'No, it's not.' 'Yeah.' 'Your motivation is, like I said, to ... My aim is not to earn this much money, it's to play as long as I can in the Premier League. None of the lads I've met are money driven. If you play well then the money comes with it. It's all about playing well and pleasing people on a Saturday.' I wondered what the fans would like their players to be paid.

Footballers might now be entertainers but that also means they have the problems of showbusiness. Westwood is like a chorus girl suddenly made a star, and with attention comes criticism. 'We lost 8–0 against Chelsea a couple of years ago,' Westwood said of one of his worst days. 'So to go home, especially in the Premiership, wherever you turn the telly on it's all football. You can never get away from it, so you just have to take it. It's in the papers, it's in ... You've got to be big and strong enough to take it.' (Nearly 14.5 million people across the world watched Aston Villa in 2013, but the fans don't seem to get to Westwood in the way the media does. I wondered who Westwood most enjoyed entertaining: the manager, the fans or the media?) Careers can be as short as eight years; 'if you get to 35 in football, you've done well'. Westwood had just signed a contract that will take him through to July 2017, but the club could loan him out, sell him, get relegated or change owner at any time. Since Randy Lerner of the MBNA credit card fortune bought a controlling share in Aston Villa for £66 million in 2006, he has spent £160 million on improving the grounds and the team, resulting in a loss of £162 million over the last four years. Only Manchester City and Chelsea made bigger losses in the 2012–13 season. The business model of most Premiership clubs makes close to no sense: money runs through the clubs without pausing. Lerner has said he wants to sell Aston Villa; attendance at home games was at its lowest for fifteen years in November 2014. Who but an oligarch or a tycoon has the means to buy such a bauble?

There are 4,000 professional football players in the UK and two-fifths of them will go bankrupt when they stop playing. Others drink or become depressed once their careers are over. 'I've thought about it,' Westwood says of his retirement in ten years' time. 'I'm into me property as well. I'd like to have a few houses, rent them out and then have a bit of coaching on the side – obviously Crewe's renowned for bringing through young players, so I will probably go back there and coach and help out three times a week. But I like me golf. Hopefully I can retire and just play golf.' He'd not been injured yet, but had seen other players break legs or their knee cruciates: 'You've got to be mentally tough. And the boys help you through that. You come in, you have a laugh.' While you play, the club supports you: personnel, welfare and liaison officer Lorna McClelland speaks five languages and will help you find a house; the newly appointed Assistant Manager, Roy Keane, who left the club three months later following a reported row at Bodymoor Heath, walks the corridors with an open box of Roses; the Christmas party is paid for with players' fines for lateness or wearing dodgy clothes. (The Arsenal fine list was leaked last year: being fifteen minutes late to training cost £500; bringing a newspaper into the dressing room cost £100; not attending a home match without Wenger's permission, even if you weren't playing, cost £1,000.) Someone called Fergus tends to the Aston Villa players' feet: 'He clips your nails for you and that. So we're like princesses! We do get looked after.'

Dr Bungee, 29, giggle doctor, Rhyl

In Rhyl, on the north coast of Wales, the salt in the air dissolves the rain as it's falling. Or perhaps that's something taxi drivers tell visitors. From the 1860s, Rhyl's promenade unfurled alongside red-brick pleasure domes: the Floral Hall, the Pavilion, the Gaiety and the Coliseum Theatres, the Marine Lake, the Roller Rink. Nearly all have since been demolished. During a February half-term in 2014, the poster for the Christmas panto is still up outside the corrugated steel successor to the Pavilion, and it's cold and windy along the prom. One of the few buildings left from the red-brick era is the Royal Alexandra Children's Hospital and Convalescent Home, built on the seafront in 1872 for the healing qualities of the rain-dissolving air. In a Victorian photo, children in ruffs sit solemnly on a rocking horse, or look through a picture book together. The top windows are opened wide.

The wards of the Royal Alex were closed to inpatients in 2010 due to health and safety measures. Now the sick children of North Wales are taken to Glan Clwyd general hospital, a twenty-minute drive out of town. In October 2014, nurses on Glan Clwyd's dementia ward were discovered to be restraining patients and leaving them in their own faeces; the BMA warned that the NHS in Wales faced 'imminent meltdown' because of a staffing crisis. Huddled around the *Ambiwlans* parked at the entrance is a woman in red-check pyjamas smoking while talking on her mobile phone; everyone else is either carrying a walking stick or a car seat for a baby. Inside, the low, narrow corridors look certain to come to dead ends, but on reaching a corner, they turn sharply and keep going. I hear Dr Bungee before I see him: a gentle, rising guitar riff. As he turns the corner, I laugh despite myself: a fez, a red star stuck to his nose, a white coat embroidered with a gumball machine and a bucket around one foot.

Giggle doctors visit twenty-one children's wards in hospitals around the UK each week. As Dr Bungee walks into Glan Clwyd's, he sees a nurse with a banana in her hand: 'Is it banana time already?' The ward is nearly empty: nurses are changing all the beds in the bay apart from one, in which a teenage girl is watching *Loose Women* with her mum beside her and the white sheet pulled up to her chin. She isn't going to be amused easily. 'What's your favourite noise in the whole wide world?' he asks. 'I don't know,' she says. 'Is it the noise your phone makes when you get a text?'

She doesn't reply. 'A seagull?' She laughs mockingly.

'JLS?' 'No!' 'One Direction?' 'No!'

Her mum helps: 'There is someone you like, McBusted? Aren't you going to their concert?' 'No! I'm not going to that any more.' 'What type of music do you like?' 'Any.'

Dr Bungee tries to find out her favourite smell (she relents: new shoes and petrol) and favourite word ('Shut up!' her mum offers), before admitting defeat and offering her a leaving present. 'If I don't, then I won't leave,' he says, 'so most people are quite keen on it.' He asks if she prefers paper or rubber, and what her favourite colour is, then pulls a sheet of tissue paper, half green and half yellow, out of one of his deep pockets. 'Beautiful or horrible?' 'I don't know – both!' As Dr Bungee begins twirling the paper into a tulip, the girl asks him a question, unprompted: 'What's that bucket doing? How did you get it on?'

Dr Bungee, or David Deanie, became a giggle doctor in 2008, when a friend told him that the Theodora Children's Charity was auditioning: 'It's your perfect job, your dream job, that you would absolutely love.' He had graduated from the University of

Strathclyde with a degree in International Business and Modern Languages (he performed magic in French for his oral assessments and set up on his own as a magician after graduating) and had been on Jobseeker's Allowance for six weeks. 'I'm going to be honest,' the Job Centre adviser told him, 'don't get a dream job, just get a job.' David had learned magic from a book his parents, who were both teachers, gave him as a boy; in 2011 he became an Associate of the Inner Magic Circle, one of only 700 to 1,000 worldwide. He charges £250 for ninety minutes at corporate gigs and weddings. In his audition for a role as a giggle doctor, he was presented with everyday objects and told to entertain the interview panel. He ignored the egg whisk on the table and picked up the pen, as he knew he could do some impromptu magic with it. 'I thought: a gift!' Once through the audition, there is a year of training. Each giggle doctor develops a character (other giggle doctors include Dr Wonderpants, a ridiculous superhero, Dr Yoho, a pirate, and Dr Scallywag, a naughty schoolchild) and attends courses on child development, how parents deal with their child's illness, infection control regimes and child bereavement. Then they are junior giggle doctors, and go on to wards for a year with a senior giggle doctor of at least three years' experience before they can make visits on their own.

David comes to Rhyl once a month; he also visits hospitals in his home city of Manchester weekly. He has got to know certain dishes at hospital canteens well (at the Royal Oldham he has eaten the vegetable lasagne many times) and learned to avoid the 'politics of milk' in the staffrooms. The Theodora Children's Charity, funded on a mostly year by year basis by grant-making trusts, corporate sponsors and individual donors, pays every self-employed giggle doctor £145 for a four-hour shift, plus expenses. Being a giggle doctor nine to five would be 'too demanding': two shifts a week is the maximum (the rest of the time they are actors, musicians and entertainers). 'It's the best job in the world,' David says. 'It's not necessarily making people laugh, which with the name giggle doctor, that's what people think. It's more about making connections, because sometimes people just don't feel like laughing. Some people are just miserable, and they are stuck here in this room, people walk past, put needles in them.' In Rhyl, he wanders, strumming his guitar, to the A&E waiting room. A straight-faced doctor in an undecorated white coat comes out of a consulting room. 'This is not appropriate,' she says and closes the door firmly behind her.

Some children are spending a morning of their half term waiting with their parents in A&E. He spots two boys and a girl: 'It's Harry Potter! And Hermione! And there ... is it? Dobby the house-elf!' All three laugh. 'It's a Harry Potter reunion! Wow!' (David described his jokes to me as 'bad dad jokes'; he became a father himself three years ago.) The waiting room is full and the hospital has made part of a corridor into an overflow room, placing chairs against the walls in a rough circle. He catches sight of the date on a TV screen: 'Waiting time is currently 27 days, 2 hours and 14 minutes,' he says. 'I'm here to make your wait longer.' He blows some sticky bubbles (ones that can be touched without popping) into the centre of the circle and small children clamber off their parents' knees and through a pensioner's legs, to the OAP's displeasure, to touch them. They bounce, unbreaking, over the adults' laps too; several of them turn, for the first time, to the person they've been sitting next to for twenty minutes.

In another room, a baby wrapped in a towel is sitting on her mother's lap while she looks at her phone. Dr Bungee makes a balloon animal for the baby's older sister, then blows some sticky bubbles. The mother doesn't look up but the baby on her lap laughs like an infant in a formula milk advert. Her sister realises the balloon can also be a fishing rod for bubbles, and so she and Dr Bungee collect them together silently, before he leaves with a last blast. (We were coming towards the end of the shift, and one of the tricks David has learned is: if you need to leave, blow some bubbles and then get out of there.) We don't find out what was wrong with the baby in the towel.

In some areas of Rhyl, half of the children live in poverty. A quarter of adults don't have work. The owner of the B&B I stayed in told me not to go into town on my own in the evening; the rape for which Ched Evans, the former Sheffield United footballer, was convicted took place in Rhyl's Premier Inn. When I asked at the train station whether they had a map of the town, I was told there wasn't much to see. Rhyl used to be a place where miners came on their summer holiday: for the lido, for the amusements, for the theatres, for the gardens. Before Rhyl's pier was dismantled in 1973, you might also have been able to walk to its end to see clowns with red noses, half-metre-long shoes and lapel flowers that squirted water. (Giggle doctors used to be called clown doctors before clowns were thought creepy.)

A nurse calls Dr Bungee into a treatment cubicle with curtain walls to distract a boy who's having a wound bathed and dressed. His routines fall flat until he asks if the boy has seen his sister. She's a chicken. He hasn't seen her for a while, at least not after he had a roast chicken sandwich last week. 'But if you see her, will you give her a message? It's in chicken. *Bock-bock-bock-ar!*' The boy tries to repeat the message, but breaks down in giggles. 'Oh no. You can't say that to her. You don't speak chicken, do you? You've just insulted her.' Dr Bungee repeats '*Bock-bock-bock-arrr!*' and the boy tries again, laughs again, tries again. The hospital photographer emerges from a side door to watch; a male nurse comes out of an adjoining cubicle for a moment too. Dr Bungee is just about to teach him something to say to his brother, the sheep, when the dressing is done. He goes to change back into his street clothes, leaving the boy with a red nose and a bandaged hand.

THINKING

scientist
question writer
professor

Aravind Vijayaraghavan, 35, scientist, Manchester

You could say that graphene, the atom-thick sheets of graphite that are the strongest, lightest, thinnest and most conductive substance in the world, was discovered outside of office hours. When the Russian-born scientist Andre Geim, who shared the Nobel Prize for Physics in 2010 with his student Konstantin Novoselov for graphene's discovery, came to the West in 1990, Friday night was reserved for the craziest experiments, the ones that made him laugh. In 2003, Geim started to wonder whether a transistor, the electronic switch which is the basis for computing, could be made out of graphite, and asked a Chinese PhD student in his lab at the University of Manchester to see how thin he could polish a tablet of it. (A rule of the Friday Night Experiments was that you couldn't work on any one project for more than a few months, so as not to derail a career barely started; this PhD student needed something to do while he improved his English.) The thinnest state the student could get to was still too thick but he had cleaned the graphite with sellotape, like a lint roller smoothed along the sleeve of an overcoat: here was graphite at an airy thinness. Since the 1940s, the existence of a two-dimensional material such as graphene had been theorised but never realised. Could this be it? Novoselov freed the graphite by dissolving the tape with acetone and floating the flakes, which are invisible to the naked eye, on to a wafer of silicon, and began testing it. Under a microscope, the flakes look like camouflage in purply shades of blue: the true purple is the thinnest part, graphene, which turned out to be the best conductor of heat and light there is. Geim, Novoselov and their team published their findings in *Science* as 'Electric Field Effect in Atomically Thin Carbon Films': the anarchic, slightly silly atmosphere of a Friday Night Experiment had made its way into the academy.

Friday Nights were about letting things go wrong – in Geim's Nobel lecture, he said there were too many failures to list on a single PowerPoint slide – but it was also about the long term. Aravind Vijayaraghavan, a 35-year-old lecturer and research scientist who works alongside Geim and Novoselov at the University of Manchester, defends the idea of playful freedom, of Friday nights and mucking about with sticky tape: 'Historically it's clear that the countries that are very strong in science and technology, that have invested in basic research over the long term, have a much stronger economy, whereas countries and economies that have taken a view to not support science struggle in the long term.' The distillation of thinking in a research paper means that in twenty years' time there could be jobs making graphene transistors to replace increasingly slow silicon ones. And in five more years' time, there could be jobs producing a graphene smartphone you can roll up like a cigar, efficient graphene solar cells with the flexibility of cling film, graphene batteries that could keep an electric car going for 500 miles and graphene biosensors that can detect cancer in minutes.

'I have to remind myself that it is work,' Vijayaraghavan said. 'More ideas have been drawn on the back of bar napkins than in lab notebooks.' At this stage in his career, work merges with life: he plays in the department football team and tacks on an extra couple of days after an overseas conference. He gets up around 7 a.m. and cycles fifteen minutes from his rented flat to his lab across from the building site for the new National Graphene Institute, arriving for 9 a.m. and sometimes not leaving until

10 p.m. His days are filled with lectures, experiments in the labs dressed in overalls, gloves and a hairnet; supervising the PhD and MSc students working in his group; or preparing public lectures and talks. His group is looking into the properties of graphene, how to make medical sensors from it as well as molecular electronics and the development of nano-devices. They recently discovered that layers of graphene can be arranged in such a way that when a laser shines on it, the graphene cools down instead of heats up, which means a future computer server with graphene transistors could be cooled with coloured light. In July 2014 his ground-floor office stored lab equipment, football kit and a computer with two screens he hadn't turned on that day: he avoids sitting at it 'like the plague'. Fifty or so conference passes hung on a hook in the corner of the room; framed covers of journals with his name on hung above the computer screens. He wore a beaded necklace around his neck, a Pebble smartwatch on his wrist and the lenses of his glasses gradually darkened when we walked out into the sunlight. He took a 'very rational view of life', one that was godless, averse to impulse-buying and politicians' lines: 'You immediately analyse it, your mind makes the connections and you realise: "That's bullshit."'

Lunch might be a vegetarian panini, but the semi-official coffee hour at 3.30 p.m. is more important. Researchers gather in a windowless corner of the lab to collect their mugs from the draining board: Geim's is dark blue with 'Andre' picked out in raised yellow handwriting. Vijayaraghavan doesn't think it would be a good idea for me to photograph it: 'We treat even the most famous people as peers. If Newton was standing on stage I wouldn't be afraid to ask him questions and criticise what he's doing, and try to pick holes in his argument, because that's what we do.' We might not all work alongside a Nobel Prize winner, but learning how to ingratiate ourselves with our superiors without demeaning ourselves and to criticise, or whistleblow, without getting fired or sidelined are how we accommodate ourselves to the modern, supposedly more open, workplace. The sort of disagreement in the open air Vijayaraghavan describes is rare and increasingly threatened by the coalition government's new funding rules for universities, which determine the worth of an academic paper by specious measures of 'impact'.

Sarah Varey, a nanotechnologist working on a PhD in Vijayaraghavan's group, organises a coffee club: £10 for twelve weeks of unlimited Carte Noire instant, sugar and milk. She puts a yellow sticker next to the late payers, escalating to orange and pink (Vijayaraghavan pays on time but certain Nobel laureates are happy to let their debt build up). The coffee break consoles, as most days scientific research proceeds uneventfully, with Vijayaraghavan hoping for the result that gives pause. 'You just do what you do and hope that along the way you stumble across something,' he said. 'It's very rare that you get this absolutely brilliant idea that no one else has thought of and you figure out how to work it. It's usually you're working, you're doing what you normally do and something unexpected comes out of it and you're clever enough to figure out what you can do with it.'

Vijayaraghavan grew up on the south-eastern coast of India, a country that officially works a six-day week. His mother worked in the home and his father worked in marketing, the 'one thing I knew I didn't want to do'. There were engineers, doctors and a captain of a ship in the family. 'If I'd have got into the top medical school, I'd have done medicine. If I'd got into the top engineering school, I'd have done engineering. It's really not because I liked engineering or wanted to be an engineer or something like that, it's that the best engineering school is better than a mediocre medicine school. You go to the best engineering school, end of discussion.' He studied engineering in Chennai, then took a PhD in Troy, New York State, before starting nano-technology research in Karlsruhe and spending a year at MIT. He arrived in Manchester to set up his lab a month before Geim and Novoselov won the Nobel. He could earn one and a half to two times his £30,000 to £40,000 salary in an engineering firm, but he likes his work enough to accept the pay not exactly keeping up with the cost of living.

Though graphene was discovered in the UK, it isn't clear that Britain will be the first to exploit it. Vijayaraghavan's work is part of 'a very collaborative global effort': the USA spends most worldwide on graphene research and development, while both the UK and China spend around 1 per cent of GDP on experimental research. In 2014, Manchester counted sixteen graphene patent publications while Zhejiang University had ninety-seven and Tsinghua ninety-two. (Geim and Novoselov argue reasonably that it is quality and not quantity that matters.) China's current five-year plan, the twelfth guideline, expires in 2015, by which time the Chinese Communist Party aim to be spending 2.2 per cent of GDP on scientific research, and are forecast to surpass the USA in 2020.

In 2011, George Osborne announced a £50 million fund for research into applications for graphene; in his March 2014 Budget speech he said he would establish a National Graphene Institute at the University of Manchester. (In April, he was photographed in a favourite costume at the topping-out ceremony: snow-white hard hat and rave-yellow visi-vest.) Vijayaraghavan's lab regularly meets with companies to advise on new applications for graphene; the Nobel win meant that the graphene lab 'went from having no money to having some money to work with industry'. Some companies come to Manchester knowing exactly the sort of experiment they want Vijayaraghavan's lab to carry out for them (they save money that way: industrial-scale experiments are expensive); others begin: 'My marketing guy told me there's a thing called graphene and I'm here to find out what it is.' The academics and the businessmen swap ideas, define an area of research, work out how it will be funded and if successful, they'll start working together. The process takes six months to a year. The UK government 'has been good to graphene for their own selfish reasons': votes aren't lost by giving money to British industry to develop a British invention. But Vijayaraghavan isn't sanguine: 'I could easily say: "Yeah, it's been absolutely brilliant. They've given us all this money and we're doing great," but that hides the overall picture' of what's happening across the country. He paused. 'The government's taken a stance where they're making cuts to areas that are already hurting, and protecting all the people who already have enough money. That's the Conservative way of doing things. Trickle-down economics, which we know doesn't work.'

If politics runs on a five-year electoral cycle, science runs on a twenty-year cycle. 'Nobody really thinks that far ahead any more,' Vijayaraghavan said. In the twentieth century, industry developed new technologies in basic labs such as Bell Labs in the USA and the IG Farben in Germany, but as companies looked to increase profit in an increasingly global marketplace in the 1970s, they began to rely on publicly funded universities for research. Long-term investment in a proprietorial lab has been replaced by short-term projects in partnership with universities or by venture capital. The sort of ten-year plan that Germany's football team had used to win the 2014 World Cup – Mario Götze had scored the extra-time winner a few weeks before I spoke to Vijayaraghavan – no longer holds in Britain. 'The UK doesn't do ten-year plans! Not in football, not in engineering, not in science. It's a pity. It is a pity. Because it's the only way you can make progress. It's the influence of the financial sector, because they deal with ... they trade stocks by the second. They're trying to balance their books every quarter or every month. It just doesn't work that way in technology and science. But that culture has permeated throughout. I think that's ruined science and tech-nology.' Vijayaraghavan thinks for a moment. 'And football as well!'

Thomas Eaton, 43, question writer, London

In 2000, Judith Keppel was the first person to win a million on *Who Wants to Be a Millionaire?* In academia, thinking can't help but be slow, failure-strewn and underfunded, but on TV, thinking must be quick, accurate and instantly profitable. Keppel's final question was more of an academic one:

> *Which king was married to Eleanor of Aquitaine?*
> *a) Henry I b) Henry II c) Richard I d) Henry V*

She didn't look panicked, with good reason: she'd covered the medieval period in her history A-level and had seen the tomb in France the previous summer. 'I do think it's Henry the Second,' she said. The audience gasped. But she was right: the studio lights began rotating, the host leaped up to put his arms around her and the doubting audience got to their feet. For the contestant, the feat is in the gathering up of knowledge – from cultural capital to book-learning – and being able to use it at the right moment. For the question-setter, there are other pleasures. Thomas Eaton, who has written quizzes for TV and newspapers for eighteen years, takes pleasure in that question's subject. 'I do quite like smuggling medieval questions into mainstream quiz shows.' Eaton was working on the Channel 4 quiz show *Fifteen to One* when Keppel became a millionaire, and remembers that the same question about Eleanor of Aquitaine had appeared on that afternoon's episode: 'Obviously that had been recorded ages before but it just happened to be broadcast that afternoon.' Perhaps Keppel had also been watching TV that day. 'Britain has a quite particular, sort-of pub quiz, TV quiz, quiz culture and over time people get pretty much well-informed,' he says, 'whether it's through attending these things or just through sort of osmosis. Generally, you can often be surprised at people's knowledge and I think quiz shows have to reflect that.'

Eaton is dressed unobtrusively in a black polo shirt, cargo shorts and hiking sandals on the hot July Sunday afternoon Andy Murray played Novak Djokovic in the 2013 Wimbledon final. Born in Harrogate, he did 'a bit of music, a bit of sport' at school, but he made it on to TV as a contestant on *Blockbusters* during sixth form. 'I got the gold run. I got a radio-cassette player that lasted much longer than it should have done. It was working until ... I went on the show in '88, and it was still working probably four or five years ago. No, getting knocked out was almost a relief. Actually being on the show was quite stressful. I hadn't disgraced myself, I'd done well enough but, yeah, it was almost a relief to have done it so I could just sit back and watch someone else playing.' I ask if he's ever lost a quiz. 'Oh yeah, yeah inevitably. Not often.' I laugh. His appearance on *Blockbusters* was a 'brief moment in the sun. I always did quizzes. I remember at my university interview, talking about my sadness that *University Challenge* had been decommissioned. It's one of my great regrets,' he laughs a light throwaway sort of laughter, 'that during my entire university career, *University Challenge* was off the air. That was one of my ambitions, to go on it – so sad to say!'

After reading history at University College, Oxford, Eaton read for a master's at Trinity Hall, Cambridge, writing his thesis on public ceremony in the reign of Henry V in the City of London. He was working in business publishing, and considering going back to study for a PhD, when he saw an ad in *The Guardian*'s media pages – 'in the days when media companies had the money to publicly advertise for things' – for a question writer on *Fifteen to One*. 'Originally I was rejected. Things like that, that don't absolutely specify lots of experience – you probably get a lot of replies, probably hundreds, but they got back to me a few months later and said they had another position, and would I want to do that? Since then, with one or two gaps, I've been moving around the quiz world, working on different shows.'

Most days he takes the tube from the house in Cricklewood he bought with his girlfriend in summer 2014 to his Central London office for 9.45 a.m., reading on the way. With a team of five – from either TV or quizzing backgrounds; some of his colleagues are Quiz League champions – he'll spend the day editing questions, stopping at 1 p.m. for an hour with the sports websites and a smoked salmon sandwich from home. By the end of the day, a writer will hope to have written between thirty and forty questions; for 200 questions a week, they'll earn between £26,000 and £35,000 a year. The company he works for is a subsidiary of one of the big TV channels, which makes the sort of fun fact programmes that fill the afternoons and early evenings of British TV schedules.

The kernel of a question might start from Eaton's general reading (he'd just finished a run of mid-century British history books: Peter Hennessy, David Kynaston and Dominic Sandbrook, whose *Seasons in the Sun* was 'a bit cut and paste') or from the *Oxford Dictionary of National Biography*, or what's happening in the world, or from daily life. 'It's not really a writing job, it's probably more of a craft in a sense. You're not coming up with anything extraordinarily imaginative, other than clever ways to use information or reuse information.' How does he come up with ideas for questions? 'I've known writers who've just basically gone through the dictionary, A to Z.' Like a journalist, Eaton talked of sources, first and second. When he started in the 1990s, the writing team used a tailor-made library; they now unwholeheartedly use the internet. 'No quiz show I've worked on has ever allowed Wikipedia to be a first source.' Questions are double-checked by their writers and the show's producers before being sent out to an independent verifier.

Question-checking protects against disputes but also against unsayability and clichés. What makes a question unbroadcastable can be both obvious – when Princess Diana died, *Fifteen to One* 'went into meltdown' and removed every question about her – and idiosyncratic. On *The Weakest Link*, certain words were avoided: 'Anne Robinson couldn't say apocalypse, so we could have no questions about *Apocalypse Now*. She couldn't say Antarctica. It's just reading at speed. She kept stumbling over them, so eventually a host, especially a big-name host, will just say: "Look, no more." I think she couldn't say Greg Rusedski. So we had a sort of small but growing banned list of topics. The South Pole. We always used to substitute South Pole for Antarctica.'

There is also question fatigue: 'You can write any number of sports questions. It's such an easy pool of things to write about. There's so much esoteric knowledge.' Certain subjects hardly come up at all: 'It's almost a joke in the quiz world that every question about Islam will end in Ramadan or Mecca or something like that.' What is general knowledge anyway? When does something that seemed specialist become commonplace? 'It's a funny fine line when you feel that something has entered the mainstream. Often with a music act, somebody will have heard of them but they won't have had any success but then eventually they turn into Coldplay or something like that.' For Eaton, one of the pleasures of his job is finding a 'nugget': 'On shows with longevity, you don't want to write repeat questions. You'll check on the database and do a search and see if it's been written before, and so many times – it's especially a problem for new writers when they come in – every idea that they have will have been done already, either two years before or the year before, but obviously there are always new things you can ask, or new ways you can ask old questions. But there are things, you know, lovely little nuggets, when you think: that is a great fact.' I wondered if he saw his questions as a stealth ennobling of the masses, smuggling in medieval nuggets alongside questions about Ryan Gosling movies: 'It's not rocket science. It's just entertainment.'

The tension between entertainment and enlightenment can be traced back to the first quiz shows, which drew on parlour games and newspaper brainteasers, sideshows, music halls and gambling. The BBC's mandate to 'educate, inform and entertain' meant that when they stole quiz shows from the American commercial channels, they resisted offering prizes. In *What's My Line?*, imported from CBS in 1951, the contestant performed a mime of what they did all day before a panel who guessed the occupation by asking yes-no questions. (One of the most memorable contestants was a saggar maker's bottom knocker, one of the most junior positions in a pottery.) The show relied on its panel – newspaper columnists, actors and a resident grump – to raise a talky quiz show played for fun into something witty. (On the US version, Salvador Dalí appeared, scorning the game by answering 'yes' to the question 'Would you be considered a leading man?' Bette Davis squeaked her answers and Groucho Marx pretended he was a German couple who had just been to the opera in Strasbourg.) A year before ITV launched in 1955, Cecil McGivern, a BBC executive, worried about the arrival of prizes along with that of commercial television: would the BBC lose viewers? They would have to offer money, he agreed in a letter to another BBC executive, but they 'would try and control it and try and keep it decent'. In its first week, ITV aired *Double Your Money*, which offered a cash prize of £1,000; the BBC developed *Have a Go!* which gave out thirty-eight shillings and sixpence.

The genre looked dead until *Who Wants to Be a Millionaire?* in 1998 (it's no coincidence Eaton found a job as a question writer that year). With a set inspired by the incubation room in *Jurassic Park*, the teasing title question, suspenseful jingles, dramatic lighting and 'shoutability', it drew in one in three of the UK population. The year 2000, when Keppel won a million, was the quiz show's modern high point as the TV schedules filled with *Millionaire*'s imitators and rivals. The fairy tale *Slumdog*

Millionaire (from 2008) would ignore the troubling aspects of offering money for knowledge – that it encouraged recklessness, as a single quiz could earn you more than a life's salary – and end the story with the clever boy kissing his girl as she reclined in his arms.

The quiz show works with the idea that an ordinary person can be extraordinary: a postman can baffle a panel of four trying to guess what he does; a mouse-haired student can demonstrate intricate knowledge of the Classical world; a grandfather can have us in stitches when he knows who Chase and Status are. Perhaps the reason *Millionaire* became so popular at the beginning of the New Labour era was for its apparent meritocracy; the most popular quiz shows during coalition austerity have staged a conflict between quiz winners and ordinary challengers. On the BBC's *Eggheads*, the public play against a team of experts (including Judith Keppel); on ITV's *The Chase*, contestants confront the Chasers, with faux-scary names such as the Dark Destroyer. Ordinary people are given a chance to upset the status quo – and sometimes they succeed! – but the dice are stacked against them.

'The show I like the most is *University Challenge*, still,' Eaton says. 'Because it just has difficult questions, interesting questions. And it's always quite refreshing to see young undergraduates with amazing ranges of knowledge. I think that's one of the reasons people like it because they see these kids, basically kids, with freakishly good general knowledge.' Quiz shows hold out the promise of something more: not just money, but that ordinary people can do more. I glimpse what Eaton would have been like on *University Challenge* when we go through an edition of the quiz he writes for the back pages of the *Guardian Weekend* magazine. One of the questions that week was: What links the Wife of Bath, Madonna, Terry-Thomas and Condoleezza Rice? 'The nicest questions are where there's a closed set,' Eaton said, 'where there's only four people who've done something: they are the nicest ones to write but they are slightly hard to come up with. When Bayern Munich won the European Cup, the manager became the fourth manager to win the cup with two different sides, so he's joined an elite group. I think I've done that "what links" question before with the existing three managers. It's a bit more pleasing to have four, and only four, names.' I imagine notebooks full of three names, waiting for a fourth; in January 2015, Eaton emailed me to say that Carlo Ancelotti had become the fifth member of the group. The link between the Wife of Bath, Madonna, Terry-Thomas and Condoleezza Rice is the gap, or diastema, they all have between their front teeth, but it's no closed set. As we left to go and see if Murray had lost the final yet, I mentioned I would be going to visit a friend in Washington DC later in the summer. 'Did you know,' he says, 'that Washington DC was the first city to use more electricity in summer than in winter?'

Marina Warner, 68, professor, London

For nearly forty years, Marina Warner – fellow of the British Academy, a Chevalier de l'Ordre des Arts et des Lettres and a Dame – has been thinking about the shapes myths take, from Cinderella to Scheherazade, Joan of Arc to Tracey Emin. In 2014, she resigned her professorship in the Literature, Film and Theatre Studies department at the University of Essex, finding that thought management in UK universities had changed. Essex was founded in 1964 as a mould-breaking co-operative where divisions between subjects would be torn down and students and teachers would hang out as equals within the hessian-covered walls, but by 2012, and the arrival of a vice-chancellor, Anthony Forster, who'd served as an army officer before becoming a political scientist, the ethos had changed.

The year before, the government block grant for teaching had been removed, £9,000 yearly fees for students were introduced and new measures for weighing thought – rewarding 'impact' instead of quality – were established. Universities were subject to a new form of work discipline with no room for thinking, dreaming, imagining, challenging. 'One of the things I most regret actually is that I no longer have time for dreaming,' Warner said when we spoke in autumn 2014. 'I remember Adam Phillips wrote a famous book in which he says that being bored is an important part of a child's life. Well, I think it's actually quite an important part of an adult's life too. Not to have every single moment programmed.' Warner, who had been asked to take on chairing the Man Booker International Prize ('impact') and offered a research fellowship at All Souls, Oxford, was promised that her teaching duties would be organised to make this possible. Instead she was told her teaching would increase. A 'workload allocation' of seventeen targets assessed bi-yearly was handed down by the executive dean of the humanities, a housing lawyer, bypassing the head of the department. She quit. 'You can't inspire the citizenry,' she wrote in her account of what happened for the *London Review of Books*, 'to open their eyes and ears, achieve international standing, fill the intellectual granary of the country and replenish it, attract students from this country and beyond, keep up the reputation of the universities, expect your educators and scholars to be public citizens and serve on all kinds of bodies, if you pin them down to one-size-fits-all contracts, inflexible timetables, overflowing workloads, overcrowded classes.'

Warner was born in London in 1946 and spent her childhood in Cairo and Brussels; she grew up wanting to be an opera singer. Her father ran a bookshop and her mother worked as a housewife and, later, as a teacher of Italian. 'There's a diptych from my childhood,' Warner said. 'My mother would be reading *Vogue* on one side of the fireplace, my father would be reading the *Times*

Literary Supplement on the other, and I was just bifurcated in the middle. I kind of did both.' After gaining a place at both Oxford and Cambridge, she went up to Lady Margaret Hall, Oxford to read French and Spanish, but the university disappointed her. 'It was very stuffy, and extremely condescending and very rigid in its concept of intellectual life.' Women's colleges had existed at Oxford since the late nineteenth century, but when Warner arrived in 1964, they had only had the same status as men's colleges for five years. There wouldn't be co-educational colleges – and 'no more hungry stares across the Bodleian', as Gillian Rose wrote for *Isis*, the university magazine, in 1969 – until the 1970s. Tutors weren't yet accepting of the changing ambitions of women; or open to combining subjects that seemed to Warner to go together naturally, like Italian and history of art; or that Warner's talents might not lie in the editing of medieval French manuscripts. Cambridge and Oxford take some pride in being the last universities to modernise. The elitism has a way also of instilling a certain sort of guilt – I know the feeling well – a low dread of doing an intellectually 'wrong' thing.

Warner became the first woman to edit *Isis* on her own and was spotted by Beatrix Miller, the then editor of *Vogue*: 'It was the 1960s; things were like that!' Warner still leaned towards the *TLS* side of the hearth, and so turned them down to take a job at the *Telegraph* colour supplement beneath a Fleet Street haze of cigarette smoke (Warner's typewriter keys were always grey with ash). She learned to write captions to an exact number of characters and was bullied by a Bluebeard of a boss. After two years, she leaned to her mother's side of the hearth and went to *Vogue* as features editor, where she interviewed François Truffaut, Andy Warhol and Bernardo Bertolucci. The first book Warner wrote was a novel, judged 'not good enough to publish' by Cecil Day Lewis at Chatto and Windus, but Day Lewis suggested she try non-fiction. (Warner's first published book was about the Empress Dowager of China.) She left *Vogue* in 1972, and then for thirty-two years she wrote, researched and thought outside academia, often barely scraping by on fees from the BBC and lecture giving.

Her first 'substantial' book, *Alone of All Her Sex: The Myth and Cult of the Virgin Mary* (1976), came out of months spent at the Library of Congress in Washington DC. She and her boyfriend, William Shawcross, had both applied for a Harkness Scholarship, and when only Shawcross got it, they married so that she could go too (with the couples' allowance). While Shawcross reported on Watergate, Warner read her way through as many books about Mary as she could – 'I wasn't exactly miserable; I just didn't have anything else to do' – and thought about the meek figure she was instructed to imitate while at St Mary's Convent School in Ascot (her family had come back from Egypt after the nationalist riots in 1952). 'Some academic language has fallen into appalling bureaucratic future-speak. That was exactly what I wanted to avoid,' Warner has said. 'I wanted my writing to aim at the vitality, and above all, the linguistic richness of fiction or poetry.' She also wanted to cross the boundaries she wasn't allowed to at Oxford and write about architecture, poetry, film, art, literature and history; she wanted to treat with rigour subjects thought to be feminine and unserious. After completing the book about Mary, she wrote a novel, *In a Dark Wood* (1977), about a Jesuit missionary losing his faith, to explore similar ideas 'from a different angle'. Warner then moved on to Joan of Arc: how could Catholicism revere the blue, veiled, mild Mary and the tomboy challenger Joan? Her books are 'all very connected in my mind because nearly every book I write arises from the one before, to do with the questions that are still lingering'. Vijayaraghavan said it would take at least twenty years for his research into graphene to come to market; it seemed to me that Warner had been following the same line of questioning for double that.

In 1977, Warner gave birth to a son, Conrad, and a pram appeared in the hall. 'I think it's very hard still for women to go out to work all day long, actually, when they have children,' she said. 'It's so tiring.' But she had to find a way to combine writing and mothering, as her marriage broke down two years after her son's arrival and for a while she was bringing him up alone. 'When Conrad was small, the fact that he was small and I was a mother didn't actually prevent me writing, because I pretty much made him part of what I was doing. So the book *Monuments and Maidens* entirely grew out of taking walks with him, because in order to keep ourselves amused we would walk around and I'd begin to notice these statues and things. So then I started directing our walks to places where there were lots of statues. And then I began to think: what on earth do they mean?' She would have him climb them and tell her about the details he found; his favourite outing was to an ice sculpture Andy Goldsworthy made on Hampstead Heath. Goldsworthy 'sort of took a sledgehammer to the ice and made beautiful things. Arches and pillars and things.' (Conrad is now Conrad Shawcross RA, a sculptor who has shown in Paris, Miami, Zurich, Beijing, New York and London.) 'It's important to try, if you're writing, to make what you do part of what you're writing,' she says. 'It's a question of not seeing them as separate so you don't get bored or fed-up because actually you can try and compost the material into your life.' Writing works well with children, because it can be done in concentrated bursts. 'It's very hard to talk directly to a child, or for a child to talk directly to one. You have to sort of lie in wait around children. You can't really come back from the office and say: "Well, how was school?" You have to be around, waiting for them to say: "What does it mean when someone tells you to take your trousers off?" Because they're not going to say some big boy tried to get me in the corridor and pull my pants down, they're not going to say that, they're going to let it out in a kind of oblique way. A puzzled, oblique way.' The eight-hour work day wasn't developed with a child's need for perplexed or distressed confidences in mind.

In 1987, she was invited to be a visiting scholar at the Getty Center, Los Angeles, and as the old journalistic model of retained, staff and star writers died away, Warner moved closer to academia. The invitations to give lectures – Reith, Clarendon, Tanner – kept arriving; in 2000, after a period of illness, she met her partner Graeme Segal, a mathematician of geometry and quantum field theory, who helped her see she was living in an 'extraordinary hand-to-mouth way'. Her books, her lectures and her familiarity with the academy over thirty years meant she was able to find a position as a professor at Essex. She went from 'earning very little' very erratically from reviews, radio and royalties – the amount never surpassed around £30,000 a year – 'to earning a professor's salary, which is high,' around £60,000 a year. 'I've never really done it for money,' Warner said. 'I always wanted to do it for enough money that I wouldn't be dependent on anyone, because my mother was dependent on my father, and that was an absolutely formative influence on my life. I remembered when I was about 14 years old hearing them quarrelling about a new overcoat my mother wanted and I resolved I would never be in a position that I would have to ask a man for money.'

Warner had taught in universities before going to Essex – Renaissance mythological painting during a visiting professorship at the University of Pittsburgh; English literature during another visiting post at Paris XIII – and found that 'although I have no training, I quite like teaching'. She remembers discovering that her class at Paris XIII had never read 'Kubla Khan' and brought photocopies of the poem to the next class. Reading it with neophytes made her see 'what a powerful poem it is'. Teaching 'does rekindle one's thirst for those first moments' with great literature. At Essex she devised a course on fairy tale that went from Apuleius to Angela Carter; it was oversubscribed every year (students would have to get up early to be sure of a place) and taught in two-hour-long weekly classes. She's proudest of the MA creative writing course she taught on 'The Tale', using stories from Robert Louis Stevenson to Elizabeth Bowen to help students find their own writing voices. 'Creative writing is a controversial subject, and many who teach it don't defend it as a proper discipline,' she wrote of her teaching in the *LRB*. 'I am not one of them, but I can see the problems. How would you mark *Wuthering Heights*? ('Emily, I think you need to reorganise the chronology.') Or assess Gertrude Stein? ('Have you heard of commas?') I try to bring in Renaissance ideas of *imitatio*, and teach by example, of past masters and mistresses.' Lecturing and teaching in front of young people every week gave her confidence, 'a bit more élan': she didn't realise before working in a university that she had been 'rather isolated' before.

Warner moved to Birkbeck in autumn 2014, taking two of her PhD students from Essex with her. I met her after her first day, in perfectly blended pewter eyeshadow and tousled hair with a skirt embroidered with flowers and sewn with sequins. She'd been worried her new colleagues would be wary of her for attacking the University of Essex, but they were supportive, as were the many letters she'd received from academics who felt the same way. Younger lecturers being forced on to zero-hours contracts, being told by their union not to fight unfair dismissals and to sign gagging orders instead, mothers returning to work to find they'd been subtly sidelined. Warner's career must seem to them as the last in a certain writerly bohemian mould, which has 'faded in England,' she agrees. 'And it faded a long time ago.' When Warner began writing for magazines, the *Telegraph* supplement retained V. S. Naipaul; when she began being invited to give talks, university lecturers weren't subject to seventeen targets and a bi-yearly review. The way Warner took is no longer passable. She sipped a cup of tea and produced two slices of cake – madeira and fruitcake – she'd slipped into her handbag during a sandwich lunch, which we shared as we talked. Her Grub Street beginning has meant she has never felt entirely at home in the academic world. When All Souls College, Oxford, offered her a stipendiary two-year fellowship in 2013, Segal had to persuade her to accept: 'I didn't feel happy. I felt that they would be thinking to themselves: "What's she doing there?"' When she was an undergraduate, All Souls was a 'locked enclave of male power and privilege, and I'd never imagined that one day I'd be invited in'. From Radcliffe Square, where one of the main undergraduate libraries in Oxford sits, the empty quads of All Souls can be seen through a railinged gap in the cream stone, like a keyhole. No undergraduates are admitted there; so there was no one to invite one in, in Warner's time or mine. But you could nevertheless gaze in.

Warner has continued to write books, lecture, serve on committees and write essays on *The Arabian Nights*, Damien Hirst, Emily Wilding Davison and Helen of Troy for the *LRB* among others, but ever since she began to teach in a university she has only written short stories, and hasn't finished the novel she's been working on about her father's bookshop in Cairo. A day at home is 'heaven'. She gets up around 8 a.m. and will take black coffee up to the study in the attic of her rose-trellised terrace house. The walls are covered with books: somehow the space is cave-like and bright. Warner's computer is on a small table and there are books and papers piled over the floor, the tables and the wooden-framed armchair; just as there are framed pictures all over the walls of the house, from Paula Rego and Tacita Dean, among others, both friends. First she must avoid email: 'Emails are my nemesis. Somehow I'm too eager to please.' She will have begun on her work while asleep: 'What I do the night before is almost always try to set up what it is I'm going to work on. So I actually try to go to sleep thinking about it. Because I believe, in a mad way, that one's brain actually goes on whirring and organising and sorting.' She compares writing to the unconscious work of learning a language (Warner speaks two besides English, in beguilingly accurate accents) or of learning your way around a new place. It is essential to have 'a porous consciousness into which things seep': thinking isn't done with the end of a pencil in your mouth but by making gaps for the brain to fill.

There are writers who arrange sentences in their head before touching a keyboard but Warner isn't one of them: 'When you write, you don't really know what you're going to write.' She prefers to get the first draft down at 'top speed' to maintain rhythm and structure and then edit the piece into shape afterwards. 'I do tend to get rather lost in what I'm doing.' If she's working well, she'll let her coffee go cold and forget to have lunch or even move – 'Numb legs! I have to stamp!' – but she'll stop around 6.30 p.m. and mark the end of the day with a glass of wine. 'I'm in the grip of wine!' she jokes. 'Bacchus has my soul!' Over the day, she has wandered around the house picking up books. As she closes the door on her work, she notices 'a sort of great circle of books strewn around me', like the arc of toys a playing child leaves behind her at bedtime.

CARING

care worker
cleaner
crofter

Rochelle Monte, 38, care worker, Newcastle

Rochelle Monte is trying to find the moment she knew she wanted to work in care: 'I remember picking up a cup and there was somebody's false teeth floating in a cup of tea! And I thought: Oh, God, no! This is just horrific!' She was 15, still at school, and at the start of two weeks of work experience; her teacher had filled in the name of the local old people's home on her form for her. 'But by the end of the week, I didn't want to leave. I just loved it. I just loved ... it's the silly things, the false teeth.' Monte started caring for older and disabled people when she was 18. Over the last twenty years, she has had breaks to have children, and tried out other jobs – working in accounts, making sandwiches, running a corner shop – but she has always returned to caring. Even the corner shop she ran became a meeting place for old ladies: 'On Saturday morning they used to come in and we used to have a little coffee morning. And they would ring us up and tell us what they wanted and I would lock the shop up and take their things to their house, you know. I was still very involved with me old ladies.' Her voice softens: 'I like me old ladies.'

The work of caring for the sick, the dying and the vulnerable has traditionally been done within the family. Those without family were cared for by the Church and then, following the Poor Laws, under the parish administration. (The structure of English society is partly derived from the idea of the rich having a duty to the poor: the English words 'Lord' and 'Lady' come from the Old English for 'loaf', as they were supposed to give bread.) In the nineteenth century, healthcare was provided under the Poor Laws but social care was administered locally and subject to charges, a blurry system which was carried through into the structure of the newly created NHS in 1948. Social care continued to be provided as it always had been: in a patchwork and piecemeal manner by charities, local authorities, neighbours and relatives. Throughout the 1950s, the nineteenth-century asylums fell out of fashion and community care became more popular; by the 1980s, local authorities began contracting out carework to private providers. There were attempts by New Labour to integrate health and social care services, and indeed politicians still talk about it: none has yet managed it. Since 2010, social care spending has decreased every year. Councils put block contracts out to tender, and award them most often to companies who can save them the most money. (When councils provide care it costs them roughly £35 an hour, while private companies try to win contracts by offering any rate from £8 to £31.) The three biggest private providers, Allied Healthcare, Carewatch and Care UK, are run as profitable businesses and owned by private equity firms.

At least 4 per cent of the UK's population, around 3 million people, need carers every day. The majority of families manage, as families always have, among themselves, though the state allows a minority of the 5.4 million unpaid carers to draw an allowance of £65.13 a week, a rate of £1.86 an hour, based on a thirty-five-hour week carers will almost certainly be exceeding. Despite the companies' profits, the growing demand, the natural dignity of the work, those who provide home care are some of the lowest-status workers in the UK. Hours are paid at the National Minimum Wage of £6.50 an hour, and change from week to week; overtime and travelling between houses aren't paid; keeping a car roadworthy, a mobile phone in credit, and the carer themselves in a uniform are up to the worker, not the company whose job requires these things. What holds the system together, barely, are the type of people who fell in love with care work in the first week: 'We're picking up the pieces: the unpaid mileage, the unpaid time, the phone, the uniform.' Monte's voice gets louder. 'By continuing to accept these terms and conditions, we are covering up, papering over the cracks in the system, because we're allowing it to continue. If everybody suddenly downed tools and said: I'm not going to go to work tomorrow! Nah! I'm sick of that! Somebody might sit up and think, but we can't do that because we care. Those people depend on us. So we have to do our job.' Monte takes a breath. 'There's cleaners get paid more than we do. We deal with the most intimate tasks. We're supposed to support people in their own homes. The trust and the confidence. No! We're definitely undervalued and definitely underpaid. I could earn more working in a supermarket than I do in my job. And it's not a menial job. It's not an unskilled job. The people I'm working with might have mental health problems, dementia, physical disabilities, mental disabilities, they could be dying, it could be palliative, there's such a wide range of conditions and complex needs, and we need communication skills, social skills, I need to know the basic task-related things, you know, catheters, stoma bags, all of the other things that go with it. But I could probably earn more in Morrisons sweeping the floor. That's wrong! But I couldn't leave. No.'

After leaving school at 17, Monte worked a desk job before getting a position at a care home in Gosforth, where she began studying for her NVQ in Health and Social Care. (The demand is high for home care in the north-east, where only 22 per cent of people can pay for their care – the percentage is 55 per cent in the south.) From there she moved to work for one of the last local authority home care schemes before having her first child at 25. Two more children and several other stopgap jobs later, she went back to care in 2009, when Northumberland County Council now used private providers. Monte worked first for Careline, for minimum wage with no mileage; then for Helen McArdle Care, where she was on £6.60 an hour and 25p a mile, and quit when she saw a payslip come to £652 for a month's work; she took a job instead that paid the minimum wage and paid 15p a mile because it was in a smaller area and she could earn more. When I met Monte in February 2013, she was working for the biggest home care provider in the UK, Allied Healthcare, for £6.25 an hour, and 15p mileage, who, like the others, didn't pay for her travel time.

There's no lack of demand or trouble finding a job, which is part of the problem: 'Anybody can walk into a job in home care. It's the fact you're working unsupervised with vulnerable people. There's something wrong about that. I've heard people claiming Jobseeker's Allowance and being told – right, we've got this job for you: if you don't apply you're going to have your benefits cut. These people don't want to care!' We see the people who don't want to care on investigative TV programmes or on the pages of tabloid newspapers, but the first set of data collected on abuse in the care sector in 2014 didn't show excessive levels: 2.6 per cent of cared-for people had been abused. The biggest cause of abuse was neglect, which one might say was a natural consequence of the conditions of work: the poverty wages, the staff turnover, the scant training. But there are other sorts of neglect too: commissioning based on price at the local authority level; reduction in council budgets on the national level.

Monte's husband Pietro works in a restaurant in the evenings, and he's spending the last of his Saturday afternoon re-ironing a shirt for work, having spotted two creases down the front. 'I have ironed it!' Monte protests. Though it's February, the children are dashing between the netted trampoline in the garden, the sofa for cartoons and upstairs for toys with a friend over to play. The sitting room of Monte's modern red-brick terrace is full of family pictures, and, for a few days more, two pink helium balloons Pietro brought back from the restaurant at the end of his Valentine's Day shift last week. Monte, in a hot pink and maroon striped T-shirt, is seemingly always in motion: making cups of tea and breaking out the Lidl – 'wonderful shop' – jaffa cakes as we talk on, peeling an orange for her daughter, finding her employment contract, or her rota, or the award she won for Support Assistant of the Year 2012. 'A bit dusty and manky, but you know.' We sit in the kitchen on stools, facing the trampoline, and can just see over the fence to the garden of Monte's 77-year-old neighbour, Margaret. A half-full bowl of sudsy water waits in the sink.

Monte gets up at 6 a.m. She'll get up, shower and dress in her uniform of a white tunic with a green logo with black trousers and come downstairs for a cup of tea; the children get up to see her before she leaves at 7.15 a.m. 'If I don't give them a kiss goodbye, say if they're asleep, ah, they cry.' Her husband gets them ready and takes them to school and nursery while Monte gets in the car and goes to her first appointment of the day. 'I hate knocking on the door for the first time. You just never know what's behind them.'

Her work days are divided into house calls, which can range from fifteen minutes to several hours, and are clustered around the cardinal points of the day: helping people get up, assisting people to eat lunch or dinner and getting people to bed. For Monte, lunch might be a service station sandwich and a packet of crisps while she's driving, or a chocolate biscuit offered as she makes tea for one of her old ladies. The longer calls of a few hours might be what she calls 'a sit', where she'll stay with the person while their carer goes out for a few hours. Even if Monte has known those she's caring for a long time, she can't know what today's visit will be like. 'I've had situations when someone's in bed, they've been doubly incontinent, I've got half an hour to get them cleaned up, get them in the shower, get them downstairs – Oh, I've got to get them dressed as well – give them their medication, their breakfast, and clean up the mess that was left upstairs. How do you do all that in half an hour when somebody's frail and can't walk? It's just impossible. But you do it. And then you have to work over, there's no option. But you don't ever get paid for going over.'

She's known people who won't go over. One colleague left one of her regulars, a man with dementia and diabetes, at his kitchen table, unfed, unwatered, unmedicated and unshod in a T-shirt in the middle of winter. 'And this man was like that: "Eee-eee-eee!" when I walked in and I was like: "God! What's happened?" As I got there, the son was arriving. I supported them to make a complaint against the company. But that person's still employed. Uh huh.' Monte took to keeping an eye on the house; if she drove past and the blinds were down, she'd call the office and ask to visit. 'And lo and behold I would go in and he would be sitting there cold, no TV, no heating, no blinds open. I done it quite a few times. And then I was told: "No, you can't. Somebody's been." "How do you know somebody's been? I've *got* to check." But they wouldn't let us go in.'

Monte works twelve days and then has two days off. She's developed her own run for Mondays to Fridays despite her zero-hours contract – on her first weeks in this job she asked clients to ring the office and ask specifically for her. She's got used to her hours changing; she gets angrier at the poor standard of care the contracts permit. (She's lucky she owns her house: workers on zero-hours contracts are being turned down by landlords for having an unpredictable income.) On Saturday and Sunday, she works a split shift: out in the morning, back at home in time for a 5 p.m. tea and then out again to put people to bed. This morning she'd received her rota for the next twelve days: 'I always go to Sunday to have a look because I hate Sunday. I do. I'm working from half past seven in the morning until ten o'clock at night – do you know what I mean? I don't like Sunday.' She's never yet arrived to find someone dead, but says death 'comes with the territory'. After a tough day, she'll go over to Margaret's for a cup of coffee and a bit of cake. 'And she sorts us out. Uh mm.' Part of caring is keeping morale up: 'You do get people who sometimes sit down and say: "I don't want to live any more. I'm 97, pet, I shouldn't be here." And I have to say, you know, you're lucky to be here, because some people don't get that opportunity and I know it's hard but you've just got to go with it, haven't you?'

A month of these days results in £800 for Monte. With Pietro's wages, child benefit and child tax credit, they're still around £24 short each month. Around £1,700 goes on fixed expenses: her husband's pension (she doesn't have one, after seeing so many of the people she cares for lose out); a window loan; phone, TV and broadband; life insurance; mobile phones; house insurance; boiler insurance; water bill; mortgage; mortgage insurance; TV licence; car insurance; the children's dinner money; food shopping; petrol; bus and taxi fares for Pietro to get home from work when Monte's got the car. And £572 goes towards paying back loans. 'The washing machine broke. You've got no money because you're paying off debts, so what do you do? Well, use the catalogue. It kind of makes sense.' She points towards the kitchen alcove: 'The leg fell off me dining room table, so that's from the catalogue. Me fridge-freezer, that broke, so that was from the catalogue. We don't have savings.' Her pink and maroon striped T-shirt? 'Catalogue!' Monte laughs. 'I haven't paid a penny towards it yet!' If Monte's travel time were paid, as a recent decision by the Employment Appeals Tribunal says it should be, her income would go up to £1,000 a month: 'You could be looking at ten hours a week, that's forty hours a month, that's a whole week's wages!' If Pietro worked full-time and Monte stayed at home they could earn more, because Pietro is paid better than she is. 'But I want to go to work. That's why we work it the way we do.'

Monte calls her daughter into the kitchen. 'It's terrible what me children think I do.' Her daughter, her son and their friend run in. 'What does Mammy do when she goes to work?''Wipe bums.''What do I do?''Errr ... wipe bums.' We all laugh.

'What do they want to be when they're older?' I ask.

Her daughter says a doctor, her friend a swimming teacher, no, hang on, a ballet teacher, and Monte's 4-year-old, who's been 'actually actually scaring' the older girls with his impression of a monster this afternoon, says: 'A knight.' What does Monte say she does? 'I get really annoyed with myself, because when people ask, I say "I'm just a care worker." I'm trying not to. Care work: we're at the bottom of the pile. We always have been. And people judge you because of it. And I suppose I judge meself because of it as well.' What annoys her most is when people think she's a home help, that she clears out the fridge and mops the floor and fetches pension money, whereas in many cases she's doing things a district nurse, if they hadn't halved in number in the past decade, would have done.

Monte's parents were members of their local Conservative Club, but she joined Unison when she started working for the council, because that's what you did. When Unison asked all their branches for information about home care in 2011, Monte decided to speak out about some of the things she's seen. She's contributed to Labour's Your Britain website and Denise Kingsmill's review into the conditions of care workers; she's appeared on *The One Show*, the Radio 4 *Today* programme, *Newsnight*; French news and Japanese news. She's even confronted her boss, Dr Richard Preece, the suited, rimless-glasses-wearing Medical Director of Allied Healthcare, about zero-hours contracts on Channel 4 News. In front of the cameras, Preece, lightly exasperated, admitted 'there is a huge issue for care workers in terms of the clarity of pay', and announced that all Allied Healthcare care workers would be offered a guaranteed contract. 'And the travel time?' Monte asked. 'We can't do everything at once.' Once the cameras were off, Monte said to him: 'You know, it's never been about money for me.' And he replied: 'Yes, Rochelle.' And then Monte remembers him laughing: 'He laughed. He laughed at us! And I said "No, it's never been about money. It's about quality care. That's all my fight's about."' Monte showed me the new contract Preece promised: 'The company will offer you work when it is available during your stated availability. Your employment with us is conditional on your agreement to work flexible hours or no hours, if the work is not available. There may be times when no such work is available for you and the company has no duty to provide you with any work at such times.' Nothing had changed.

Monte is courageous on screen, with an animal-print scarf and a smile once it's over, but speaking out has consequences. Monte's rule is that she 'doesn't knock the company'. She argues what she sees as the truth: the system is to blame. Does she worry? 'Of course I do. I've got a stupid name! I just think how on earth would I ever get a job with somebody else! Rochelle Monte? Oh, that rings a bell! Oh God.' The dread remains. 'I feel like I'm waiting for some kind of backlash ... That's when they wash their hands of you, isn't it?' A month after I spoke to Monte, she was suspended by Allied Healthcare for being a 'safeguarding risk', and for two weeks, she knew nothing more than those two words. Had she given someone the wrong drugs by accident? Had someone died? 'I was just broken,' Monte said. Her GP prescribed diazepam.

Allied Healthcare eventually revealed that they'd been unhappy that French TV had apparently filmed her washing a client's legs. When Monte, with Unison's help, explained that it had been a neighbour who had given their consent, she was reinstated, but she couldn't face going back. 'They didn't want to employ me.' Now she has a job with a private provider, Home Instead Senior Care, who pay between £7 and £9.35 an hour, doesn't schedule calls shorter than an hour, and who ask her to provide companionship as much as care: walks along the beach, trips to the theatre, even a shift that involved sleeping for £8.35 an hour. Monte's new employer is proud that she's invited to Parliament to speak to MPs about her experiences in the care sector; Monte herself is finally confident in the quality of the care the company provides.

Henry Lopez, 35, cleaner, London

For two weeks in July 2013, the floor of Manchester Art Gallery was swept not only at night but also at lunchtime in plain sight of the gallery's visitors. The cleaners worked in a swarm, chasing small slips of paper in red, yellow, green and blue across the parquet with dry bristle brooms. The lunchtime sweepers weren't real cleaners: they were instructed by the California-born performance artist Suzanne Lacy, and the slips, which talked about the living wage, were swept into a tote bag to be littered again the next day. The performance continued once the cleaning was done, as sweepers, professional and amateur, gathered to talk under *Work*, Ford Madox Brown's painting from 1852–65. *Work* shows a group of navvies digging up a Hampstead street. They are constructing the sewers that would prevent typhus and cholera; mounted aristocrats, suited intellectuals and orphaned urchins look on. Madox Brown was thought radical in his time for putting workers at the centre of his view of society. Henry Lopez, who earns a living cleaning offices and portering at the University of London, sat underneath a muscled arm throwing rubble out of the sewer trench in the painting. He remembers talking about 'how we feel when we are there in the morning with no people around and just on our own – basically feel, if you like, invisible. There is no one around. And basically we talk about how in the day it can be the same. There are people who ignore you completely because you are a cleaner and they don't know what you're going through.' Lacy had invited him because the summer before he had led a campaign to improve the conditions of his fellow workers, which won them the London Living Wage.

Cleaners perhaps serve a sort of psychic function for the rest of society by taking away the dark, dusty, imperfect results of living, like the navvies making a channel for our shit to flow underground. They are the ones who keep up the illusion with bleach and borax and soda crystals; when they remove the dirt we can believe there wasn't any dirt in the first place. Cleaners make waste disappear, and then they disappear. We invite them into the most intimate parts of our homes, and send them away cash in hand, no questions asked. Perhaps we require that they disappear because of what they remind us of. One of Lopez's slogans during the campaign for cleaners' working rights was: 'We are not the dirt we clean.'

In 2011, the University of London outsourced the contract for the cleaning of university buildings and halls of residence to Balfour Beatty, a private company who employed women and men from Latin America, Eastern Europe and Nigeria (and a few from the UK) on the minimum wage. The university had recently announced it would be implementing the London Living Wage, but as the cleaners were employees of Balfour Beatty (as at the Lincoln call centre, as for the Newcastle care provider), they were loopholed out of that agreement. By spring 2011, after back wages hadn't been paid for several months, the cleaners went on a wildcat strike, and within three days they had won the payment of missing wages and voluntary recognition for Unison, their union at the time, which meant they could open official negotiations on the remaining issues. It might have seemed like a victory, apart from the fact that they still weren't receiving the London Living Wage. Lopez saw an article in the *Evening Standard* on the bus home about workers at the University of London who were campaigning for the London Living Wage: 'I didn't know what was the London Living Wage. I didn't know anything about anything. So I was reading, reading. I saw that SOAS already had £8.30, Birkbeck already had £8.30. I was thinking to myself: what is this SOAS getting £8.30 and at Senate House we're getting £6.15?' He took the article home with him. 'This is interesting. I'm going to take this newspaper to my work colleagues and say these guys are campaigning: why cannot we?'

By July 2012, further strikes brought the University of London to agree to raise the outsourced cleaners' hourly wage from £6.15 to £8.80. Unison were satisfied but the cleaners wanted to continue to fight for what they began calling the 'Tres Cosas' (Spanish for 'three things'): sick pay, a pension scheme and paid holidays. Cleaners employed directly by the university already had these things; Balfour Beatty offered none of them.

To the cleaners, asking for the three things that would bring them a dignified working life seemed fair, but to Unison it looked like too much to ask. It's not a new problem: 'There's been unions in this country for years,' Lopez said, 'but they never care about these workers.' The documentary film *Nightcleaners* (1972–75) showed what cleaning offices at night looked like – a hoover's buzz echoes into a roar; a cardboard tube of bleach is shaken into a shiny toilet bowl; a lonely cleaner waves from a skyscraper window – as well as revealing that traditional union organising didn't serve non-traditional workplaces. How can nightcleaners attend a 6 p.m. union meeting in the pub, when their shift starts then? Unions are less practised at recruiting and campaigning for agency and outsourced workers, and the cleaners of the University of London in 2013 needed a more agile, technologically adept, responsive union. They didn't want to negotiate, but to resist.

The cleaners were mostly Spanish-speaking, middle-aged

women with sensible hair and rimless glasses, who worked split and short shifts around other caring responsibilities. Lopez arrived from Ecuador at the age of 22 in 2000, joining his father who had emigrated the year before during the 1998–99 banking crisis. 'My situation in Ecuador was really bad. That was the time that they changed the currency, and the time they overthrew the government – maybe it was like three governments in the year.' His mother, brother and sister eventually came to the UK too. He arrived with no English and no papers; he wouldn't be official for nine years. He didn't exist so he did work that we like to think doesn't exist: cleaning for £4 an hour, cash in hand. 'When I came, there was no other option. I couldn't speak English, I have no papers, I have no CV or anything, so the only job is cleaning. There's no other job. I cannot even do catering because that is something that is a bit better, you can say in a way, but I couldn't do that because I couldn't speak the language to talk to people. So I used to work in hotels cleaning. And that's the reason most of the people do cleaning in this country, basically. Because most of the people that learn English they leave the job because it's a hard job.' When his English got better, he worked in catering. The problem with cleaning wasn't 'just the job – which is hard – it's about the treatment you receive from these people. The conditions you work in, you know. Sometimes you don't even get paid for the job you do. And I experienced it myself at the University of London: that's why we started all this. But sometimes you have to accept it because you don't speak the language – you don't have any other option.' When he got his papers, he kept his best, most flexible cleaning job – hoovering and cleaning desks in an office, a two-hour job that can be done in less and that fits around his other work – and got an official position at Senate House in the University of London as a porter, where his father also worked. 'In life, there is a reason for something,' Lopez says of the way he ended up getting involved in the Tres Cosas and

London Living Wage campaigns. 'And for me, my destiny was to be here. Because it wasn't planned.'

In April 2013, 120 cleaners, porters and security guards who worked for the University of London broke away from Unison and joined the International Workers of Great Britain – a small independent trade union that describes itself as organising 'the unorganised, the abandoned and the betrayed' – and started to campaign for the Tres Cosas. Students joined them for a summer of action, keeping promises made during the 2010 student protests. Konstancja Duff, who was studying for a master's in philosophy at Birkbeck, was arrested for chalking 'SICK PAY HOLIDAYS PENSIONS NOW SUPPORT THE CLEANERS STRUGGLE' on a university foundation stone and was charged with criminal damage. (She was eventually found guilty and fined £1,010, long after the rain had washed the chalk away.) The university also tried to forbid political protest on campus, but the cleaners went out on a two-day strike in late November, with drumming, homemade signs ('Prohibited: Get Sick, Get Old, Visit Family', 'Trabajadores de los Gardens'), red balloons, a tea bar and gentle dancing. Delivery vans were successfully persuaded not to cross the picket line and drove away to whoops and cheers; a strike fund rose to £5,000, more than enough to compensate all of the workers for two days off. At the end of the second day, the campaign Unison thought was too much was triumphant: Balfour Beatty announced in November 2013 it would give the cleaners 'sickness absence pay, improved holiday pay and access to the company pension scheme', bringing working conditions close enough to the workers' demands. The cleaners' breakaway union, the IWGB, hadn't yet been formally recognised by Balfour Beatty, but they had proved that bringing a new, defiant energy to traditional labour organising could work. 'Now that we've become visible, everything has changed,' Lopez said. They had uniforms now, with boots and gloves. 'Even the managers, bosses, they say

"Good Morning" to everyone. They are aware of what we do. Everything has changed.' Fighting back had transformed the atmosphere into a more caring one.

On 21 December 2013, the Tres Cosas campaign held a Christmas party in a series of rooms over a shop on the Strand. We crammed in, passed around plastic pint glasses of beer and watched the children of the cleaners, in ponchos and circular skirts, sing and dance. The eldest girl, in red lipstick for perhaps one of the first times in her life, giggled when an 'Arriba!' went up from the crowd. Grandmothers clapped along; fathers filmed on iPads; I caught a few people collecting empty beakers and putting them in bin bags while the party was still going on. The performance ended to terrific applause, but not from the little brothers who had got bored and had planted their hands over the steamed-up windows. The children were taken home to bed and turntables were set up: everyone salsaed in couples and cheered on others in a spontaneous dance-off. 'The way we do trade unionism is with happiness, not just as a business,' Lopez said, as he took a pint glass of water into a quieter room next door to cool off. That politics could be done with exuberance perhaps seemed normal to someone brought up in Latin America. His friends teased him for stopping dancing. 'She's going to make me famous!' he said.

In the mornings, Lopez works his two-hour office cleaning job from 5 a.m. to 7 a.m. He just puts music, 'all kinds, mostly Latin', in his ears and gets on with it. He then makes an hour-long bus journey to the university, where he works as a porter from 8 a.m. to 3 p.m. setting up rooms, preparing the projections and computers, and packing up books. After work, he reads for a degree in social sciences at Birkbeck, and hopes ultimately to do something related to social work. He earns £1,200 a month for his two jobs, but money's 'not interesting. What makes me happy is more interesting to me. As a human being, you have to enjoy your life.' He never knew what he wanted to be when he was younger: he just took things 'as it comes' but he hopes that his nephew and niece won't have to work as he has done: 'Let them benefit from what has happened to us.' 'We don't ask for anything special,' Lopez said. In the New Year, they would have to fight for the university's recognition of the IWGB in order to begin talks on remaining issues, including the redundancies being planned following the closure of one of the student halls for a long refurbishment. The union would have to be strengthened with more members: 'We have created something so good and important that we need to maintain it.' But for now, it was Christmas, and he invited me to dance.

Donald MacSween, 29, crofter, Outer Hebrides

Farming in the Highlands is ancient, although the system of crofting itself dates from the 1700s. Hebridean clans used to farm communally before the Highland Clearances, when the aristocratic owners of the land decided it would be better used for raising Cheviot sheep, and gave individual farmers strips of land of questionable quality – crofts – to work instead. (It wasn't until the Crofting Act of 1886 that the farmers finally secured their right not to be evicted at the laird's whim, to be compensated for improvements they made to their crofts and to be charged a fair rent.) When the American reporter John McPhee visited Colonsay, an island south of Lewis in 1969, he accompanied a crofter on rent day, the one day of the year a crofter met the man who owned the land he worked. The crofter paid his rent, the laird murmured something about the year's farming and then poured two drams of whisky which they drank together. Now much of the land on the Hebrides is owned communally following the Land Reform Act – brought in four years after the Scottish Parliament was established in 1999

– which gave crofters the right to buy the land they farmed at any time. There's no longer whisky on rent day, just £35 handed to the land's trustees. Modern crofters take care of livestock but also of the welfare and future of isolated communities, of the Gaelic language, of the idea that Sundays aren't work days.

Nessmen, or *Niesochs*, come from Ness, on the Isle of Lewis. 'No Nessman of working age ever died in his bed,' they say here on the top tip of the Outer Hebrides. A Nessman might have a heart attack cutting the last peat of the summer, but not beneath a feather duvet. Ness is a network of tarmacked roads studded with houses with strips of croft land behind. Each strip is divided into square after square until they reach the *machair* where tiny purple, yellow and white meadow flowers bloom on sandy soil, then the fine pale sand fades out to the Atlantic on the left or the Minch on the right. The fields are lumpy and peaty, and watched from a window, they always seem to be moving: rabbits bounce up, birds alight and take off, wind moves through foliage, a cow or sheep trudges gently to a fresher part of the field. You don't notice the fences at first, but they're there; occasionally, they are studded with barbs. I was told that people down south get mixed up and call the house built on the croft a croft. The house is just a house: the croft, those seven acres or so, is the thing.

The Comunn Eachdraidh Nis, or Ness Historical Society, holds a grey archive folder for each croft. For that of Donald MacSween, the 29-year-old who works the seven and a half acres known as 20 North Dell, the ownership can be traced back 200 years to his great-great-great-grandfather. Donald's mother, Annie, one of the founders of the Historical Society, showed me the family tree in the library. 'We have the croft going back to the first tenant that we know – this guy was born in 1807,' Annie said. 'Now, his daughter was my great-great-grandmother. So if you go down the line – this is me, that's Donald, who you've been talking to, that's my father, his father, his mother, who was the daughter of that man.' She turned the pages. 'And then, we have photographs pertaining to the family.' The first photo showed Murdo Macdonald, the great-great-grandfather, caught stiff-backed for posterity in a portrait studio. Then a snap of the great-grandfather outside on a chair with Annie as a baby sat on his knee. 'We try and do that for every family, and people come from all over the world to see ...' Here's the grandfather Murdo in blue overalls waiting for his flock to be dipped, and finally the croft itself can be seen. 'I'm turning the pages because I want to show you – that's me – I want to show you the last photo here ...'

I couldn't help laughing. The last photo was of Annie's tall, dark and strapping crofter son as a boy, his fine, shiny baby hair swept into a side parting. 'Oh how sweet he was! Look that those eyes,' I said.

Annie laughed. 'Yes, he *was* sweet, past tense!'

Every crofter I spoke to on Lewis knew Donald MacSween. The owners of the recovery croft, which was worked by people suffering from mental illness, had sold him pigs. A Harris Tweed weaver newly come to Ness had asked him for help to manoeuvre a ton loom into his weaving shed; MacSween turned up with several other Nessmen to heave for an hour to get it in place. I read about him on the football pages of the local paper, *Fios*: 'A few minutes from the final whistle, Ness keeper Donald "Sweeney" MacSween saved an Andy MacLeod spot kick.' Even the owners of the B&B I was staying in knew him from his hospitality to some American girls staying there earlier in the summer.

He picked me up from the B&B too and took me to Ness FC Social Club. As well as being the goalkeeper, he's on the social club committee and is currently working with them on an application for lottery funding. (*Fios* seemed to run a lot of stories about winning funding of one type or another: money for a play park near the Eoropie Sands or for a spoken edition of *Fios* for blind people.) Inside the TV was on and a group of men were congregated around the bar: they all joked that Donald had no 'work ethic'. MacSween also presents the sheepdog trials on the Gaelic-language channel BBC Alba, and being on TV doesn't look like work (he didn't entirely think it was work either). He lifted a can of Irn-Bru to drink, and the rolled-up sleeves of his Ness FC hoodie revealed red midge bites all over his forearms.

MacSween told me that he bored easily, which is why he liked crofting: 'Crofting, historically ... you were never going to make a living out of being a crofter, on its own. It would sustain you, but not more than that. It wouldn't allow you to live outwith poverty basically, so crofters were always crofter-weavers or crofter-fishermen, you know, always doing something else – odd jobs, driving, and doing a bit of this, bit of that and I think it's the same kind of ... I've got four or five income streams, I could lose one or two of them and I'd still be OK.' We went through his income streams: crofting, TV, working for the council on a project to keep young people in the Hebrides, Gaelic translation and interpretation, writing the Gaelic page in the *Stornoway Gazette*. They might seem very different to collecting seaweed, but 'I think the way I live right now is very much the old-school crofting mentality, although I think the new word for it is multi-skilling. So you're doing lots of different things. That's how I see it anyway and I don't like being told what to do, I don't really like working nine-to-five jobs, kind of have to, but this gives you a taste of harder, harder work.' He worked for the council, mostly in an office in Stornoway, Lewis's capital, during the working week. Everything else had to be fitted around that: in winter, MacSween would be out on the croft in headtorch for the pitch-dark hours before work; in summer he was out with the midges in the early evening.

At the Ness Historical Society the next day, we were also crofting. MacSween was working with a group of local teenagers to make an app, as part of the council project to show young people it's cool to stay on the Hebrides. They had £4,000 funding to develop an interactive tourist map of Ness. One running joke pretended that Michail was having a bromance with Spencer, the eager tech developer in Glasgow: a draft email began 'Dear Spencer xoxoxoxo'. But talking to the developer had them entertaining a crofter thought: could we do it ourselves? 'It would be better,' MacSween agreed. But they kept with Spencer for the moment. MacSween's role was that of enabler: he hid behind his phone a little. While we paused for tea and cake in the café run by Nesswomen, the conversation ran away with itself. Would you prefer fingers as long as your legs, or legs as long as your fingers? Or to see babies as muffins or muffins as babies? MacSween had a good answer to the first: fingers as long as legs, so that he could cover more of the goalmouth.

The teenagers didn't speak Gaelic among themselves, and although they had a Gaelic word for an email password, they had to ask MacSween to spell it for them. For Annie Gaelic was the language of the playground; for her son, it was the language of crofting. 'My first memories are feeding sheep with my grand-father on the croft, and lambing. So my grandfather died in 1988 when I was 4, so my first memories are of … I remember being at their house all the time, and I remember going in with him lambing. These are my first memories. The pictures in my head are of a sheep lambing and the lamb coming towards me. A newborn lamb and it's trying to get on its feet for the first time and it's looking for its mother. And it came to me. And me being a 3-year-old or whatever, I'm like "Oh the lamb's coming to me, it's great, look it's my friend, it's my friend," and my grandfather pulling me back and saying "No. You can't do that. It's got to go to its mother, don't let it come to you." So I remember that. But it would have all been in Gaelic of course.' To describe the rhythm of the year on the croft, MacSween had to use Gaelic. 'I don't speak English when it comes to my animals.' I asked him the Gaelic word for tupping, the six to eight weeks in October to November when the ram mates with his ewes, but I pronounced

'Gaelic' as 'garlic'.'Gallic gallic gallic!' MacSween laughed. 'I correct a lot of people when it comes to that. The word for tupping is raihock.' MacSween pronounces *reitheachas*, the Gaelic for tupping, throatily and confidently.'Ray? No.' I give up on my first half-attempt.

He breaks it down for me: 'Rai. Hock.'

I try again, but it comes out sounding German: 'Ray. Hoch.' 'Raihock.''Raihock!''Yeah. That's when they go to the ram.'

Gaelic is not just the language he talks about his animals in, it's also the language he talks to them in. More practically, it's the language crofters talk among themselves: 'I don't think you can be a real crofter if you don't have Gaelic. Because there's a big communal side to crofting here anyway still because we're all working with small numbers and when it comes to dipping and shearing and things like that we all bring our sheep together and we'll do them all at the same time. Gaelic is the language of the fank – the fank is where we collect our sheep – everybody will be speaking Gaelic in the fank. And I don't think you can be a real part of that community if you don't have Gaelic. For me Gaelic is the same as the crofting, it's not something I think about ... it's just part and parcel of living here.' MacSween said that he didn't understand people who came from far and wide to seek their Hebridean roots: 'I don't romanticise it,' he kept saying. He might sometimes look up while on the croft and realise that people had been doing the same thing as him on this spot for thousands of years, but it wouldn't disturb his day. 'I'm a Niesoch and a Lewisoch and I'm a Scot. You're asking me what I am, these are the three: Ness, Lewis, Scotland. I wouldn't go any further than that.' He knew who he was, and what he cared for, because he knew from where he came, what language he spoke and who his great-great-great-grandfather was.

MacSween began a blog of life on the croft after putting a photo of a lamb that had been born without a head on Facebook which the social network removed. Looking after sheep means spending one toxoplasmosis spring burying stillborn and deformed lambs every Saturday (the Highlands and Islands have an exemption from mainland rules for the incineration of dead livestock). Looking after sheep means coming home to a sheep on its back, dead, with its eyes pecked out. Caring for sheep also means sometimes killing them. 'It's not easy, it's tough at times when you're losing animals. You're not a bloodthirsty killer.'

MacSween buries his animals with little fuss, but when a Nessman dies, most of the community's men participate in the lift of the coffin. MacSween's father is an elder in the Free Church of Scotland, a Calvinist denomination. The Isle of Lewis is also one of the few places left in the UK where the Sabbath is formally observed. (There is a place or two open and the ferries and planes run for tourists, but that's it.) What does a day without work look like? 'I feed the sheep, I'll feed the chickens, give them water if they need it. I won't handle them, I wouldn't shear a sheep, I wouldn't drench the sheep, you know give them wormer or anything like that. Anything you could do on another day I wouldn't do it, basically.' He doesn't think the religious arguments for keeping the Sabbath stack up, but 'in terms of our way of life' it's a good idea. 'My mother always used to say that we've got the Calvinist work ethic, which is work your backside off, basically, six days a week, which is what we all do. If it wasn't for Sundays, I'd be burned out. I'd have been burned out a long time ago, because of just working working working working working. So, in a way, you really do need your Lewis Sundays.' When he's on the mainland he doesn't hold himself to Lewis standards: 'Last time I was in Glasgow, two or three weeks ago, I went to the museum, then I went to the cinema, then I got some food and I went home. Not exactly rampaging around the city.' Because crofters have always patched together a living, working in the evenings and mornings when the light allowed, one day off a week didn't seem too much. He makes £1,000 a year on the croft: about the same as he receives in subsidy.

Other crofters felt differently about Sundays. Some were happy to advertise their working Sundays by hanging their clean washing out to dry. It is part of Lewis's charm that it is so itself, but if you haven't grown up there, you might find it wearing. You notice certain names again and again: there is Macleod & Macleod the makers of fine black pudding, Macleod IFA the accountant, Macleod the operators of a refrigerated truck. There are eleven pages of Macleods in the phone book. Ness men and women have tackled the pointlessness of the official phonebook by writing their own, arranged by village and nickname. The nicknames are practical but they also, as in Tolstoy, either tie you to the community or show that you're newly arrived in the country. Annie's nickname is Anna Murdaig, an old-style patronymic as in Imperial Russia; MacSween's is, in the newer style, just Sweeney. People talked of 'outwith' the island, or of 'on the mainland'; only the outsiders named themselves 'incomers'. Incomers don't speak Gaelic, don't have the right sheep, or no sheep at all, and they spend a lot of money on replacing broken fences. Families who have been on Lewis a long time might deduce that they don't know what they're doing. MacSween lowered his voice to talk about a new crofter: 'They haven't a clue about crofting ... They're just making a mess ... Yeah. I'm not going to say too much.'

He drove me to see his croft, waving at people along the way. (It was like this every time he gave me a lift; I took to waving as if I knew everyone myself.) The croft stretched out from the house: in the first square there was a hen house with twenty or so chickens and a brood of week-old chicks that already knew to leap out of my hand as I tried to hold them. In the next pen were the white sheep, recently shorn. MacSween called to them: '*Trobhad!*' I was wearing a red dress and they wouldn't come; MacSween said they might be spooked. He doesn't use his sheepdog Bud to get the sheep in as they generally come when they hear his voice, though he admitted 'they're *seòlta* ... how would you say ... they can be crafty'. He pointed out his favourite, which he'd hand-reared, with a deeply curved back and no horns. Beyond them was the ram, in a separate pen. In another field behind the house there was the 'wee team' of a blind sheep and a one-eyed sheep. With a single eye between them they moved together around the field, the blind sheep's head on the one-eyed sheep's hip. They listened intently – you could see it in the way they held their heads, just slightly cocked – as he called to them, but they too didn't come. Bud watched from the back window of the house.

It was a quarter to nine and still light: the so-called blue hour that comes in deep summer before the sun goes down for good. It doesn't get dark until 10 p.m. in July here. As we turned to leave, MacSween picked up a low clucking in the long grass. A hen sitting on hatching eggs. He lifted her up and found several chicks, black and lemon yellow, as well as eggs that hadn't hatched yet. He wasn't as happy as I thought he might be. On top of writing a blog for the Scottish Crofting Federation, making a packed lunch for next day's trip to St Kilda and getting to bed before midnight, he had yet another thing to do. He would have to move the hen and chicks into his parents' barn, or the chicks would die in that night's rain. I heard next morning that they had.

REPAIRING

rabbi
army major
nurse

Benjamin Simmonds, 48, rabbi, Bury, Manchester

On Friday 18 July 2014, Shabbat, the Jewish day of rest, began at 9.09 p.m. The lighting of the candles marked an end to cooking, writing, driving, doing the housework, carrying things, cutting the stems of flowers, tearing paper, turning a light on, checking your mobile phone: anything that could be understood as work. (Jewish law bans thirty-nine activities on Shabbat, including threshing, spinning, ploughing and building.) The sky was a pale summer blue over Bury on the north edge of Manchester and men dressed in black and white walked home from the Stenecourt, the Manchester Great and New Synagogue, pausing to talk to friends in the road. I had been invited to Friday dinner with its rabbi, Benjamin Simmonds. I held my gifts of a potted pink gerbera and pack of cards for playing Snap and started to feel too hot in my trench coat, buttoned-up blouse, calf-length skirt and black tights. He wasn't back yet. Across the road from his red-brick terrace house, a man in a T-shirt and shorts opened his front door, stretched, and took a long draw on a cigarette. The rabbi arrived, with two of his sons, walking fast, in grey-tinted glasses and a small black tallit on top of a black suit with a white shirt. Rabbi Benjy had told me on the phone that Orthodox Judaism's modesty rules meant he couldn't shake my hand, so I didn't offer it. 'Have you been waiting long?' he asked. Inside the table was set: the white tablecloth woven with semicircle menorahs was covered with a clear plastic sheet and seven places were laid, each with a tumbler with a darted pink paper napkin tucked inside. The house was filled with leather- and gold-spined books from floor to ceiling; stuffed toys had been tied into the bannister and many soft, primary-coloured faces looked at you when you came in. Rabbi Benjy and his wife Rebbetzen Anna were 48 and had eight children and an infant granddaughter. 'Shabbat is just amazing,' Simmonds had told me when I first met him in February 2014. 'I don't think of it as a negative at all. You don't have your phone on, no emails, nothing. We just enjoy the time with our families and we do things which we never have time to do the rest of the week.' Like Sundays on Lewis in the Hebrides, Shabbat stands against the idea of seven days' work without a free moment. Some activities are encouraged on Shabbat: sleeping, going to the synagogue, reading the Torah, spending time with family and friends and spending quality time with your husband or wife. The seventh day is when the parts of us worn thin by the working week are repaired.

The dinner begins with the scripture, Genesis 2:2, which inspired Shabbat: 'And on the seventh day God ended His work which He had made; and He rested on the seventh day from all His work which He had made.' Then there's a song to welcome the rest day and honour the lady of the house: 'She riseth also while it is yet night, and giveth food to her household, and a portion to her maidens,' it goes, describing 'a woman of valour' and the ideal of wifeliness. 'I'm not sure I live up to it!' Anna said. The parents bless their children, taking their heads in both of their hands in turn and kissing the crown (Anna tweaked her 12-year-old son's nose after he wriggled). After the Kiddush grape juice is blessed, sung over and drunk, everyone in turn went to the kitchen sink to take the two-handled green plastic cup and pour water over one hand and then the other. Simmonds uncovered the Challah bread, plaited and glossy, sliced it, dipped the first bit in salt and shared it among us. It tasted like brioche. Blessings are made over the food in front of you in a Jewish household: Simmonds told a story about a time Jonathan Sacks ate with John Major, who asked him to say grace. After a moment's visible panic, Sacks caught sight of a bowl of grapes on the table, and blessed the meal. When Major later asked what had happened, Sacks said: 'You bless what you are about to receive, we prefer to receive it first.'

Anna, who trained as a chemist and works mornings as a lab technician in the local Jewish school, begins the work of preparing the Shabbat meals when she makes the Challah dough on Thursday. The rest of the food – a stew for Saturday that could sit a long time on the stove, and Friday's dinner – was made on Friday before sunset. We ate clear soup with flat ears of pasta and carrot while we talked about Harry Potter (the books were thought much better than the movies); then after a shot of chocolate Israeli liqueur there was chicken, roasted vegetables and potato gratin. The children remembered their favourite Shabbats: the one where they'd had a food fight with plastic fruit and veg; the one where they'd stood on their chairs to sip 7 Up through foot-long straws. Conversation was also directed. The lesson that day was about the importance of taking risks and of keeping promises made in extremis. The children aren't allowed sweets in the week – 'I'm hungry for sweets!' the youngest daughter said before the soup – but fizzy-sour jelly snakes, giant cola bottles and triangles of dark kosher chocolate studded with nuts arrived in small glass bowls for dessert. It was 10.30 p.m. and the sky had turned Quink blue; my taxi arrived. The sweet-seeking daughter was in bed, and the others would follow. Tomorrow's Shabbat service at the synagogue began at 7.30 a.m.

Rabbi Benjy's days begin earlier than 7.30 a.m., even when it's not Shabbat. He wakes up at 5 a.m. naturally – 'there's no great shakes in it. I'm not saying I'm anything special. I've been that since I was a kid' – and spends the first hours of the day on his work for the Shul. (Shul is the Ashkenazi word for synagogue; the Ashkenazim originated from Central Europe and make up 74 per cent of Jews worldwide; Kafka, Einstein and Anne Frank were Ashkenazim.) He'll walk to the synagogue – it 'clears your mind' – and lead the first prayer meeting at 6.30 a.m., returning home for 7.45 a.m. to see his family, before driving through the backstreets to the local high street solicitor where he's worked for twenty-four years, arriving early at 8.30 a.m. At work, he specialises in employment law, suing, accident and medical claims (though he reduced his hours in November 2014 when his responsibilities increased at the synagogue).

He held to the Jewish work ethic, which he described as a 'very very strong work ethic in the ethical sense – in the way you work. If you're employed to work for a day, you work for a day and you have your tea break when you're supposed to have it, and you don't sit at the computer playing games.' He might have to interrupt his work to take a phone call from the Shul; he'll either go to the synagogue at the end of his road or to an upstairs room for afternoon prayers. 'Work is work, for me it's partially enjoyable, some of the time, but it's mainly just like any other job. Whereas being a rabbi is a different thing altogether.' He'll leave the office at 5.30 p.m. or so and have dinner at home before returning to the synagogue on Mondays and Wednesdays until 10.30 p.m. Saturday is Shabbat but on Sunday he might conduct a wedding in the busy late summer period before Hannukah. He works thirty-five hours a week as a solicitor and thirty hours a week as a rabbi, but rabbis don't clock off: 'If someone rings you up at nine o'clock and says they've got a problem you can't say ring me back in office hours. You can't do that.' There are jokes about it. A rabbi gets a call at 3 a.m.: 'I'm making a Bar Mitzvah in five years' time,' the caller says. 'Can you tell me which part of the script my son has to read?'

When Rabbi Simmonds was 12 or 13, he wanted to be a

politician. 'There's a saying about politics: "It's not a good job for a Jewish boy."' He was born in Manchester in 1966: his father served in the RAF, trained as a printer then became a wicker-ware salesman; his mother looked after the family at home. The family attended Stenecourt and Simmonds went to Jewish schools in the area before getting a place at 18 at the Gateshead Yeshiva, the largest Talmudic school in Europe. 'It's like Oxford for Jewish scholarship.' At Yeshiva, he worked from 8.30 a.m. to 10 p.m. for two years, began doing a bit of community teaching and realised he liked it. He then did a law degree followed by a year's qualification and a year's training to be a solicitor. After marrying, he worked as a lawyer by day and towards becoming a rabbi in the evenings. His calling didn't come in the form of a flash of light, but he remembers a feeling of heat 'building up' and becoming convinced he 'would be missing something very very big from my life if I didn't do it'. He became assistant rabbi at Stenecourt in 2001 and was voted rabbi in February 2014 on the retirement of Rabbi Brodie. Stenecourt is an Orthodox community – women rabbis aren't permitted; a banner saying 'Stenecourt supports Israel' in blue and white hangs in the entrance hall; women cover elbows, clavicles and knees – but 'we're a bit different: we're an observant community, but everyone in this community will be involved, will be working, will be very much outward-looking, with very moderated views'. There are 700 families in the Shul who pay a subscrip-tion of £550–£600 per year that provides, among other things, contributions towards burial costs, and Simmonds's salary. The average salary for a rabbi in the UK is £20,000; most rabbis, like Simmonds, have a second job: 'It's all very nice being a rabbi, but you've got to have an income.'

The hardest part of being a rabbi is dealing with members' expectations of him: 'You can't do everything. I've said to people: "I'm not the Messiah."' Weekday services are well attended and well attended to: 'You're dealing with people who've got a lot of passionate involvement. And they've got an opinion about everything. You know what they say: two Jews, three opinions?' His work in the Shul is in some way similar to his legal work – at Stenecourt he helps with questions of Jewish law – but he is more personally involved. 'You're also a bit of a social worker for people who are in crisis, sometimes.' He gave a 'famous or infamous' sermon on Passover 2013, around the time the coalition government's bedroom tax came into force. The changes have been 'very very very socially divisive': 'There's a widespread misconception that everyone who's Jewish is rich and it's just not true. I can tell you now: I'm dealing at the moment with a lady who's having her house repossessed. I'm doing it using both hats: my legal hat and my rabbi's hat.' She lost her job, can't get benefits for a 'ridiculous reason' and is facing a repossession hearing against the housing association. 'There is genuine poverty.' Rabbi Benjy cares for her state of mind while Benjamin Simmonds legally delays the repossession so that she has time to find a job. He also sees clients in his work as a solicitor who need other sorts of help: 'Without breaching confidentiality, I have a client, a young woman, not Jewish, I feel so sorry for her but alcohol is the root of her problem. It upsets me to see a lovely young person just having her life ruined because of alcohol. And I can't do much about it, because all she comes to me for is legal questions, which is all I can do. I can't do anything about it.'

The first Jews came to Manchester in the 1740s, selling small items and treating people's teeth and eyes. (William the Conqueror invited Jews to England in 1070, Edward I expelled them in 1290 and Cromwell allowed them to come back, but they came slowly, warily, often bringing up their children as Christians or living quietly among themselves.) Nathan Mayer Rothschild, who established a Europe-wide banking dynasty with his four brothers in the nineteenth century, was the first of the brothers to leave the Judengasse in Frankfurt and come to England in 1798. He started exporting English cottons to the Continent from Manchester in 1799, as well as indigo, tea, grain and jewels when cotton was too cheap. In 1809, he moved to London and began to deal in bullion, using his money to support Wellington against Napoleon. He was strictly Orthodox and had seven children; when someone hoped at a party in 1834 that his children wouldn't be too ruthlessly commercial, he said: 'I wish to give them mind, soul and heart, and body, and everything to business; that is the way to be happy.' His son, Lionel, carried on the business and became the first Jewish Member of Parliament in 1858, the same year that the Great Synagogue in Manchester, the original of Stenecourt, was founded.

In 1871, there were 3,500 Jews in Manchester. Many of them carried on their trades – tailoring, cap-making, waterproofing clothes – in the Red Bank quarter by the River Irk that Friedrich Engels, sent to Manchester by his father to work in the family textile business, saw in 1845: 'A planless, knotted chaos of houses, more or less on the verge of uninhabitableness, whose unclean interiors fully correspond with their filthy external surroundings.' Michael Marks, the Jew who founded Marks & Spencer in Leeds's Kirkgate Market in the 1880s, came to live in leafy Bury New Road in Salford in 1898; eight years earlier Jews had finally been admitted to all public offices (apart from that of monarch). Eventually things improved: by 1914, there were 30,000 Jews in Manchester; during the Second World War 6,000 refugees from Nazi Germany were accommodated in the city, and today the Manchester Jewish population is around 30,000 in a city of half a million. The 2011 census put the Jewish population in the UK at 0.5 per cent; by comparison the UK is 59 per cent Christian and 5 per cent Muslim.

The fastest-growing version of Judaism across the UK is more orthodox than Stenecourt's – the Haredi community, who keep men and women apart, grew 48 per cent, mostly because of a high birth rate, between 2001 and 2011 in Salford – but Stenecourt's style of orthodoxy is evolving differently. There are 400 full members of Stenecourt and the synagogue has seen a 'modest' increase in strength since Rabbi Benjy has been there. In January 2014, an Eruv was created which meant that within a certain area, some Sabbath rules could be broken. Now Shul members can carry their glasses or house keys to the synagogue instead of using a belt; people in wheelchairs or babies in pushchairs can come out too. 'Five weeks ago, my granddaughter would not have been able to come to us on the Sabbath,' Simmonds said in February 2014. 'It's already made a vast change in the community.' Since Simmonds was elected to rabbi of Stenecourt, the constitution has been changed so that a woman could become an executive officer of the synagogue, helping to run the building. 'We thought there would be a fight over it, but there wasn't.' The role of women in the Shul has changed enormously; the rabbi used to be able to rely on the ladies' guild to cater for social events – 'You can't do that now! They're all working!' – so now they have to buy food in and charge for it. I sat in the ladies' gallery of the synagogue, which, though modern and light, smelled of both strong perfume and the stale warmth of my grandmother's house, for Rabbi Benjy's first sermon after he'd been elected, with 77 per cent of the vote, to the highest role in the synagogue. He asked everyone to put the differences of the election period behind them and build a 'Mishkon', or community, 'in their hearts'. Some had already done so. As we left the building, a passing family called out: 'Everyone loves you!'

Other things stay the same. In February 2007, Rabbi Simmonds was punched as he walked home from a party on a Friday night: 'It happens, but it's not too often.' (He did a self-defence course afterwards.) In July 2014, while the Israeli Army carried out Operation Protective Edge in the Gaza Strip, he told Stenecourt members not to walk home alone; at the end of that month, the Community Security Trust, a charity founded in 1994 to protect Jewish communities across the UK, had counted 304 anti-Semitic attacks in the first six months of 2014, a rise of 36 per cent on the same period the year before. There were twenty-three incidents in Bury and forty-two in nearby Salford. 'We made our contribution,' Simmonds says of the 200 people from his community who died in the Second World War. 'We're as much British as everybody else. We pay our taxes and we're not entitled to be treated in that way. That's wrong.' Stenecourt has bomb-proof windows, CCTV, security on a Saturday and a door lock whose numbers are in Hebrew. In July 2012 Mohammed Sajid Khan was given an indeterminate sentence for planning to bomb the streets around the synagogue. 'There's a threat which is always hanging over us. It's happened in various communities around Europe. Thank God nothing's happened in Manchester.' On Sunday evenings every few weeks, Simmonds goes to interfaith meetings, knowing nevertheless that the people plotting his death aren't the ones who are interested in interfaith dialogue. 'We're not armed; we can only do what we can.' Not everything can be repaired easily. As a rabbi, Simmonds hopes he's 'adding value to people's lives, in a way. You hope that's what you're doing. Adding spirituality to people. Because it's a rough old world out there.'

D, 30s, army major, south-west England

It's Friday, or Poets' day (Push Off Early Tomorrow's Saturday) at the army barracks and the corridors are clean and empty. Major D comes to meet me at the gates of his barracks with a sunburned face underneath his beret. Yesterday he was on exercise with his company, who teased him for putting on sunscreen; today he's less pink than some. His office is, in some ways, entirely ordinary: institutional carpet, a corner desk with a computer, a whiteboard, a grey metal filing cabinet. But a camouflage rain cape hangs on the pegs by the door and his barrelled knapsack with helmet and gun sits calmly beneath it; the orange-toned photo collage is of a tour to Iraq. Out of the window, I can see the flag of Major D's battalion flying.

Major D joined the army as an officer at 23. His father was an estate agent and his mother a physiotherapist; on leaving home for boarding school, he told his father he wanted to join the army. He wasn't scholarly and his father told him to look into the family regiment, which he joined after getting a 2:2 at university. His summer jobs included a day as a dustman and a spell at a mushroom factory, slicing off juicy ones for Waitrose and warped ones for Aldi (both jobs were picked as a response to his father's accusation of laziness on finding D one day on the drawing-room sofa). After a year at Sandhurst and six months' infantry-specific training, his first posting was to Salisbury Plain, the 'super garrison' area in Wiltshire, of which the Ministry of Defence own half (including the secret military science park, Porton Down). What does Major D think his work is for? 'I exist for the benefit of 123 men who rely on me for their welfare, their pay, their career, the welfare of their families, their moral upbringing.' He reminds me that the Sandhurst motto is 'Serve to Lead'. 'And on operations,' he continues, 'we're safeguarding the ability to go down to Waitrose and fill up your cars with food, and then go and fill up your petrol tanks and drive home and live with your families, in what we would call normality. The government has used us in really misguided ways in the past but ultimately we're there to safeguard our national way of life.'

A normal day begins early, around 5.30 a.m., when his two nursery-age children wake up. He leaves the house at 6.20 a.m. and arrives at the barracks for 6.50 a.m. where he'll quickly check the officers' mess (where he's in charge) before starting work at 7 a.m. Every week is timetabled in advance: his soldiers might have a swimming test, a session on standards and values for a test they'll need to pass that year, a weapons-cleaning session, a first aid lesson, a four-mile run, an afternoon's training to fight in an urban environment. Every Wednesday, they have a sport afternoon; his men recently tried to convince him that snooker, played in a pub, was a sport. 'I don't think it's an army-encouraged sport: beer and snooker!' He laughs. 'Ha! Good boldness for asking.' They'll work until tea at 10 a.m. At 10.30 a.m. they'll start again until lunch at 12: in the officers' mess, there's soup and fish or an omelette with salad but no dessert. The afternoon lasts until 5 p.m. for the soldiers and until about 6.30 p.m. for Major D, when he'll drive home listening to Radio 4, back in time to hear his 'little people' splashing in the paddling pool in the back garden. He'll cook dinner, and then sit in the garden with his wife, who worked as a teacher before having children, over a glass of wine and talk about the day. He's had 'no bad day' since becoming a company commander, only busy or frustrating ones. For officers without families, the evening begins in the officers' mess at 7 p.m. with sherry, then four courses – starter, main, pudding, cheese – and coffee afterwards while sunk into a leather armchair or contorted around a Twister board. (Some online chat rooms insinuate that this is often done naked.)

He keeps the door to his office open. If one of his soldiers comes to see him with a personal problem, he'll sometimes remove his rank slide from the front of his fatigues, or call a soldier by their first name or a nickname to put them at ease. 'I love them to bits,' he said. His work in camp is about the development of moral courage in his men. 'I did one of those online surveys you can do, and they said you should either be in the services or you should work with special needs children. And some of the people I see, I question, why do we give these people guns? Because they're just ... some of their stories are heartbreaking. Most of them, as I say, haven't had much of an education, some of them have been abused as children, sexually as well as physically, and they come with the most hideous stories. Some of them have got nowhere else to go other than here. They don't go home at the weekends because they've got no one to go to. And they've just been let down by the people who are closest to them.'

Soldiers start on £17,500 a year, rising to nearly £30,000 after two years in some roles, and receive a bonus while on operations which Cameron doubled when he came into office in 2010: a six-month tour of Afghanistan attracts a bonus of £5,280. 'When you come back from tour, you always see a lot of Range Rover Sports,' Major D says, but the cars often disappear back to the dealers after a while. You can join the British Army at 16 – the average age of a soldier is 20, and a third of the force is under the age of 30 – and earn an income more disposable than most of your peers, because of the accommodation and facilities the army provides. There are around 82,000 men and women in the British Army, of which 17.5 per cent are officers. The force is half the size it was in 1980, and despite getting smaller, the responsibilities haven't lessened. (Major D said that servicemen were 'triple-hatting' jobs.)

The Ministry of Defence doesn't collect data on the background of its recruits, but a small-scale study in Cardiff in 1998–2000 found that most soldiers had come from a 'broken home' or a 'deprived background' and hadn't gained any qualifications at school. It's been estimated that 30 per cent have a reading age of 11 or less; 40 per cent in Cardiff joined up as a 'last resort'. A third of recruits drop out before completing basic training. A soldier in Major D's company will have to leave the army because he joined his friends in taking cocaine on a night out and got caught; another was AWOL; yet another had built up such a degree of debt with a bank and a payday loan company that he had only £50 a month to live on out of a £1,200 monthly salary. Major D and the platoon commander set out to repair the situation: they went to the bank and spoke to the manager, and the interest was cleared. Then they spoke to the loan company, 'who were very good' and wrote off their interest. The soldier should be free of debt in six months. Major D's brother, who works in banking, tells him that sort of pastoral care is unheard of in his workplace. 'I don't think there's many other organisations that will do that. For the army, that is absolutely expected, and if I hadn't done that my boss would have been saying: "What sort of leadership are you practising in your company?"'

The army's concern for its men isn't altruistic. 'Everything we do in camp to try and help people is about that moral component. So that when we then go on operations and you have to then look someone in the eye and say: "Go and destroy that" or "Go and kill those people", they know that you're not doing it because you've got a bloodlust, you're doing it because it needs to be done and you wouldn't waste their lives, and they have a trust in you that you develop with them because they know that you've got their back.' There's a boom of a gun discharging in the background and Major D looks over to the photo collage of his tour of Iraq. Downtown Basra. A covert operation overlooking an enemy stronghold: 'If they had found out we were there we would have all got on Al-Jazeera.' An ambushed vehicle covered in bullet holes. A shower block wall hit by a rocket. 'It was just horrible. Friends were bleeding to death on your lap, just terrible. And I came back and I was just really angry with everything. Particularly because I thought there were circumstances out there where there was nothing you could do. People were dying and you could not do anything about it. And, in that environment, you'd have all these conundrums put in front of you. You'd be in an armoured vehicle and you'd come to a crossroads. And there were two insurgent tactics. The first one was they'd put bombs on the crossroads and if you drove across it, even in an armoured vehicle, you'd blow up and you'd all die. So to get out of that, three or four people would jump out and they'd go and look for the bombs around the crossroads on their feet. If they couldn't find any, you'd drive across the crossroads. But because we started doing that, they then covered the crossroads with snipers. So as the guys jumped out they'd get shot in the head. The first two or three patrols we did I thought I need to set the standard, so I'd get out – people were being physically sick in the vehicle because they were so scared, it was very much like *Saving Private Ryan*; it's just so accurate – so you'd get down from the turret of the vehicle, you'd go out the back and people would pat you on the back and say "Good luck" and you'd put your webbing on and out you get and look for the bombs in 50 degrees of heat. You're sweating, and you couldn't find anything, you get back in again, and then you'd cross over and finish your patrol. I did that three or four times, and then I thought if I do that I'm not leading my platoon because I'm out on the ground. I've got four vehicles and thirty people: I need to lead. I've done my bit now. I'd peer down the turret and I'd look at people I loved in the eyes and say: "Corporal Smith, Corporal Jones, go and do it." And you just saw them all thinking: "Don't ask me, don't ask me, don't ask me." They went anyway; they never said no. That was hard, for six months, every day, things like that.'

After coming back from Iraq, he signed off for a year, uncertain he wanted to come back. He knew he was suffering from post-traumatic stress disorder, but it was harder for someone of his rank to admit it, or even recognise it, 'because at the time no one really talked about it'. Things are better now: his soldiers congratulate each other on having gone for a psychological debriefing, and Combat Stress report that soldiers returning from Afghanistan are coming to them within eighteen months instead of after thirteen years. In 2013, there were as many army suicides as there were soldiers killed in Afghanistan; the Ministry of Defence says that the rate of suicide in the serving military is lower than in the general population, but researchers at the University of Manchester found in 2009 that young ex-servicemen were three times more likely to commit suicide than their peers. The army doesn't manage to repair all its men: in London, 10 per cent of rough sleepers are thought to have served in the military, around 13 per cent of soldiers misuse alcohol on their return from war. Major D told me about an unsigned poem that has done the rounds of his regiment: 'When I came back from Iraq one of the things I did to get me through not feeling terribly good, I sort of changed it and added a few things to it.' It's framed in the colours of his regiment on the walls of his office, above the photographs of Iraq. 'Reluctantly, I accepted the promise of eternal guilt, should I fail those that I served. / I felt terror, glimpsed hell and drowned in the sense of loss.'

The effect of modern battle on the soldier was noticed in the First World War, where 10 per cent of officers were said to have 'dreams that drip with murder', as Siegfried Sassoon put it (Sassoon was himself hospitalised at Craiglockhart in Edinburgh, where he met Wilfred Owen, another 'emotional case'). 'Shell shock', as the soldiers were calling it, was first thought to be caused by damage to the nerves. Charles Myers, the then Royal Army Medical Corps psychologist, clashed with the men at the top of the army who felt that discipline would be the best cure. He tried to repair riflemen who couldn't feel anything on the right-hand side of their bodies, sergeants with a persistent tremor and a pulse of 102, stretcher-bearers who jumped when cotton wool touched their shins. Myers found that early psychological intervention to help them accept and reclaim their memories as well as an expectation of recovery helped, but not all returned to 'light duty'. There were some whose right arm still trembled eleven months after they'd returned from the front; others were accused of malingering or cowardice. In 1942, Churchill was arguing that 'it is very wrong to disturb large numbers of healthy, normal men and women by asking the kind of odd questions in which the psychiatrists specialise'. Now PTSD is recognised as a psychological condition, and treated as such.

Major D has happier memories of Iraq: his mother-in-law sent a Fortnum and Mason's hamper to Basra, and 'my platoon and I sat down and had foie gras and some sort of cheese thins. It was amazing. We had some really lovely jams and some leaf tea for a few days.' The empty basket was used for storing hand grenades. 'When you get a Liverpudlian taking the piss out of a Mancunian, both of them ganging up to take the mickey out of a Fijian, they're hilarious. And they're the salt of the earth.' He reached for a photo album: a cricket match in whites against the sparkling green grass, a 'Days of the Raj' themed ball where someone in black tie is wearing a stuffed toy snake around his neck, a group in plus-fours with toboggans before doing the Cresta Run in St Moritz. There is a ball in the summer and at Christmas; a grouse dinner every September. He turns the pages, pointing out himself in black tie and a friend 'who's out now'.

A major in the army is paid £52,000 a year with a final salary pension that can be claimed after sixteen years' service. Major D is a year off receiving his £40,000 lump sum with £800 a month for life. 'If you want to do well in the army, from this point onwards you have to make a lot of sacrifices,' he says. 'So you have to work really late every night, you have to volunteer to go all over the world for two or three years, you have to move around, you have to hit every timeline, you have to do a lot of sort of political wrangling: it's a very political game because the triangle gets pretty thin closer to the top. It's very cut-throat. And against that I've got two children, and we wanted to buy a house and settle down and that's not conducive with a career that's taking me there. I'm going to leave the army so that my family can be my main effort.' He shows me one of the photos his wife sends every day of his children: today his daughter is wearing a yellow fireman's helmet lopsided. He can't receive daily pictures easily when he's on operations, as connecting to the internet on your phone can show the enemy where you are.

Does he think about the lives he's saved? 'I probably think

about the lives I've taken. That's something I think about more.' He has Iraq in mind. 'I think about that maybe too much. The people you've saved – if you weren't there maybe someone else would have been there. Usually you save someone's life by taking someone who would have killed them off the streets. So in Basra we took horrible people off the streets, but we'd never meet the people who we'd protected. But there's no escaping from someone who you've killed. And you ask yourself: did you really need to do that? Was there another way around it? However many times you come to the conclusion that it was absolutely the right thing to do, and I'm pleased to say I have got that certainty, you still think. You're not born to kill people, are you? For whatever reason.' How does he deal with it? 'I don't think twice about picking up my weapons systems and doing the job now, but I used to be into shooting. I don't shoot any more. So I would prefer not to go into an environment where people take pleasure from guns. I try not to think about it, to be honest. If my children ever asked me, I'd never tell them. But I wrote a diary. It's all in the diary. Probably, when I felt it was right, I would let them read my diary.' His son wants to be a lorry driver at the moment. 'I don't think he's going to be a soldier! I hope not!' And then Major D adds in a quieter voice: 'Well, I'd be proud of him ...'

Major D walked me to the front gate and left me with the pair of soldiers on patrol while I waited to be picked up. They checked the cars that came in, drawing up the barrier for each authorised visitor. A woman officer in a brown peaked cap drove out in a small car; one of the top brass in a black, shiny 4x4 drove in. The soldiers chatted in between the intermittent raising and lowering of the barrier: one liked meat on the bone, the other hated it. Their friends drove out for the weekend: 'Who's she?' they asked when they saw me sitting in the hut next to the barrier. The patrol kept open cans of Coke in the hut to sip throughout their watch; on the floor were handwritten sheets soldiers had signed to confirm they were sober enough to drive. The barrels of their guns were pointed at the floor as they defended their barracks. Occasionally, they'd pause, legs wide, arms on their weapon. And then one would ask the other: 'Do you prefer the sweet chilli sauce or the honey mustard dressing?'

Julia, 48, nurse, High Wycombe

'The most frequent comment most women make is "you're being so nice",' Julia, a registered nurse in the High Wycombe clinic of the British Pregnancy Advisory Service (BPAS), explained. 'Almost they kind of want you to be horrible to them. Most clinic days I get the tissues out, because I've upset someone. Not in a horrible way – they're just like "you're being so nice".' A third of British women will have an abortion, usually in the first three months of pregnancy, by a nurse administering a pill in GP surgeries, hospitals and specialised clinics across England, Wales and Scotland. (In Northern Ireland, abortion remains illegal unless three doctors agree you are a suicide risk: Northern Irish women with unplanned pregnancies generally travel to the UK, often to Liverpool, for treatment.) Having a private abortion costs around £500, but the NHS pays for 98 per cent of terminations, mostly via charities such as Marie Stopes and BPAS. In 2013, 185,331 abortions were carried out in England and Wales, the lowest number in sixteen years; since 1989 around 20 per cent of conceptions in the UK end in abortion.

Three times a week, BPAS takes possession of a handful of rooms in a GP practice on a business park, among workplaces for Hovis, the bread maker; Biffa, the rubbish collector; and Jewson, the building merchants. High Wycombe, surrounded by beech woods, was already known for furniture-making in the 1680s, eventually producing millions of high, round-backed Windsor chairs, but in the early 1990s recession G Plan went bust and seven years later Ercol moved to Princes Risborough. Between 2004 and 2009, Wycombe lost more jobs than anywhere else in the country. Inside the GP's surgery, the blue pleather chairs turn tacky in the heat. The nurses are wearing summer clothes today: a badge and a green lanyard (which reads 'don't lose it until you're ready') are the only ways of telling who they are. Julia manages to look harried and happy at once as she wheels her scanner to where she wants it. She wore scrubs when she worked on a children's intensive care ward, but here 'most women would prefer that we didn't, they don't want it to seem so clinical'. Carol, the lead nurse, and Paula, who manages the practice, work alongside her.

In the morning they see new clients (no one refers to them as patients). Paula will take their details – 'Your title – is it "Miss"?' 'Were you born in England?' – and ask: 'Would you like an abortion?' If they say yes, they're asked: 'Have you been forced?' They can speak freely; no accompaniment is allowed for this first interview. Stories come spilling out, anxious and jumbled, sad and bare. A woman in her early twenties had discovered the father of her unborn baby was sleeping with two of her best friends, then a scan showed the baby was small for its age: she had wanted to bring it up right, but circumstances were against her. She had a 4-year-old already; her previous partner (now in prison) had once made her drink bleach while pregnant, causing a miscarriage. 'I do pick 'em!' she said, as her large black glittery earrings bobbed in the hot air. The next appointment is with one of the nurses. Julia's room is divided by a blue fabric curtain: client and nurse talk in one half and Julia scans their stomach to find the foetus in the other half.

Being a nurse in an abortion clinic is similar to being an ante-natal nurse: Julia is studying for an MA in foetal sonography, learning the same skills as the nurses on the maternity ward. Scanning a small foetus is 'quite an art', and getting a good picture becomes a collaboration between nurse and client. Julia chats at the beginning of the consultation – 'I write the date all day and still don't know it,' she says to one client; she commiserates with another about her 2-year-old waking up at night (her 11-year-old son did the same too) – and so when it comes to the cool jelly, the electronic wand and the otherworldliness of the first scan, the clients are calm. 'Bit cold, bit slimy... sorry,' she'll say. 'Sorry I'm fiddling about.' 'That's fine, I'm in no pain at all,' one client replies. Julia prints the picture and brings it back to the desk face down, where she'll later staple it, still hidden, in the file. 'In America, they make the women look at the scan. We give the women the choice. So if a woman says "Can I see my scan?" then we just note that down and let them have a copy if that's what they wish, but on the whole we don't really show them much about scanning.' Out of seven clients that morning, no one asked to see the scan.

Some don't get further than this. Julia described one woman who wanted to know the date on which the baby could have been conceived. 'And you can't say to them "this is the day you've conceived" – it doesn't work like that.' She was back two weeks later for treatment: she'd been having an affair and couldn't tell whether her lover or her husband was the father. A Muslim girl, one of their regulars (High Wycombe is one of the least white places in the generally wealthy, strongly Conservative home county of Buckinghamshire; 16 per cent of the town is Asian), is comforted by the idea of a scan: 'She's having sex with a boyfriend, using condoms really consistently, but she's absolutely petrified of being pregnant. She's come to us about four times – never been pregnant – and this time she hadn't even done a pregnancy test. But everyone was sort of alerted to her. I said to her: "You haven't done a pregnancy test." She said: "No." I said: "Well, I'm going to get you to do that first" – she was almost getting on the couch to have a scan. I said: "I'm not doing this, there's no point." So I had to have quite a long session with her, talking about contraception and what would be acceptable and that she can't keep using us as a service because she's so scared.' The test showed she wasn't pregnant, but she wouldn't believe it: 'I was on Google and ...' 'No, no, no, no, no.' 'But what about implantation bleeding?'"So you've had a period since then?' 'Oh, yeah.'

That day, a 16-year-old in a Mickey Mouse T-shirt and her mother spent a long while talking about what to do after the scan: the young woman wanted to keep the baby, and her mother didn't want her to. The mother promised that if they booked an appointment for treatment next week, she could cancel if she changed her mind, no questions asked. BPAS don't chase people who don't turn up for their abortion: 'We're just like: "Fine, thank you for letting us know, that's great."'

Seeing that the pregnancy looks like a pale, hazy smudge can help women make up their mind: 'Some women will say they want to see the scan because if it looks remotely human, they wouldn't go ahead. Whereas if it looks like a blob – which a lot of them do – they just say: "I can do that."' Julia said that it 'would be a bit of a struggle' to assist in late-term abortions. Does it change things for her when the scan reveals a blob? 'I think it does for me. But then most pregnancies that are conceived don't go to implantation and certainly don't go to full term. Most implantations are lost as a period anyway, so most people wouldn't even know they were pregnant in the first place. So to me, I don't think it's viable until post-twenty-four weeks, when if someone did go into premature labour then those babies have got a chance to survive. Before that, you can't be someone in your own right because you can't survive without the mum. A lot of people are saying that the woman should have less rights than the unborn baby. How can you figure that? She's alive, she's breathing, she probably has a job and has other children. If her mental health or whatever is going to be totally destroyed by having another child, then the two that are already here have lost their mum, effectively. And I've worked in a neo-natal unit. When you're seeing them born at twenty-three weeks, they don't survive. And it's horrible. All the heroics that go into trying to save this one little person that if you do manage to get him to survive, what have you let him in for? A life of oxygen, and feeding tubes and ... You just think, mmmm.'

The abortion happens a week after the first appointment so that the clients have a chance to reflect, and the clinic can obtain the two doctors' signatures UK law requires. Julia explains what will happen when they come back for the abortion, going through a BPAS booklet they take away with them. She can't be sure that everyone who comes to see her can read it. There are several methods based on the stage of the pregnancy and what the client can face doing: the abortion pill, or a surgical abortion under either local or general anaesthetic. The 16-year-old who came with her mother thought that if she were to have an abortion, she'd prefer it to be carried out while she was asleep. Julia said they could bring a friend, that they should stay at home the day after and 'get other people running around after you', that they should bring sanitary towels. The pain is like a bad period, and if it's any worse than that, they can call the BPAS helpline any time of day or night, or go to hospital. And although the mood is serious, it isn't sombre: 'You'll say to them no sex for two weeks after the procedure. And then they all go: "I'm never having sex again!" I just joke with them and say: if I had a pound every time I've heard someone say that I'd be a rich woman. They all say it.' Even if there have been tears, the idea is to send them away comforted: 'I do think we laugh more than cry, and if they cry hopefully I'll make them laugh afterwards.'

In the five-minute gap between patients, there is a paper file to complete, the bed to cover with fresh paper towels, the computer to update, and a pause: 'You never know what will come through the door.' In the waiting room an Asian man in a long pale blue tunic and matching trousers walks around bouncing a baby; a blonde emerges from one of the consult-ation rooms and pauses by a waiting man, who follows her out without a word. The clinic stops entirely for lunch: everyone camps in Paula's room with sandwiches, pulling in chairs from the waiting area and grabbing a cup of tea from the tray. Julia has stolen a smoothie pouch meant for her son's lunchbox to go with her sandwich, and there is a lot of talk about each other's children: 'I think people believe if you work for BPAS you hate babies. It's utter rubbish. No. No. I love babies, I love children. But I also believe when you're done you're done. I've got two, I wouldn't want any more. I've done my bit. They're growing up, and I hope to have a life again at the end of it all.'

Julia had begun her career as a dental nurse. Her school had suggested she became a secretary – 'Who'd want to do that? It's so boring' – but she was bored mixing up fillings too, and left to train as a hospital nurse. Julia was one of the first 'diploma nurses', who trained for eighteen months at college and eighteen months on the ward. She was regarded with suspicion: 'Oooh God, you're a dip-*lo*-ma nurse! You ask too many questions!' She worked on wards in Leicester and Reading, but decided to change direction after 'a critical incident where a child was born really really sick – I think he died – and as a result of that I was like "I need better training,"' and so took a job on the children's intensive care ward at Guy's Hospital in Central London. After six years there, she moved into school nursing in Nottingham – immunisations, child protection, sexual health – and so enjoyed the teaching part that she trained as a contraceptive nurse and joined Buckinghamshire County Council, where she gave sexual education lessons in schools. When 'all the massive cuts came to all public sectors, particularly education', she was invited to apply to BPAS after meeting them at a health fair in August 2012.

Julia also works in the BPAS head office in London on a

schools programme for the charity two days a week. (Fridays are kept for her family.) The idea of BPAS going into schools is to discuss abortion in an unbiased way, 'because at the minute in schools abortion will be debated in religious studies and it always becomes a bit of a for and against, whereas actually young people need factual information about where they can go, what they can do and often how they got to be pregnant, which sounds a bit strange but unintended pregnancy is very complex.' There has been a rise in pro-life groups offering to come into schools for free: the Society for the Protection of Unborn Children, for example, was discovered in March 2012 to be telling 14- and 15-year-olds in a Cambridgeshire school that abortions caused breast cancer, infertility and death, and that even abortion after rape wasn't a good idea because it consti-tuted a 'second trauma'. There aren't any pro-life campaigners outside the clinic in Buckinghamshire, but she's seen them at the BPAS HQ. Often on a Wednesday afternoon – 'we've never worked that one out, why Wednesday afternoons?' – a nun and two men will stand on the pavement, staring. This atmosphere makes its way into the consultation room: during Julia's scanning seminars she learned about Ian Donaldson, the Scottish doctor who developed ultrasound for pregnancy. He regretted that his machine was being used for discovering abnormalities: 'I myself would not like to feel I had contributed to a Huxleyian Brave New World.' Julia must tell every woman who takes Misoprostol, the abortion pill, that it is actually gastric ulcer medication being used 'off-label', because its manufacturer, Pfizer, will not license it to terminate pregnancy.

After lunch, the nurses go to the medicine cabinet and sign out tablets, including Misoprostol, for the afternoon appoint-ments. The orange plastic jugs are refilled with water, and a fresh supply of plastic cups is placed upside down by the jug. The waiting room seems calmer now, with a woman in a headscarf and another with a baby in a plastic bucket-like car seat on the floor. A young couple come into the consultation room together: she's in a lumberjack shirt and he has neon-framed sunglasses in his hand. They're students who work at a pub together; she stopped taking the pill when it made her migraines worse and became pregnant. Carol checked whether she still wanted to go ahead, and asked if she had had any bleeding. Then she gently took her blood pressure and her temperature, poured a glass of water and pushed the Misoprostol out of its plastic blister. 'Can't go back now,' the boyfriend said, with a heavy lightness, as she swallowed it. 'I'm just dreading tomorrow, to be honest,' she said.

Swallowing can be the hardest part for some, because of severe morning sickness: 'We've got girls, they can't stop throwing up,' Julia said. 'If you're a princess, or whatever she is, Kate Middleton, that's fine, you get looked after and put in hospital for three weeks. If you're a normal person, vomiting every minute of every day is not doable. Especially if you're very young. This one girl couldn't get through her treatment because she was just being sick all the time. In the end we had to send her for a surgical treatment the next day, she couldn't keep her tablet down ... Her mum said: "She's been like this for weeks now, it's awful." You just think, poor kid.'

Once the abortion pill has been given, there is an opportunity for the nurses to care for any future children the women may have. With a fingerprick blood test, the nurses can determine both whether they are anaemic and might bleed a lot and whether they carry antibodies that might cause the body to see a future pregnancy as an invasion, and bring about a miscarriage. The test says to their clients: you can't go back, but things can be repaired. 'Our motto as BPAS is to do ourselves out of work. We don't really want people to come back to us. That's why we give out contraception. I don't want to see any of those women ever again. In the nicest possible way.' Carol goes back to the medicine chest to find a contraceptive pill with a different balance of hormones for the woman in the lumberjack shirt and I'm left alone with them. The boyfriend is surprised how low-key it is. He'd expected protestors outside the clinic: that's what you see in the movies. When Carol comes back with the right pills, he asks her: 'Do you tell people what you do?' Carol replies, without a beat: 'I'm careful ... I'm selective.' Julia wonders what her fellow commuters would think of her if they knew what she did: 'I sit on the train and think: Mmm. People would probably lynch me if they knew.' Did she really think so? 'Probably some would, yeah. I suppose in a carriage full of people half would and half wouldn't. Depending on their own circumstances.' But 73 per cent of Britons think abortion should be allowed if both parents agree. Wouldn't it be more like 70/30? 'I don't know. Maybe because I get on the train in Buckinghamshire. And I think: very white middle-class. So I don't know.' At one religious school Julia was asked: 'Do you consider yourself a murderer?'

The girl in the lumberjack shirt accepted a box of correct contraceptive pills, her boyfriend put his sunglasses on and they left. On Wednesday morning, when she came back, she would be encouraged to put the second tablet in her vagina herself, and sent away with painkillers, antibiotics and a pregnancy test to be done in three weeks' time.

Julia first cared for someone who'd had an abortion when she visited a friend she thought was ill. When she got there, the friend told her what had happened: 'I was like: "A what? What? What?" I couldn't even get my head around it all. "But your boyfriend told me you had just got a bad cold." I was so shocked.' 'I kind of see it from all aspects,' Julia said over squishy fish finger sandwiches in a quiet pub. 'I am an adopted person, I was born in 1967, which was just as the Abortion Act had come in, so I can see the pressures that young women were under back in the 1960s. It was all supposed to be about free love but you were punished for being pregnant with someone you had no intention of marrying. So obviously at the time my biological mother couldn't go down the abortion route unless it was an illegal one, so I was adopted. So I see it from both sides.'

In 1966, at the cusp of the change of the law, abortion was supposedly legal if the mother's life was in danger, but in practice, this meant well-connected women knew to go to a certain doctor on Harley Street for a stint in a maternity home and a 'diagnostic D and C'; the women who could afford it went for a box of Dumas's Paris Pills, 'whereby a maximum certainty of producing the desired effect is absolutely assured'; and the rest were left with knitting needles, drinking iron filings dissolved in a glass of beer and vigorously cycling uphill. The more desperate ate the heads of matches for the phosphorus that used to be in them, or put potassium permanganate inside them. If they bled, or developed ulcers, that just proved it was working. (In Germany after the Second World War, women believed that drinking the powder from an 8mm cartridge dissolved in a glass of warm water would do it.)

When the homespun remedies didn't work, they turned to the nuns in the nursing home, like Julia's mother did, or to friends. They might know someone: a factory forewoman, a former nurse, a retired dressmaker. In 1963, the Howard League for Penal Reform spoke to abortionists in Holloway prison. Half were housewives married with children, grandchildren and even great-grandchildren in one case. They felt 'women have to help each other' and they said they wanted to do it 'for the love of it' as well as for the need. One said: 'They used to drive me mad – telephoning, pestering.' And the abortions, sometimes paid for with a bunch of flowers but usually with £10, were pragmatic, English affairs: 'Two girls, friends, were operated on at the same time in the furnished room which they shared, while another girl looked on. The abortionist said they were all talking and laughing, and made cups of tea.' Their method, known as 'bringing a period on', was to inject a weak antiseptic solution into the uterus with a rubber syringe, which would irritate and cause a miscarriage. There was a distinction, as in the old common law, between that and destroying life. They were in Holloway because someone had died, or held a grudge and called the police; but they weren't social outcasts. When the factory forewoman was on trial, her girls collected money for her.

Julia found herself 'unintentionally pregnant when I was ... I'd just bought a flat in London, I was working at Guy's Hospital. I'd missed one pill because we used to go out and fetch sick children from all over the countryside. I was out fetching a sick child and thought, "Oh! I've left my pills at work." Completely forgot about it, and I found myself pregnant.' On her twenty-week scan they found her left hand missing. So at my twenty-two-week scan they said: "So, what do you want to do about this?" "I don't understand, what do you mean?" She said: "Well, do you want to continue with the pregnancy?" "Of course I do! You said it was just her hand, or its hand." She said: "Yes." And I was just thrown because I was really surprised that she offered it that quickly. And then the doctor actually said to me: "Well, people want perfect babies, don't they?" "I don't know, do they?" So now Amy's here, she's 15. So I can see it from all sides.'

Amy has gone on to compete for Great Britain as part of the Paralympic air rifle shooting team, and is aiming for Rio 2016 if Julia has anything to do with it. Amy 'doesn't think it's cool'. She just wants to fit in: 'And she'll often go: why did you even have me, 'cause of *this*!' Julia raises her hand as her daughter does to her. 'She did say to me: "Why did you have me?" "Because you're amazing! You're absolutely amazing! Why wouldn't I have had you?" And she went: "Because of *this*!" And she hates it but I said to her: "Well, you're amazing. You've done wonderful things, you're beautiful, you're gorgeous – you're hard work and you're challenging – but that's what kids are supposed to be for." So I can see the whole debate from all sides.'

Julia saw what she did as a 'positive' job: 'For me, it's about women's choice. I think you do what suits you at the time. Not "I've got this plan." And I have had friends that have gone "yes, at 25, I'm going to have my first baby, at 28 ..." And you just think, God, how do you do that? It was all so "I'm going to try for a baby here and going to have one here." Oh God, life's not like that. And then the women we see some of them have got six children, some of them have got no children. Some of them are university students who say "this would absolutely end my life", others are 46-year-old women that go "I thought I was in my menopause, obviously I'm not." Some women really wrestle with their decision, and you have to send them away and say you're not ready to make your decision yet, so go away and come back when you've decided, and others are just "Yep. I'm doing this, I have to do this, just don't talk about it too much to me, I've made my decision."' How do the nurses feel at the end of the day? 'I feel I've done a good job because the women didn't want to be in that situation,' Julia said. Carol said she felt 'wrung out'. Nurses on hospital wards get cards, chocolates, flowers, but they don't.

STARTING

apprentice
intern
technologist
unemployed
on workfare

Candice Devine, 19, apprentice, City of London

How do you start a career? The idea of an apprenticeship – of a number of years' work in exchange for bed, board, clothes and tuition at the beginning of someone's working life – is old, but first recorded on paper in 1230. A medieval boy would leave home at 10 or 11 and wouldn't be free of his apprenticeship until he was 21. The apprenticeship system showed society's faith in the future. A blacksmith whose own son wanted to be a furrier would take on another man's son to teach in the forge, creating a second hereditary line, a work family. People sometimes talk about a company as a family but at the Assay Office of the Goldsmiths' Hall in the City of London, there is a virtually complete family tree, in a register with illuminated letters kept in the library, and it goes back to 1578, when the first goldsmith's apprentice signed his curlicued name.

Long before trade unions were founded in the nineteenth century, craftsmen formed livery companies to regulate their trades and defend them from charlatans and foreign competition. The goldsmiths were the bankers of their day: they ensured that gold really was gold, introduced the hallmark to certify it as such and put the country's coins to the test once a year at the Trial of the Pyx. The livery companies were ranked by wealth in 1515 and the goldsmiths came out fifth: they are one of the 'Great Twelve' guilds – the others are the mercers, the grocers, the drapers, the fish-mongers, the merchant taylors, the skinners, the haberdashers, the salters, the ironmongers, the vintners and the clothworkers

– and were one of the most important groups of workers in early modern London. The red-carpeted, chandeliered Goldsmiths' Hall is still richly hung: oil paintings in which the artists' attention has been concentrated on the hands and the jewels on them cover the walls of the banqueting hall; the triangular head of the leopard, the goldsmiths' symbol, with two dagger-like teeth poking from the top lip, is everywhere. Many of the ancient livery companies have lost all links with their trades (understandably, given the number of wheelwrights and basket-makers left) and have effectively become grand dining halls. The day I visited, the hall was being transformed into a 'Belgian Palace' for a movie, but the company is one of the few that keeps links with its craftsmen. In 2012, the company built the Goldsmiths' Centre, a training centre with workshops not far from Hatton Garden in Clerkenwell. Every October the company hosts a fair for working goldsmiths in the hall, and they also fund apprenticeships.

I go past the set-dressers carrying gilded chairs and through a heavy wooden door to arrive at the white-painted walls and lino of London's Assay Office. Nearly every wedding band, christening cup and pair of Christmas cufflinks in the south-east of England will have come through these doors. (There are also Assay Offices in Birmingham, Edinburgh and Sheffield.) The word 'assay' comes from the Latin *exagium*, meaning 'examination, trial, test'; the Assay Office is where every piece of gold or silver is tested and then rejected or hallmarked. The sequence of hallmarks has changed over the years, but the minimum legal requirement is for the assayer's mark, the leopard's head, to indicate the piece has been tested; a fineness mark to give the percentage of gold, silver, platinum or palladium; and the sponsor's or maker's mark. (The Goldsmiths add two more: the traditional fineness mark, as the EU-decreed one is just a number instead of the familiar prancing lions, Britannias, orbs and crowns; and a letter indicating the year the item was tested and hallmarked.)

Candice Devine, 19, an apprentice in the Assay Office, works in a bright workshop at the top of the hall. She gently rubs a ring on a touchstone, a small tile of sheeny black stone – schist or jasper – and then rubs a sample of pure gold from her set of touchkeys alongside it, and then another line of touchkey brass alongside that. She swipes a pipette of nitric acid through all three: the ring and the pure gold go a rusty brown, but the brass disappears altogether. The ring is genuine. The acid test (the process is the origin of the phrase, along with that of 'touch-stone', 'hallmark', 'coming up to scratch') isn't the only way to test metals. There is an X-ray spectrometer in the corner, and a lab at the back for fire tests, the oldest and the least popular test with the trade, because it confirms purity by destruction, but 'there's just something about the touchstone I prefer', Devine says. It's the first thing she learned in her apprenticeship and the foundation for her career.

Devine went to the Assay Office straight from school at 17. She 'never wanted to go to uni. I've never liked the look of that life. My cousins, all of my cousins, all went to uni. And they've all come out with a big debt, no job, find it really hard to get a job – and one of them's now 32 and he's only just paid off his uni debt. And it's like: ooh gawd, I don't want that!' She had dreamed of training dolphins and whales as a child but as she grew up she enjoyed making jewellery, applied to the Goldsmiths for an apprenticeship and was offered an interview at the Assay Office, which she had to google to find out what it was. When she came to her interview, in a dress borrowed from a cousin, shoes lent by her sister and a letter from her headmaster, she looked up at the grand staircase of the hall and thought 'I'm going to try my best, but I'm never going to get this job.' But the idea of the Assay Office immediately grabbed her. The same thing had happened to David Merry, her master, who had wanted to be a gunsmith but became an apprentice here in 1971, having looked up 'Assay Office' in the dictionary. In Devine's interview, he remembers his colleague leaning over and saying she couldn't see Devine with a ten-pound hammer in her hand. So Merry asked: 'Can you see yourself with your arms rolled up bashing away at a piece of metal with a big hammer?' Devine replied: 'Of course!'

Devine comes to work four days a week, and on the fifth day she goes to the Goldsmiths' Centre in Clerkenwell for tuition in engraving, silversmithing and other metalwork techniques. In her spare time she engraves, and is working on a set of playing cards in copper and silver which will be her masterpiece at the end of her four years. (A masterpiece is no longer a require-ment, but Devine wants to make one anyway.) She arrives at 9 a.m. on the Central line and leaves at 5 p.m.; has learned to take tea at 11 a.m. and 3 p.m.; not to walk too far in her lunch-break and that it's cheaper to bring sandwiches from home than buy them every day. She's moved around the Assay Office from testing, to sampling and handmarking over the past two years. She goes slower than the normal salaried workers, doesn't have a target, and gets help from Merry or the other apprentices who are further on from her. 'If I do something wrong, I am really scared,' Devine says, when I speak to her and Merry in the staff common room, across from an exotic-looking board game that colleagues have been playing for weeks. 'Like that one time I actually marked something that was hollow. I did feel I was going to cry. That one time I did cry. I was so upset with myself. Because obviously you know – I've been trained, I should be better than this.' Merry, who teaches his apprentices in the way he was taught, sees it differently: 'Doing something wrong is part of the learning process, do you know what I mean? What tends to happen here is if you do do things wrong, you tend to learn more from them than if you do things right all the time, strangely enough. Innit?'

In the early modern period, apprentices and masters would come to their guild's hall to be bound to each other in a ceremony, and at the end of seven years, the apprentice would be made a freeman, and could set out on his own as a journeyman, and eventually become a master. The Goldsmiths' Company agreed on the match if certain requirements were met. It was usual for the master to take the apprentice into his house, feed him, clothe him and teach him; the apprentice had to prove he wasn't a bondsman, and so engaged to a feudal master, and to be obedient, studious, keep his seven-year term and not mind sleeping under his master's bench. The company also required that the apprentice wasn't to be sent to fetch water (there were supposed to be servants for that) and that the apprentice could read and write, which they would have to prove by writing in the apprentices' register during their binding ceremony. The company would resolve disputes: if an apprentice protested that the master's wife beat him or if the master complained that money had disappeared, the hall would mediate between them. One apprentice who fell in love with his master's maid and stole money to buy her clothes was dressed up in her lace and silk and put in the stocks to be laughed at, but he was later made a freeman of the company. Women were occasionally apprenticed – Brigies Cross appears in the Goldsmiths' apprentices' register in 1614 – but usually they did lower-skilled work such as burnishing, and only if they were married to a metalworker. They disappear entirely in the nineteenth century. The first female apprentice goldsmith of the modern era was in 1979, when Wendy Cook was taken on by Garrard to learn engraving.

Merry and Devine were bound together for four years at the hall in February 2012; Devine came with her father and all three signed an Apprenticeship Deed in which she agreed 'for the duration of her apprenticeship to faithfully honestly and diligently serve the Master and obey all the Master's lawful orders and requirements and will not do or knowingly suffer to be done any damage or injury to the Master or his property and will in all respects conduct herself as an honest and faithful Apprentice ought'. Merry remembers her father not letting go when he shook his hand; Devine thinks her dad would have liked to work in the Assay Office when he was younger.

Merry says he is like a 'surrogate father' to Devine. As she talks, he'll add in detail ('you were a strong swimmer') or a dad-like comment ('I'm going to interject here. She's a bit of an overachiever'). The bond made at the ceremony is more than a contract. Merry is still in touch with his old apprentices; he wants more for Devine than he had for himself: 'I've always said she could be the first female Superintendent Assayer here.' Every year on Good Friday, there's a big lunch in the grand hall for all the staff, with three courses and port, and everyone gets dressed up. (It's at Easter because October to December is the Assay Office's busiest time, hallmarking Christmas presents.) Last year he remembers talking to Devine about what it meant to him to be elected to the Institute of Goldsmiths, 'a huge bloody honour'.'We get quite teary with each other at times, don't we, having those conversations?''Yeah. It's kind of embarrassing really! It's like at the staff lunch, we had a bit of a moment there, didn't we?' Devine adds.'It's just problems, and stuff like that. But we iron them out.'

An apprentice/master relationship can be tender because it is meant to be for the long term, and for the good of the profession. And as a mark of that, it is properly paid. Devine started the apprenticeship on a salary of £16,000, immediately earning more than her elder sister, a hairdresser. They are 'probably about the best-paid apprentices in the trade,' Merry says. 'Whenever the old guys get together, we always sort of talk about the apprentices now and then.' When Merry was bound 'we were on horrendously low amounts of money. About £8.50 a week or something stupid ... My disposable income was probably about £1.50' – around £20 in today's money – 'Seriously. It was horrendous. By the time I'd paid my mum, I got two pints of beer and a packet of cigarettes.' The minimum wage for an 17-year-old apprentice is £2.73 an hour, but the worth of an Assay

Office apprenticeship seems to have risen. Devine remembers being shocked when Merry told her the salary; 'If I've got £50 to spend, it's like: "Oh, what shall I do with this £50!"' When interns work unpaid and graduates can't find jobs, a starting salary of £16,000 when you live at home – still £10,000 below the UK average wage – and a promise of more isn't nothing.

In 1971, there were 218,000 apprentices in the UK, but by 1990 the number fell to 53,600 as the British economy shifted away from manufacturing. The 'long wait' (an old trick: go to the workshop, apprentices are told, and ask for a 'long weight'), a salary while training and a trade for life fell into obsolescence. Apprenticeships became shorter and rarer. The Youth Training Scheme devised in 1982 was supposed to provide on-the-job training for 16-year-olds, but allowed employers to let the state pay for a worker and to supply little training in return. It was described by a young man in Chelmsford at the time as 'a year's slave labour. Not assured of a job at the end. Thatcher junta not going to get me.' By the late 1980s, it was thought that young people should stay in education: National Vocational Qualifications were created in 1987 but it was soon obvious that they weren't valued by employers or trainees. Higher Level Modern Apprenticeships were established under the Tories in 1993 and were adjusted throughout the New Labour era – Blair boasts that he 'more than doubled' apprenticeships – and remain in place today. Genuine apprenticeships persisted in a few traditional areas – engineering, goldsmithing, building – through informal relationships between a company and a young person. One of the most successful schemes kept young people out of the workplace altogether. The Education Maintenance Allowance – £30 a week as long as you stayed in further education – encouraged disadvantaged students to continue acquiring skills. The coalition government abolished the EMA in 2010, and students went out on the streets in protest.

In 2011, three years into the downturn, there were 247,000

people starting apprenticeships, but the age bar had been lifted, and the average length of an apprenticeship had shrunk from ten years to twelve weeks. The biggest provider of apprenticeships in the UK is Elmfield Training, which runs twenty-eight-week 'apprenticeships' for the supermarket Morrisons; the most common discipline is business administration, and the day reserved for study has shrunk to an hour or two a week for training. By contrast, BAE Systems and Rolls-Royce release their apprentices from the workshop for at least a day a week. This quality of training costs Rolls-Royce £70,000 to £95,000 for the three to four years it takes an apprentice to learn their trade, so competition is strong, stronger than for a place at Oxford: twenty to one versus six to one. Each place at Rolls-Royce requires a minimum of five GCSEs, including English, Maths and Science, at grade C or above, but the adverts also stress 'dedication', an 'interest in and passion for cars' and a 'collaborative spirit'.

At the week-long summer school for Goldsmiths' Company apprentices in August 2014, Devine is learning how to enamel. The basement of the Goldsmiths' Centre in Britton Street, Clerkenwell is kept purposely cool, and the apprentices are discussing their sawblade scars as they watch Ros Conway, an enameller for forty years whose work is held by the V&A, show them how to grind lumps of coloured enamel under water to a fine sand. Like the blue scars Orwell noticed on the foreheads of Wigan's miners (from coal dust which had got into a fresh cut), an old wound can be a storied rite of passage. 'All jewellers have sawblades in their fingers,' Ros says. Ben Pritchard, a 20-year-old apprentice diamond-mounter with Emson Haig, an Essex-based jeweller, has one on the pad of his thumb. Devine has a long white trace on the inside of her forearm from a trampolining accident: 'I win at scars,' she says. Conway is still grinding. 'Can you hear it getting finer?' she asks, and passes the pestle and mortar around so that they can feel as well as hear the grain.

Devine is the first back in the workshop after lunch, grinding blue enamel, then green, then the pale base colour called Flux. All seven apprentices are grinding now, boasting to each other that theirs is as 'fine as flour'. 'No!' Ros says, 'You can grind the colour out!' They are only teasing: more than one goes to Devine with their enamel to ask if she thinks it's ready. Pritchard is slightly ahead of the others. He has spread his medal with Flux using a tiny trowel, 'like white icing on a wedding cake'. It's now ready to be put in the kiln for the thirty seconds needed for it to fire hard: first it goes dark, then it looks like orange peel, and when it looks wet, it's done. The yellowy colour will fade to a more opalescent white as it cools. The firing has gone well, but it needn't: 'You learn by your mistakes in this game,' Conway says, 'or in any game really.'

C, 23, intern, London

For the London Symphony Orchestra's concert at the Barbican on Sunday 23 March 2014, the audience arrived early. Grey-haired couples in fleeces sipped coffee from paper cups while they waited for the doors of the concert hall to open. John Eliot Gardiner would conduct Mendelssohn's Italian Symphony and Ruy Blas Overture that evening: the programme notes explained that Victor Hugo's play *Ruy Blas* is about a servant who takes revenge after being tricked. On the final pages of the programme, they would find the names of the LSO's interns. They had worked for six months from 9.30 a.m. to 6 p.m., plus evenings 'as required', for not much more than complimentary concert tickets.

The Future Interns, a protest group formed in late 2013, sat on the floor on the mezzanine of the Barbican. Last November, they had dressed up as Santas and walked through the Serpentine

Gallery with a banner that read: 'ALL I WANT FOR XMAS IS PAY'; weeks later, the gallery announced it would begin paying its interns. Three members had come on the bus from Gold-smiths, University of London, sharing a bag of toffee popcorn and talking about Beckett, Lefebvre and Marx. One had been at the Barbican since two in the afternoon; the others arrived in ones and twos from the outer edges of London. An MA student on the documentary film course at Goldsmiths had brought her camera. In August 2014, around a fifth of young people in the UK aged between 18 and 24 didn't have a job, weren't at university or weren't in other work training, including graduates. How are they supposed to start work if there aren't enough jobs for them to start in? Create their own? The Future Interns joked that they, not the government, were the job creators: they had created paid internships at the Serpentine Gallery, after all.

Harry, who had circled her eyes in white kohl and dressed in black, had made cardboard masks of Wagner, Bach and Handel for the protest. In 2006, she was locked in the dungeon of the Houses of Parliament (not much of one; it was full of broken chairs and old computers) for waving a CND flag from the public gallery during the Trident debates; in March 2011, she was arrested at Fortnum and Mason during a protest against austerity. She wasn't nervous. The Future Interns use absurdist humour, letter-writing, social media and embarrassment to make their point. They had rolled up their flyers – the LSO's advertisement for an intern, which they'd angrily annotated – to look like musical scrolls, and fastened them with curling ribbon in shimmery midnight blue.

The day before, the interns had met at the Richard Hoggart building at Goldsmiths to paint a banner for the LSO protest and roll up flyers. (The college was founded in 1891 as a 'Technical and Recreative Institute' for the people of New Cross by the same Goldsmiths' Company Devine is apprenticed to.) A rectangle of sea-blue fabric was pinned to the wall and a PowerPoint slide with the slogan 'LONDON SYMPHONY ORCHESTRA – YOUR POLICIES ARE OUT OF TUNE – PAY YOUR INTERNS' was projected on to it, so that the letters could be traced with black paint. I sat with C at the silver MacBook, whose job it was to keep pressing the space bar so that the projection wouldn't disappear.

C had found the Future Interns online. She had spent the two years since graduating from a prestigious South Asian university going from unpaid internship to unpaid internship at international NGOs across the world. She was now 23. After South-East Asia and Scotland, the UK appealed: 'I wanted to experience something new, I wanted to go out of my comfort zone.' She was 'impressed' by what the Future Interns did at the Serpentine after reading about it online. During one internship, she had written an article about an NGO's programme to help young people get work in the developing world; the biographical note didn't say the writer was unpaid. She remembers sitting in on a meeting about an organisation's underspend (under-spending is as bad as overspending for an NGO): 'And I was just sitting there quietly, nodding my head. I know where you could spend it! It was always just like really funny for me. I didn't take it personally, because you know.' 'Each team has a constant vacancy for an intern,' C said. There seems to be a pre-career career ladder in the NGO world: volunteer, intern, paid intern, entry-level job. 'People are happy to have internships. I'm happy to have an internship. People who are sad about their intern-ship and end up suing the company – that's just a minority. Most people are happy to have an internship, if that makes any sense? But what's really depressing is "Oh my gosh, this is like my third internship!" And when you're faced with the choice of unem-ployment or internship, I chose internship. Because it drove me crazy to be unemployed.' C spent five months in the summer and autumn of 2013 unemployed, writing an individually tailored application every weekday. She sent out her CV over 100 times. When she couldn't find a paid job at an NGO, she applied for internships again, and immediately got one. 'It hasn't really sunk into the older generation that you are all exploiting young people. They think we're being lazy! Hello! Give me a ... They complain that the UK has unemployment, and they complain about young people being lazy and not doing anything – but there are no jobs! How about you sort that one out first and then give us jobs so that we don't have to ... It's really funny.' 'Funny' didn't seem strong enough for what she felt, but she kept using it anyway.

Unpaid interns are used across the charity sector, TV, film, journalism, publishing, politics, fashion PR, photography, marketing, digital start-ups, scriptwriting: the sectors millennials have grown up revering. Dreaming of being an intern at *Vogue* might be today's equivalent of a 1950s boy wanting to be a fighter pilot. C's tired not of the work (though solidarity among interns is tempered by competition) but of the cycle: 'Oh my God, when do I get a real job?' She relies on her conservative, religious parents for support: 'I'm gay, but they don't know that I'm gay. I've been out to my friends, for example, for three years now. But they still have no clue. They don't know that I drink as much as I do. They think that I sip wine! It's very difficult for me to balance, because I don't have a close relationship to them. I have a very "How's your day? Good" kind of relationship with them. But I try to maintain it because I'm not financially independent yet. It's not like I don't love them, I do. I'm really so happy about the support that they've been giving me but it's just so hard to reconcile that. Shit – I'm taking money from people who do *not* approve of my lifestyle, basically. But I guess it's just a pill that I have to swallow, for my own survival. Once I get a permanent job, for example, then I just plan to say it all to them and say: "Well, if you don't want none of it, then fine, that's fine with me because I'm going to be independent already."' She forgets to push the space bar and the banner painters turn to her.

C didn't make it to the Barbican the next day; she had an

interview for a paid internship on Monday: 'They call it Commu-
nications Assistant (internship).' At ten past seven, the doors
to the concert hall had opened, and ushers were selling bags
of Maltesers. The Future Interns began handing out masks to
put on and scrolls to hold, as well as partially unfolding the
banner and walking down to ground level. They were no longer
incognito; could the security guards be conferring? By the Costa
Coffee stall, there was an impromptu huddle: 'Boom boom good
luck!' The banner was unfurled, masks were slid on, and the
group dispersed among the coffee-sippers, beginning conversations with 'Can I give you this?'

There was no hallooing, no megaphone, no music or chaos.
The two banner holders were slightly blocking a throughway,
I suppose. The two people stood at the LSO stall turned to each
other: 'What does it say?' said one. 'It's about paying interns,'
the other replied. 'Who's doing that?' One older gentleman took
a scroll, decided he didn't want it and balanced it on top of the
rucksack of one of the protesters. A few people came to look at
the banner. Others slipped off the florist's ribbon and put their
coffee to one side to read. A flyer had even made its way to the
LSO stall. A short man in a grey suit and an orange Barbican
badge arrived with a walkie-talkie. 'You're very welcome to
protest,' he said, but the Barbican complex was private property.
They could stand outside the main entrance, in the cold night,
where there would be no one to look at their banner or take a
scroll. A protester in a Bach mask handed him a scroll: 'Would
you like to read this?'

The banner-holders didn't move. The man in the grey
suit told the documentary student to turn her camera off and
erase the footage (perhaps he didn't know the second request
was illegal). The banner-holders still didn't move. No one had
stopped giving out scrolls either. 'I have had to warn the police,'
the man said. 'They are coming.' The banner-holders conferred
and walked out with him, refusing his request to roll up the

banner. Once over the line of metal studs on the pavement outside, the man was content, and stood on the other side of the rubicon, facing them.

Two policemen arrived. One of the banner-holders muttered 'pigs' under her breath. One policeman talked to the man in the grey suit and the other to the Future Interns: they offered him a scroll, which slipped out of a Future Intern's hand before he could get a grip on it. 'Now you're littering!' he joked, picked up the scroll and tucked it into his flak jacket for his wife. He doesn't even have to tell the protest to move, because it's already moved, and so both policemen leave: 'Good luck with your protest, guys!' one said. 'Good luck – cheers!' the other said.

A man in a tux carrying a trombone case wouldn't take a scroll: 'That's the way of the world!'; a group of young people said they'd look the Future Interns up online; a man with a walking stick declared that internships are a racket – 'None of the politicians care a damn!' It was too cold to wait until the interval and so they went off in search of a pub, hoping to find a Wetherspoons for cheapness but settling for one showing Real Madrid v. Barcelona near Spitalfields. I'm buying: they drink cider, gin and tonic, Guinness and IPA.

One of the Future Interns tells a story from earlier. She was giving out scrolls in a queue when she recognised the HR director of the LSO from the photo on her LinkedIn profile. They began talking but when their exchange became heated, the protester came out with: 'What about you? You did an internship at the BBC!' The HR director's boyfriend stepped in at that point, saying it had got too 'personal'; and a male protester came over to calm things down too. Entanglement – that most people hiring interns have been interns themselves – is part of the problem. The workers who have made it into paid jobs understand an internship as a rite of passage instead of as an illegal arrangement that swallows up entry-level jobs. An intern is the opposite of an apprentice: short-term, unpaid and with no relationship with their employer. I worked for free in magazines and publishing when I was 22, when my MA grant money hadn't yet run out and I could stay with my boyfriend with London; I didn't question it at the time. Protest, we understood from the million-strong and entirely unheeded Iraq march of February 2003, wasn't effective any more. And so there was a collective gritting of teeth I don't see in the Future Interns' generation. When I visited the student occupation of UCL in 2010, there was a memorial site with melted candles, faded roses and placards: 'EDUCATION: The Fourth Deathly Hallow'. The Future Interns are also from a generation brought up on the Harry Potter-promise of education as a way to good, well-paid work, or, at the very least, work. My generation's promise was kept; theirs wasn't. But at least for them protest works again: a few weeks later after the Barbican action, the LSO announced that they would be paying their interns from autumn 2014.

Anne-Marie Imafidon, 25, technologist, City of London

'As each day passes, it becomes more and more true that entrepreneur doesn't mean necessarily that you've started your own business. It's a set of behaviours,' Anne-Marie Imafidon says. I catch sight of a black rubberised Jawbone around her wrist, which electronically tracks her movement and sleep. 'Obviously I am an entrepreneur because I've got a business, dah, dah, dah, dah-dah, but it's not that that makes me an entrepreneur. It's the starting stuff. And having that fearlessness.' At school, Imafidon started a business teaching people to make websites. Between university and beginning work she started a social media consultancy. Once she began work she put on and ran dating events with a friend. Then she ran networking events.

These businesses exhausted themselves before she started the project she runs now, Stemettes, which encourages women to pursue careers in science, technology, engineering and maths by organising hackathons and panel events sponsored by O2, Starbucks, Accenture, Deutsche Bank and Microsoft among others. On top of Stemettes she has a job at Deutsche Bank, running their internal social network. 'I'm constantly aware that I might not be fulfilled,' she says. 'So I kind of pre-empt that by just doing other stuff.'

In May 2012, the coalition government announced that loans of £2,500 would be made available for entrepreneurs aged between 18 to 24 to start their own businesses before April 2015. The prime minister said: 'Start-up loans are an important part of my mission to back aspiration, and all those young people who want to work hard and get on in life, so this country competes and thrives in the global race.' By January 2013 £1.5 million of the £82 million made available had been lent out; the government's notion that the downturn wasn't structural but down to a lack of entrepreneurial spirit clearly wasn't right. By dismantling the structures that help businesses get going – Business Link, a free consultancy for small, local businesses evaporated – the money proved useless.

Imafidon started businesses because she didn't think conventional work would be enough for her. Her father came to East Ham in London from Nigeria in the 1980s to study ophthalmology, and her mother came with him and raised five children while working as a TEFL teacher. 'We didn't come from money and we didn't have rich grandparents or anything like that, so it was like you work and you get it done.' Anne-Marie, the eldest, passed GCSEs in Maths and IT at 11, was accepted at Keble College, Oxford, to study Mathematics and Computer Science at 17 and is one of the youngest people to have been awarded a master's degree from Oxford. She thought she would take GCSEs early because she saw her 16-year-old cousins doing their exams. 'It's not that it was normal,' she says of her genius-track school career, 'but you don't understand how weird it is.'

When she was very young, she told her mother she'd like to be a weather girl, but a careers questionnaire she did at school at 13 suggested she would make a fine management consultant: 'I saw how much they earn and I was like "Wow!"' As part of a programme for ethnic minorities run by Deutsche Bank called 'I have a dream', Imafidon interned at the bank in the university summer holidays (she was paid around £2,000 a month) and moved into a job there once she graduated. 'It's not a secret that you have to work hard,' she says, legs jiggling, hands talking. 'No one ever goes: Oh, it was easy!' She hasn't completely shelved her ambition to become a millionaire, but her plan now 'is that when I wake up in the morning I can do what I feel like doing. And that's pretty much it. As long as I've done that, then I feel like I'm winning.' Imafidon didn't seem to be a gamer, but the language of life-hacking and game-playing seeped into the way she spoke.

Imafidon doesn't keep to a schedule and arranges her appointments on her iPhone: 'Every Tuesday doesn't mean anything to me.' But she's noticed a work pattern: cycles of ten to fourteen days of work, followed by 'downtime', which will mean binge-watching *Parks and Recreation*, the US version of *The Office*, or *Suits* on her iPad; or coding a website: 'I find it quite therapeutic ... It's almost like meditation. I kind of zone in on code.' (E. P. Thompson argued that this cycle of intense work followed by intense leisure was probably a natural human pattern.) With two phones, an iPad and a MacBook Air in her Stemettes-logoed tote bag, Imafidon can work wherever she is, and as her day job at Deutsche Bank is target-led, so as long as she's reachable and gets her work done, she doesn't need to go into the office every day. She likes things 'to be different and change every day'; she works 'smart' as well as hard; she can do her make-up 'in one tube stop'. She's been looking to buy property for two years, giving up buying a new handbag every quarter to save for the deposit, but she has placed an offer on eleven houses, and each has fallen through. She earns around £50,000 a year at Deutsche Bank, and corporate sponsorship covers her expenses for Stemettes.

Her work with Stemettes has taken her to Buckingham Palace and Downing Street and lunch with Tim Berners-Lee: 'The archetypal geek. Fantastic ... He's like Jack Dee, almost, but not as miserable.' She started Stemettes because there were only three women on her course at Oxford (and two in the year below and one in the year below that), but sees that being an untypical geek has worked in her favour: 'As much as it might have held me back as in people see me and think a certain thing, because of everything I've got it's almost like that completely ... it's almost like I'm not a black woman. Like, I'm just basically not.' Her view was that 'you can count everything as a disadvantage, but there are people who don't have arms. And bloody David Blunkett is blind. Cry me a river.'

She sees worklessness in the same way: 'So one of my closest friends is unemployed, and has been for ages and we've been wanting to employ her for Stemettes and it was just like ... Even putting her through the interview process was like: this is why you're not being hired. You can't live life like that. You have to be more self-aware just of what you say, what you're like. And I'm not saying change yourself, I'm just saying if you're going to function with other human beings you have to be a certain way. Me and you have been best friends since we were little so I understand you, but there's a whole world out there that wasn't there when we were little. You know, you have to function there, you have to get on the bus, you have to talk to them, that kind of thing.' Imafidon made me think of what Norman Tebbit is supposed to have said to the unemployed after the 1981 summer of unrest: that they should get on their bikes, like his father did in the 1930s, and keep looking for a job until they find one.

But what if a lack of jobs is a structural problem? Capitalism will always require a proportion of the population to be unemployed, for wages to fall, for working conditions to weaken. And what if the reality is simply – seen in statistics, felt by many of the people I spoke to – that decent jobs are scarce?

She continued: 'You do make your own luck. We both were at sixth form together at the same time, we both did A-levels at the same time in the same country in the same situation, so why has she ended up that way and I've ended up this way? It's something else around what she is, what she's like. And it's funny because even looking back, there's some times then when I'm like: "God, I hope she grows up – what's it going to be like when she's older?" I dunno. She's like had a heart attack because she got 16 out of 20 on this coursework. Literally had a heart attack. And you want to be a doctor – as much as I love you, I hope you won't be my doctor, because what if I actually have a disease, do you know what I mean, and you have a panic attack, and won't be able to treat me properly?' Imafidon spoke with a big sisterly, telling-it-like-it-is tone. 'I'm not apologetic at all, actually. Partly as well because I'm not in charge of what's going on with Stemettes if that makes sense, so I catch the balls as they come, so it's not even that I've sat down and planned it. I've just had the right attitude around it and she's been here the entire time and seen what I've done. Sometimes she's questioned it: "Why don't you sit still? Why are you doing this? Der der der der." But it's like: "OK, cool, if I'm doing that then why don't you *not* sit still, rather than complain to me and being like, oh you're so lucky." I'm not lucky – you were here! I'm not lucky. I dunno.'

In Imafidon's London 'most of the roles that you want to apply for are well-paying graduate roles, and the degree is the minimum. Not: because I've got the degree I'll get the job, I can only be in with a chance for the job because I have a degree, and I have this and I have that. But it's not rocket science. There are loads of schemes around to help you out. You have to kind of get up off your butt – jobs aren't going to look for you. Why should jobs look for you?'

R, 24, unemployed, Basildon

In R's south Essex, youth unemployment is higher than anywhere else in the south-east of England. He took me to a pub near Basildon train station in June 2013, and we talked under the coloured glow of the game machines and the sound of empty alcopop bottles crashing into a recycling bin. He then showed me around the town, a walk which he said made The Specials' 'Ghost Town' play in his head: 'So many shops down there have gone.' A young mother pushed a child in a buggy with a red carton of McDonald's fries in the plastic tray across the seat. R had noticed on Twitter that the government was encouraging young people to start their own businesses and create jobs for themselves: 'So many independent businesses in this town have gone bust. There's a shop the other side of Laindon that was open for fifty years and it shut a couple of months ago saying we can't compete with the internet, expensive rents, other competition. So setting up a small business – if it worked, why are 20 per cent of small businesses boarded up at the moment?'

R had gone to a local comprehensive school, got straight As in his GCSEs, achieved 3 As at A-level and won a place at a Russell Group university to study politics, gaining a first-class degree 'with ease', as one of his tutors put it on graduation day. Only 3 per cent of young people in Basildon get that far. After an internship with an MP in Westminster, many job applications, and a few job interviews, he is unemployed at 24. He had studied for his A-levels while Lehman Brothers tottered, and remembers being told that if he worked hard, all would be well: 'Everything that I've been working towards for several years now, it does feel like one big lie.' He was told a good degree would change his life. 'We were sold going to university as a ticket to the middle classes and it's just not true. At least in my reality.'

R worked in a supermarket for a year before university to earn money, but commuting to Westminster every day was work as he hoped it might be. His parents liked being able to tell people he was working in the Houses of Parliament. After an interview in the summer, R began in the autumn, opening and sorting post, writing letters and making casework notes in an MP's office for three months on £8.30 an hour. (Internships in Westminster weren't always paid, and some placements still aren't, though advice issued in May 2012 makes it clear that when any obligations are placed on the intern, the intern becomes a worker and must be paid the National Minimum Wage.) He used to get the 8.07 train to London in the morning in an M&S coat he'd bought for the commute. 'I really miss that structure.' At the end of the internship, he went to buy a round of drinks for his colleagues in the bar of the Houses of Parliament, and a colleague said: '"Interns don't buy drinks!" I would have liked to have bought him a drink, 'cause it would have made me feel that I was ... that we were equals, when you know, actually, I was just a here today, gone tomorrow intern. So. Yeah. So that's why I kind of want a full-time job.' R had a pragmatic, perhaps downbeat way of looking at the world; I wondered what advice Imafidon would give him. He also knew his parents – his father had worked in an oil refinery and his mother works at a school – wouldn't accept him working for free for six months with no prospect of a job at the end of it. 'I don't want to become a kind of perennial intern. I want the status of a full-time job where I know that I'm going to be there in six months.'

R had signed on in February, not so much for the money as he lives at home, but for help with finding a job. (Jobseeker's Allowance is worth £57.35 a week if you are 24 or under and £72.40 a week if you're over 24.) In the first week, he had to prove he'd applied for three jobs. As the weeks went on the Job Centre's requirements become labyrinthine to the point of despair. 'It gets to a stage you're applying for jobs you're not qualified for, jobs that frankly you don't even want.' His grandfather worked in the Labour Exchange in the 1950s: a man could come in for a job on Monday and walk out with one on Friday. R decided to sign off entirely after three months, when he was having to meet a target of twenty-five to thirty job applications a week and felt it was stopping him from applying for the jobs he wanted. 'I think I started off with some quite naive, middle-class views about how the welfare system works. It sounds very patronising, but now I've experienced it first-hand I've realised actually the system's really broken.' R's views, handed down from his grandfather and father, were reminiscent of a postwar moment – sometimes called the spirit of '45 – when it was thought that failures in the system ought to be compensated for with welfare. Like Irina in Chekhov's *Three Sisters*, our culture is simultaneously fascinated by, disgusted with, worn down by and desiring of work. Yet it proposes that the answer to a crisis of work – too much for some, too little for others – is more work. Being on Jobseeker's Allowance in the UK in 2014 resembles nothing so much as working for a particularly demanding and unpredictable employer.

R was reluctant to detail how his days went. His days would still start like work days, at 6.30 a.m., but didn't continue like them. 'My alarm will go in the morning, but there isn't actually a reason to get out of bed. I can get up late and do my job searching in the evening, can't I?' He found himself helping his dad in the garden, doing the ironing for his mum, reading a book or watching his *X Files* boxset. 'You could go three or four days only speaking to the postman. You've got no money so you can't go out. You need money to have any kind of life, so you just kind of stay in, do applications.' He'd applied for eighty jobs in a year when I spoke to him; a pie chart he'd made showed the most common response was 'no response'. Getting an interview is the rarest outcome: 'Because interviews are so hard to come by by themselves, there's so much pressure on you when you get an interview. You've got to really throw everything at it.' He'd recently got out his graduation suit and watch for an interview at Ofcom which he thought had gone well. 'The only questions I struggled with are where you would actually need to have done that job to know the answer. So I said: "Well, you know, that's something I would pick up within a week of doing the job." I got the sense that wasn't an acceptable answer. It's something of a catch 22: I need the job to be gaining the skills, but unless someone gives you a job then you can't gain them.' The next day, he got a rejection note. 'I actually like the rejection email in a way. One: you feel acknowledged, and second: you can say well, tough luck, move on to the next one.' He chases up every rejection with a phone call. One interviewer told him that there had been 500 applicants for an entry-level, minimum wage job at YouGov, the pollster. 'He said a First and an internship isn't enough to stand out. I'm not entirely sure what I've got to do to stand out now.'

One study in July 2013 found that 40 per cent of unemployed young people no longer felt part of society; yet nearly three-quarters thought they could offer something if they were given some support. R had the impression he'd run out of leads. The Job Centre 'said that my accent was unusual for the type of person they normally get in Basildon Job Centre'; school had lied, and his university had shined the truth. 'We were given one civil service talk – and the public sector is cutting back considerably. And we were given one talk when graduates who had succeeded came back and they said: "Well, I've got a politics degree from here." An Irish lad who went to work for Jimmy Carter. So we all looked at that and thought: "Wow! That's what we're going to do because we've got a politics degree from here!" and you realise just how unrepresentative those people are.

They are the people who have succeeded. I've got friends who are pulling pints – they're not going to be invited back next year to talk about how their politics degree has helped them pull pints in suburbia.' R still had a soft, boyish face with pale short brown hair; he had got out his wallet to pay for our glasses of Coke, even though I had said I was buying. 'I think there is something in the *Daily Mail* types who say we send too many to university. I think we do.' One friend had graduated from Cambridge with a degree in Natural Sciences – 'Isn't that the course Newton did?' – and hadn't found anything. 'He's not doing as well as people who left at 18 and got a job.' He 'really respects' the friends who resisted his school's relentless focus on UCAS forms and university league tables and left school at 18 to do on-the-job training: 'They have far better job prospects.' None of his friends had done an apprenticeship. A year of applying for jobs had left R exhausted, baffled, lacking in the confidence that he would find his way. I wondered how he came across in the seven minutes interviewers say they take to decide whether someone is employable: 82 per cent of managers value the ability to hold eye contact; 73 per cent judge someone on their personal appearance; 60 per cent rate someone on the quality of their banter or small talk; 55 per cent decide on the strength of the candidate's handshake.

He'd had just enough experience of work to know what he was missing. The flatlands of south Essex are filled with twice-a-day, forty-minute commuters: 'Aged about 14, 15, I thought: "What a terrible existence, a kind of commuter drone!" Yeah, now I'm at the stage that I aspire to it!' He couldn't go on the lads' holiday; he can't go for an Indian on the weekend. 'I miss … you know … the phone ringing and saying "Let's go for a drink." We used to go to Shoreditch, where all the hipsters are. Having the money and going for a drink of a Friday night. Nothing particularly excessive, but that kind of social … I miss that.' A period of unemployment at the beginning of someone's career has been shown to have 'scarring effects' on a working life. Unemployed graduates are twice as likely to take antidepressants as employed graduates. R's not at the sort of parties to have to give an answer to the supposed ice-cracker 'What do you do?' but social media demands he craft himself: 'You kind of feel you've had your identity taken away. So all your focus has been on doing well at university, so that's taken away from you, and what do you put in your Twitter bio? That's one of the issues I've found with friends. After a while they put in their Twitter bio "unemployed graduate". Which is what you are, in essence. I would like to be able to put something in that Twitter bio other than "Politics Graduate".'

I lost touch with R. He didn't reply to my emails; he closed his Twitter account, possibly after the Basildon Job Centre began tweeting him. But over a year later I found a profile for him on a new site About.Me. He describes himself as 'University Graduate, Class of 2012'.

John, 56, on Mandatory Work Activity, Surrey

The letter arrived in July 2014, when John had been unemployed and on Jobseeker's Allowance since 2008. 'What is Mandatory Work Activity?' appeared in bold at the top. The first paragraph explained:

> MWA is aimed at JSA customers to help them gain a better understanding of the discipline and focus that is required for work by attending on time, carrying out specific tasks and working under supervision, whilst at the same time making a contribution to the community. It consists of a four-week work placement for 30 hours a week and could consist of manual, administrative or retail related duties.

At the end of the letter, Seetec – the private contractor arranging workfare placements on behalf of the government – explained what was meant by mandatory: 'It is a condition of getting Jobseeker's Allowance (JSA) and/or National Insurance Credits that you must start your placement and continue to attend, when asked to do so, unless you have a good reason.' John would lose benefits if he didn't turn up to his placement, or if he didn't ring before 9 a.m. to explain his absence, or if he was dismissed, or if he didn't do the work he was given. He turned up.

His four-week placement was at the Vine Project, a charity and social enterprise in Surrey which refurbishes old furniture and sells it. On his first day, arriving at the Willow Lane Industrial Estate in Mitcham – 'parts of it were OK, but the part where this was, there was quite a few empty units nearby and it's all a bit of a mess, you know' – he was one of a group of eight: two women and six men, ranging in age from 18 to 50. 'They were all mandated, they were all not really keen to be doing it.' Other workers, as at the charity shop in Dover, included true volunteers, who kept themselves to themselves, and paid employees. People with learning difficulties used to come a few times a week too. On the first day, John asked someone: 'How long have you been here? 'Two weeks to go,' was the reply. 'It was just the right side of being sent to prison, really,' John said.

The women were sent to do administrative work; the men were given hand tools and presented with old furniture – 'some of the things you were getting were really nasty, actually: partly rotten' – to break up into parts. 'It was quite a hot period in August. Yeah, it was ... Breaking up upholstered furniture is not a lot of fun. You've got to work out how to do it, the best way to do it, and that always takes a while. So for the first couple of weeks, you're just struggling to find the way. There was a Rasta there who'd been there a couple of weeks longer and he'd worked out a few good ways ... first strip all the material. It all tends to be stapled on now, which is really quite nasty, you had to just use a screwdriver – we didn't have any special equipment – we just had screwdrivers and hammers. You just had to get all the upholstery off and then the padding, but not break up the frame. Keep the frame together. Then keep on all the metal – it had springs in. Quite difficult to get those off sometimes.' They used crowbars to loosen the springs. 'Fortunately I didn't have any accidents while I was there but they have these great big metal springs, when you'd release them, they'd ping up. The staples as well: they gave you protective gloves, overalls, work boots, so you were OK. It was pretty basic. They clearly didn't have money – there were a few power tools and things.' They took the frame apart once it was bare. 'Some were built more well than others. It would take a long time, the ones that were well built. To do a whole sofa would take an hour.'

The day started at 10 a.m. and finished at 5 p.m. with twenty-minute breaks in the morning and afternoon and an hour at midday. At lunch, John would keep his grey cotton overalls and steel-capped boots on and talk to Kevin, another mandated worker who had lived on the other side of the industrial estate all his life. 'He showed me how you could get down to the river, because the River Wandle goes through there. And we used to go down there, most of the time. Have sandwiches. It happened to be a nice bit of weather and it was nice to go out of the building. Otherwise you're just spending the whole day in the building. Yeah, it was nice. Did that most days.' They would talk about work: first Kevin had been mandated to a charity shop, but he didn't like it, left without permission and had his Jobseeker's Allowance removed for four weeks. They're no longer in touch, but Kevin was a 'very sweet guy. He didn't seem to hardly go out of that area. If you talked to him about even somewhere like London Bridge, he'd say: "I went there once, I think." It's extraordinary! But he was nice.' All the mandated workers had to pay for travel themselves (it cost John £26 out of the £72.40 he had a week), and were then reimbursed on Fridays, when someone from Seetec arrived, 'literally with some bags of money', and they queued to show their travel tickets and be refunded. 'You never knew precisely when they were coming in,' John said. 'They didn't do it by name or anything, in any order, you just had to sort of be aware that they were coming in that day and keep your ears and eyes open.' The work wasn't undignified, but became boring after the second or third settee. 'It was just physically quite tiring. I felt OK at having efficiently broken up a sofa.' I thought about the Rasta and Kevin and wondered if there was a sort of Workfare camaraderie, or even just gallows humour. John pauses. 'There was generally, shall we say, a fairly subdued atmosphere.'

Did he think he'd got anything out of it? 'Yeah, a little bit. I wouldn't completely knock it. No, definitely not.' But he wouldn't have done it voluntarily? 'No, and that's the difference. Even if they gave you £20 or something a week extra, it just would have made that tiny bit of difference, that they would be recognising that you were actually putting in the effort.' Seetec is paid £400 by the government for every person they place on workfare; the company made a profit of £10 million in 2011. For four weeks of dismantling furniture, John received £289.60. 'I sort of accepted that I had to do it. I didn't agree with it but I had to do it.' When John received the 'What is Mandatory Work Activity?' letter, he took it to his Job Centre adviser: 'People at the Job Centre themselves, your advisers, they are being put under pressure to make these sanctions and to mandate people and so on. I argued the toss in a fairly reasonable manner, not losing my temper or anything. First of all I emailed her to keep it somewhat impersonal and she said: "No, you've still got to do it, this is it." The next time I went into the office, again I said: "Look, you're still saying I've got to do this even though I'm in my 50s and my background is in architecture. This is not really going to make any difference. Four weeks!" She said: "Yep, it's been decided." I said: "Who's your manager?" The manager comes out, someone I've never seen before, much younger than the adviser, I said to her: "You're insisting I've got to do this?" "Yes." I said: "Are you sure it's lawful?" Her response was: "You can speak to your MP about that."' The UK's courts are still deciding whether workfare schemes such as Mandatory Work Activity are legal, as legislation bounces between the High, Appeal and Supreme Courts to Parliament and back again, but the government's own pilot study showed that of all those receiving unemployment benefits, those on workfare did no better in finding a job than those who simply received benefits while looking for work.

John's father came to England from Poland in 1940 and served in the RAF for seven years before running a corner shop; his mother looked after six children at home. John remembers his father working a great deal; his mother 'was the one who had less conventional ideas about what were and were not the most important things in life. She didn't think that work was the be-all and end-all of life.' John trained as an architect at Manchester Polytechnic, came to London in the 1970s and played in post-punk bands, rehearsing in abandoned houses in Hackney: 'It was one of these streets they'd earmarked for demolition but they never quite demolished them. We just used to borrow the electricity from some neighbouring house, you know, with their agreement.' He did some painting and decorating for money, but he also signed on: 'I didn't really think in terms – in any way – of getting this stuff released, or you know that any one ... It was just not going to happen so I didn't particularly aim ... I just did it. You could just about survive on the dole in those days as long as you were pretty frugal, so I just did it.' Once his daughter was born, he worked in sound engineering at the BBC, then on freelance and zero-hours contracts for architecture firms. He signed on between 1991 and 1995 when work was hard to find, and then again in 2008 when new building slowed following the credit crunch. He's worked off and on since then, always less than the sixteen hours a week allowed under JSA rules, and often for himself. 'I'm not desperately looking for another job in architecture,' John said. 'I don't like what they do any more. I don't want to work on the Battersea Power Station: it's complete madness what they've done to it. Those flats are being sold off-plan, unbuilt, just as speculation, already. It's only an extreme example. It's been going on for a long time now in London. It doesn't appeal to me any more working in that area; it contradicts everything that I think is worth doing. Unfortunately, it's the only area that I've got any expertise in.'

How has dealing with the Job Centre changed since the 1990s? 'There are security officers on the doors, not literally on the doors, but as soon as you come in, there are security guys. That just didn't use to exist. The first person you see is a security guy now.' You feel, he says, 'as if you're coming into somewhere you're not meant to be. You just get out your little appointment card, and again, that's all you've got now. An appointment. If you come in ten minutes before that appointment, you can't even go up the stairs, so you have to go and sit down somewhere. You always time it exactly right so you don't have to wait too much.' John comes to the Job Centre once a week; sometimes that visit will include an event. The speaker at a recent motivational talk said he had 'an MBA from London School of Business or something and you think: "Well, maybe you have, but why are you doing this then?" He was quite, not aggressive, but he was quite, shall we say, I felt he was completely overdoing it. He said you must always go to the top of any organisation, as high up as you can go. Don't just send your CV in; there's no reason you shouldn't phone up the Chief Executive and ask them for a coffee. Ask them for an informal meeting. Even if it doesn't get you a job it'll be a good thing to have done.' John didn't say anything but the woman sitting next to him did: 'What are you talking about?' she said. 'That is completely ridiculous what you're saying.' Other courses have begun with asking the unemployed participants whether they've considered working for free. 'There's a sort of tension about the whole situation,' John said, 'which certainly wasn't like that even a couple of years ago.'

In January 2014, the European Council called the UK's unemployment benefit 'manifestly inadequate', as it fell below 40 per cent of the European median income. Living on the dole, as John did in the 1990s, is 'not feasible any more. It's just impossible now. It's just too worrying. I've got an electricity bill outstanding, which is just really worrying because I can't pay it – I mean they wouldn't demand it all in one go, but if they then wanted to take, say, £10 a week or something it would be a serious issue. It shouldn't have to be like that.' John had had his benefits removed when the Job Centre brought in a new computerised job search, and he hadn't yet grasped he had to interact with it weekly. He was given a letter during his Job Centre appointment and the money stopped a couple of days later: 'I just couldn't believe it. It seemed to me extraordinary that they could do that.' His brother sent a voucher for Asda; a friend lent him money. 'I still don't quite know what the rules are.' Perhaps they are changing. 'It's just accelerated,' he said. 'This idea of it being a median safety net, it's going. It's not quite gone, but it feels like it's going.'

The Thatcher government, impressed by the spread of workfare programmes across the USA, first introduced workfare to the UK. As an incentive, the dole was topped up by £10 a week. In 1996, John Major argued for his 'Project Work' scheme by saying that 'people receiving unemployment benefit ultimately have an obligation to accept reasonable work on offer'. Blair's New Deal in 1998 used companies like Seetec and A4e to train and then place unemployed people in work. It was rebranded in 2009 as the Flexible New Deal and essentially became the coalition government's current suite of workfare schemes, which range from the Mandatory Work Activity John was made to do; the Work Programme, which can last for two years; and the Community Action Plan, involving a minimum of six months' work.

What is primarily useful about workfare for the coalition government is that those on the scheme are counted as workers: 1.5 million instantly disappear from the unemployment figures that way. But workfare also allows the state to express its view on the place of work in twenty-first-century British society, or at least on the place they wish it held. The Department of Work and Pensions have released 'Work Programme Real Life Stories' that pretend workfare doesn't exist, and argue that jobs in a weak economy can be found with judicious retraining and bootstraps enthusiasm; a dyslexic 25-year-old from Weston-super-Mare did two weeks' work experience at a brickworks and got a job as a hod carrier at the end of it; a 41-year-old mother of three from Worcester, who had lost her confidence after eleven years out of work, got a job as a sales assistant at Clarks following retraining; a former drug addict was sent on a Railtrack safety course which led to a job repairing rails damaged in the West Country floods in the winter of 2013. None of the stories say a workfare placement helped them get a job. When mandated workers were used at a Homebase store in Haringey, North London, full-time workers had their hours cut by half: workfare replaces the sort of jobs it was meant to get the unemployed into. Being forced to work for benefits doesn't help someone without a job to get one, it replaces low-skilled work, it gifts profit-making companies labour and it promotes unfairness. Work experience can build confidence and eventually secure someone a job, but the emphasis on workfare ingrains the idea that every citizen of the UK is simply a past, current or potential worker.

There are other ways of organising work as a society. In Thomas Paine's *The Rights of Man* (1791), he proposed a guaranteed minimum income as a right of every citizen, who could then choose how they wished to contribute to the world. John agreed with Paine. Replace the benefits system 'with a basic income and a means to live, and then they can work, or not. And most people – I still believe they would choose to work. It's only a basic income, it wouldn't give you much of a ... you couldn't go on nice holidays and buy all these things that people want. I think most people would seek out a job or find a way of creating an additional income.' The idea of giving every citizen an allowance in return for their taxes – enough to avoid poverty – was tried out in Manitoba, Canada in the mid-1970s. New mothers used it to stay at home for longer with their children; young men put off getting their first jobs, stayed at school and saw their grades go up. Very few people stopped working; when made redundant, they held out a little longer for a job that used the more sought-after of their skills. A citizens' income set at the right level – £320 a week is the current estimate – would kill off the sort of unproductive 'bullshit' and low-paid jobs that have proliferated since 2008 in the UK. Despite the fact that giving every citizen an allowance each month could be expensive and might prove unthinkable for a swathe of the population, the Green Party count it as a 'long-term aspiration'. Leftist parties across Europe – from Greece's Syriza to Spain's Podemos – also support the idea. It's a way of reimagining our relationship to the state: work would no longer be so important. John's pint glass, streaked with amber and deflating white foam, was nearly drained. 'I just don't think your job necessarily defines who you are,' he said. 'During the time I was breaking up furniture, I wasn't a different person. You know, I wasn't a furniture decon-structor. That's what they call it: deconstruction.'

AT SCHOOL

THE WEEPING WILLOW at the school's entrance had been felled but the scent was the same. I first arrived at Connaught Junior at the age of 7, and I hadn't been back for twenty-one years: the dust from the playground, kicked up in the summer heat, still drifted into the classrooms and made them smell like the field we used to play rounders in. Bagshot, where the streets are lined with commuting cars, is a village just over an hour's drive from London, and Connaught Junior was judged 'good' by Ofsted in 2012. Thirteen per cent of its pupils are eligible for free school meals, half the national average. I find that I hold myself to a old standard of behaviour: instinctively keeping to the left as I walk along the shrunken corridors to the girls' loos, which also seem to have got smaller. (I realise later that I had gone to the children's loos automatically: the teachers had to point out the grown-ups' toilets to me.) I'd returned to find out what today's children wanted to be when they grew up. After months of hearing from workers across the country about failed strikes and poverty pay, boredom and depression, I wanted to hear about dreams. Work shapes (or flattens) us as adults, but what did we think it was when we were still too young to know what it entails?

The twenty-eight children I spoke to had started school at 4 and told me proudly that they were 8. They wanted to work in a chocolate factory, or be a 'baby doctor', or a policeman, or a singer. Three wanted to be teachers, but worried about how to deal with 'naughty children'. Two wanted to be pilots. Four wanted to work with animals in one way or another: one girl wanted to be a vet because she already had seven stick insects, six fish and two hamsters; another girl wanted to be a 'pony rider', the third wanted to work for the RSPCA and the fourth wanted to be a zookeeper. Two poor souls wanted to be authors. One boy, memorably, thought he wanted to be in the RAF, but then changed his mind and said 'sniper'. He ran to the corner of the classroom and laid down with arms supporting an invisible shotgun, as if to practise. The only drawback would be that he 'might die'. One girl wanted to be a 'great ballerina': the best thing would be having a biggest fan and the worst would be doing the splits. A girl wanted to be an archaeologist because she would get to go to Egypt; a boy wanted to be a palaeontologist but didn't look forward to getting lost. But by far the biggest number of children – six boys – wanted to be footballers. 'When I grow up, I want to be like Ronaldo,' they said. 'I would have awesome skills like Rooney.' It would be fun, and you would get the best seats for your friends to come and watch you at games. Also you would get a lot of money, three boys said separately, and a car. What would be the worst thing about it? Three couldn't think of any disadvantages, as well they mightn't: where's the flaw in achieving every boy's dream? But three others thought about it and said: you could get injured, tackled, or worse, subbed.

The first few times I heard this I asked them what team they played for and what position they played and who their favourite player was, but when I heard it the fifth time, I added a question: 'And what would you like to be if you couldn't be a footballer?' One boy hesitated and then replied: 'window cleaner'. What did his dad do? He was a window cleaner too. Perhaps it seems a stark choice – do you do what you dream of or do you settle for what your father did? – but I wonder if those are the two extremes we naturally hold in our heads as we try to strike out on our own. Where in the middle will we fall? I imagined the boys trying to maintain that they could still become Premiership footballers while choosing their A-levels: soon enough it would dawn on them that doing something they're both half-decent at and quite enjoy would be enough. And I tried to imagine them at a twenty-year reunion, laughing at their youthful callowness, and talking of the good pay of the work they do, the decent work–life balance it offers, the freedom they have to make or do something of their own.

What part does accident play in what we spend our lives doing? Rochelle Monte, the care worker in Newcastle, ended up in care because she was sent to a nursing home on work experience. What if she'd been sent to a prison? Or local government? If Lord Somerleyton hadn't been to the manor born, he may have been running a chain of Middle Eastern restaurants. In a 2013 survey carried out for the government's commission on social mobility, three-quarters of the British public agreed that family background had a significant impact on life chances. Half of medical consultants, FTSE CEOs and journalists were among the 7 per cent of children educated in the private system. Perhaps we don't get to choose what we do. The parents of the dreaming children at Connaught Junior worked in airports and storage companies, walked dogs and knocked down houses, fixed coffee machines and did scientific experiments. What had they wished to be when they were little? Three did one of their children's dream jobs: two flew aeroplanes, and one was a doctor.

Not one of the girls offered that they'd like to stay at home and look after children, and I saw them in neat skirt suits like Susan Rice, unaccepting of the idea that home and work couldn't be balanced. (In a 1948 survey for the Central Office of Information, 73 per cent of girls aged between 10 and 15 opted for a 'realistic' career – which meant leaving school at 15 to work, then leaving work to have a baby – over a 'romantic' one, like acting or sport.) The girls of 2014 were more likely to say artist – biggest problem: running out of paint – than sniper, and less likely to say that the advantage of their dream job would be the money they earned, though the girl who wanted to be a baby doctor winningly said that not only would she be able to deal with 'cute' babies all day, but she would also get to be rich and go home to a big house with a swimming pool. One boy looked to the future and announced he wanted to be a programmer. He would be able to make games and websites from scratch; he would earn money and be able to buy a McLaren P1 (he was specific). What would be the worst part of the job? 'I don't think there is a worst,' he said.

Even though I didn't hear about how wonderful it would be to drive a train or to put out a fire, the children's dreams were analogue dreams: they wanted to spend their days with other football-mad boys, or strokeable animals, or cute babies. And they weren't very different from the childhood dreams of the workers in this book: Anchor maker, who makes pointe shoes at Freed, wanted to be a pilot as a boy in Cyprus; Candice Devine, the apprentice, wanted to learn to train dolphins; Phil Reilly, the spad, wanted to be a novelist; S, who worked at Pret, wanted to be an astronaut; Susan Rice wanted to be an architect. Some had achieved their childhood dreams: Nathalie Harrison, the ballerina, had wanted to dance; Ashley Westwood, the footballer, had wanted to play football; Major D had wanted to be in the army since he was 3. Others had never known what they wanted to do: Aravind Vijayaraghavan, the graphene researcher, said what he wanted to be changed every day; Henry Lopez, the porter and cleaner, said he had 'just taken it as it comes'; Julia, the nurse, had no idea: 'nothing really'. The ones who didn't impose dreams on themselves were happy with their lives; the ones who had achieved their dreams were alternately sanguine and scathing; the ones who rejected their dreams laughed at themselves. None of us can avoid negotiating with ourselves about the work we choose, or have to take: what can we bear? What can we achieve? Who are we if we do this job?

The Protestant work ethic has shapeshifted along with history: in the eighteenth century we told ourselves we worked for religious reasons, in the nineteenth century we said we worked to better our position, in the twentieth we thought we worked to express ourselves and now we might maintain that the best work gives us meaning. If my interviewees won the lottery, I asked them, would they still work? The sex worker, the pottery decorator, the spad, the legal aid lawyer all would. Rice, who is already past retirement age, said: 'I think, and I once heard someone say this as well, that work is actually core to human happiness. I think we need to work. I think that's how we're made. And so it's lovely to sit and relax and put our feet up and read a book when you're on holiday or something like that – which, you know, I will do – but not to do that for ever. I think we do need to be doing stuff. And so if you're doing stuff, and engaged, and you get some fairly positive comment from others who think you are adding some value, why wouldn't you continue?'

But there were also those who would enjoy slacking off if there were millions in the bank. Daniel, Butterfly maker at Freed, would tell his boss: 'Right Darren! Ha ha ha! Whee! You know what! I'm only going to do 20 pairs a day! I think I would tell him, you know what, I don't want to be there all day, I don't have to be there all day, I still would love to do it, but I'm only doing half!' And those who enjoyed the thought of never having a boss again: 'I think I would open me own care company,' Rochelle Monte said. 'Uh huh. Yeah I would. And that way I could guarantee that everything was done properly.' Katherine, the charity shop volunteer, and S, who worked at Pret, both wanted to go back to university. Caroline Pay wouldn't stay in advertising: 'Fuck no! Oh my God no! I want to be a teacher! I want to be a teacher who earns a quarter of a million pounds a year! That's my ideal job.' It's a thought experiment that tells us something about the resourcefulness, independence and fuck-you-ness that gets dampened down by the need to pay the bills.

One of the mysteries of the economic downturn since 2008

is that unemployment in the UK has never reached startling levels. In 1931, unemployment got up to 21.3 per cent; in 1982, it hit 13 per cent; in 2009 it touched 8 per cent; but by October 2014, it was back down to 6 per cent. Self-employment has gone up, as have numbers of casual and zero-hours contracts. Median wages are lower than they've been for a decade; overall wages have fallen 8 per cent since the crash. Nearly 5 million workers in the UK earn less than the living wage. The conditions of work have become less stable: companies keep employees on agency contracts to avoid paying for sick leave, councils don't pay care providers enough to give their workers a guaranteed number of hours of work a week, charities hire unpaid interns who have to rely on parental handouts to keep smiling through the coffee runs. At the top, technology has eroded the distinction between working and not-working, and longevity in a career increasingly means continually learning new skills. Workers' share of national incomes has been falling around the world since the 1980s. Work and its rewards are unevenly distributed across the population, and it's an inequality that compounds all others because work is supposed to allow us to escape poverty.

The 2015 general election couldn't be fought on unemployment, because the problem wasn't that there was a queue undulating its way out of the Job Centre. It's subtler than that. Work is now one of the ways we understand ourselves, how we give our lives meaning when religion, party politics and community fall away. So we hold faster to its pleasures and ignore its unfairnesses: hymning businessmen and women and allowing workfare programmes to continue. Wages in the UK won't return to growing as they did in my youth until at least 2018, when the children at Connaught Junior School are 13. By 2030, they'll live in a world ten years recovered from the current crisis, where demand for food and energy has grown by 50 per cent and the jobs of their childish dreams are increasingly automated: they will work as climate change reversal specialists, old age wellness managers, nano-medics, verticalf and quarantine enforcers. Will they be able to choose what they want to be?

As I spoke to people in fields, in offices, in factories, in cafés, at home, in pubs, on protests, in dressing rooms, in markets, in hospitals, on the streets and in court, and as they told me stories that made me laugh and ones that made me angry, I most often wished for the way we work as a society to be organised more fairly, and hoped for more resistance to the way it's organised now. I wondered how each of the people I spoke to would arrange their working lives if they had a basic income and could afford to lessen their hours if a parent was sick, a child was small, if they wanted to learn another language or hold out for a job that used their talents. I also noticed how many of the conversations I had quickly veered away from tea breaks and workplace politics and towards what work enabled them to do, feel or be. The good life might involve work in a way that doesn't mean being subsumed by it. I remember an old teacher telling me that Dorothea's fate in Eliot's *Middlemarch* was pitiful: that she, who could have contributed to the world in her own right, put her energies into marriage, children, everyday life. But even if Dorothea's tomb remained unvisited and unlaurelled, her 'effect on those around her was incalculably diffusive: for the growing good of the world is partly dependent on unhistoric acts'. When we ask someone: 'What do you do?', we're not asking who they are. If nothing else, I hope this book shows that we are all more than what we do all day.

REFERENCES

All quotes from interviewees are taken from recorded interviews and contemporaneous notes.

In Dover

Marx's words are taken from *The Critique of Gotha* and the quotation from *Tess of the D'Urbervilles* from the late section of the novel called *The Woman Pays* (1891, Penguin Classics edition of 1998 by Tim Dolin). The figures for average hours worked and earnings are from the Office of National Statistics' provisional results for the Annual Survey of Hours and Earnings for 2014. The Rowntree Foundation has calculated that the cost of living has risen 25 per cent and the National Institute for Economic and Social Research has found that wages have gone down 8 per cent.

Making

The announcement of Prince George's name, via Twitter, was widely reported by the BBC and *Telegraph* among others; Britax announced their involvement with a press release, still available online. G.H. Hurt and Son spoke to the *Daily Mail* about their woollen baby blankets in an article called the 'Prince George Effect' published on 25 July 2013. Emma Bridgewater's comments about her mother appear in her 2014 memoir *Toast and Marmalade and Other Stories* (Saltyard Books, p 8–9 and p 98). Bridgewater's trade trip to Mexico was reported in the *Guardian* of 20 June 2012; her house near Witney was reported in the *Oxford Times* and her lunch with Cameron in an *Oxford Mail* column by Bill Heine of 2 May 2014. Bridgewater told the *Financial Times* in 2014 that she votes Green or Lib Dem. Matthew Rice's comments on Stoke and Afghanistan were reported in the *Telegraph* of 23 November 2010 in an article by Nick Britten called 'Stoke-on-Trent like Afghanistan, says Pottery Director'. E.P. Thompson's essay appeared in *Past and Present* 38 of December 1967. The *Stoke Sentinel* reported that 250 people came to an open day at which 25 jobs were available in the edition of 1 February 2013. Bridgewater recorded her first impression of Stoke in her memoir on p 183. The BBC reported that Stoke City Council were selling houses for a pound in an article of 23 April 2013, and the *Telegraph* reported the Wedgwood estate sell-off in an article of 11 June 2014.

Toni Bentley wrote an account of her visit to the Freed factory for *Smithsonian* of June 1984 and my account of Marie Taglioni's life is taken from the *Oxford Dictionary of National Biography*'s 2004 entry written by J. Gilliland and of the early history of the Royal Ballet from Jennifer Homans's *Apollo's Angels: A History of Ballet* (Granta, 2010). The history of Freed can be read on the Freed of London website. PricewaterhouseCoopers estimated that manufacturing jobs in the UK have diminished from 1 in 4 to 1 in 10 in a report of April 2009 called 'The Future of UK Manufacturing: Reports of its Death are Greatly Exaggerated'. The *Manufacturer* magazine classes the UK as the eleventh biggest manufacturer in the world using figures from the World Bank and Wikipedia, and my definition of the Mittelstand is borrowed from the *Financial Times* lexicon. Details about Gaynor Minden and Grishko's shoes can be found on their websites.

The myth of Pygmalion first appeared in Book Ten of Ovid's *Metamorphoses* and the quotes from Capek's play *Rossum's Universal Robots* come from Acts One and Three of the Dover eBook edition. Details about the Unimate can be found in the *New York Times*'s obituary of its inventor, George Devol, and about the magnetic drum that was its first memory in *Popular Science* of 1962, searchable on Google Books. The Stanford Lab have published details of the Stanford arm and details of the first robots at Lordstown can be found in the *Implementation of Robot Systems*, p8. Much of the history of industrial robots I've taken from the International Federation of Robots's own history, available as a download from their website. I've relied on *The First Five Years: A Progress Report* by the Pressed Steel Company from February 1960 of which Kimberley Ragousis made me a copy for my account of the beginnings of Plant Swindon. Swindon in the recession has been thoroughly reported by the *Huffington Post*, the *Independent* and think tank The Centre for Cities. BBC Radio 5 Live's Wake Up to Money on 4 October 2013 reported that people were using PPI payouts for downpayments on new cars. The figures for workers at Swindon in 1965 were taken from an English Heritage Conservation Bulletin, the current figures from *The Manufacturer*, the ratio of robots to workers was drawn from articles in the *Financial Times* and *The Manufacturer*. Bob Crow shared his view on robots during a Lunch with the *FT* interview of 25 March 2011, and the price of a robot was taken from the *FT*. My account of what robots can and can't do comes from Erik Brynjolfsson and Andrew McAffee's *The Second Machine Age* (Norton, 2014). The video introducing the idea of 'Fully Automated Luxury Communism' can be seen on Novara Media's YouTube channel.

Selling

I've drawn my account of Belfast's markets from the Belfast City tourism website and a short BBC archive film from 1959, 'Roving Reporter: Smithfield Market', available online. I took details of the Herring Moratorium of the late 1970s from an article in *Fishing News* of 12 February 1999 and the date of the Common Fisheries Policy from a European Parliament publication 'The Common Fisheries Policy: A Practical Guide'. A useful list of endangered fish can be found on the Marine Stewardship Council's website. The Ulster Architectural Heritage Society has detailed the renovation of St George's Market on their website. Barbara Herrick appears in Studs Terkel's *Working: People Talk About What They Do All Day and How They Feel About What They Do* (1974, The New Press edition, 2002), pp. 66–72. You can watch the Bailey's 2014 Christmas ad on YouTube and accounts of how it was made can be found at The Drum online in an article of 20 November 2014. *The Grocer* reported the falling sales of Bailey's. Ira Blankenship delivers her line about masochists and sadists in *Mad Men* season four, episode nine. For my brief account of the Toxteth Riots, I relied on an excellent post by Gerry on the That's How the Light Gets In blog from 4 July 2011 as well as an episode of Radio 4's *Thinking Allowed* from 13 July 2011 as well as *Liverpool '81: Remembering the Riots* by Diane Frost and Richard Phillips (Liverpool University Press, 2011). Hazel Tilley is quoted in an article by Oliver Wainwright in the *Guardian* of 27 November 2014. The BBC reported the Thatcher cabinet's decision to let Liverpool slide into 'managed decline' on 30 December 2011. The quote about the purpose of the Housing Renewal Initiative comes from a Commons Library Standard Note of October 2013 by Wendy Wilson and the £152 million figure from a Commons Standard Note on HMR Pathfinders 2002–2011, SN/SP/5953. The details of Liverpool's scheme come from an interview with Anthony Mousdale on 16 December 2014. Hilary Benn's figures about the unequal cuts to local councils were reported by Andrew Sparrow in the *Guardian* of 25 August 2014; the quote from Jack Thorne's *Hope* appears on page 55 of the Nick Hern Books edition of 2014. The figure of 635,000 empty homes is from the Department of Communities and Local Government from February 2015, from the policy web page 'Increasing the Number of Available Homes'; Oliver Wainwright also reported on community-led housing schemes in Liverpool 8. The Bar Council have established that there are 150,000 barristers in the UK while the Law Gazette has counted Solicitor Advocates. I reported on the changes to legal aid in 'Who will get legal aid now?' which appeared in the *LRB* of 20 October 2011 and the *Guardian* reported on the Bar strike in their edition of 3 December 2013.

Serving

I used the 2012 Penguin English library edition of Elizabeth Gaskell's *Mary Barton* (1848); Esther speaks on p 191 and p 284 and I refer to Garry Marshall's 1990 film *Pretty Woman* and Belle de Jour's 2005 memoir *The Intimate Adventures of a London Call Girl*. Information about migrant sex workers can be found in a government *Review of the*

Literature on Sex Workers and Social Exclusion and an ESRC project on migrant sex workers from 2012. You can see reviews on PunterNet – if you dare – online. The Ugly Mugs project is also online. The Soho Raids of December 2013 were documented by the Sex Workers' Open University at The F Word online, on the English Collective of Prostitutes website and the *Daily Mail*. The *Guardian* reported the ECP's protest against the Soho raids on 9 October 2013. The ECP announced the re-opening of the Brewer Street flats on their blog. The *Independent* reported the government's proposal of the Swedish model of state organisation of sex work, and the *Spectator*'s Coffeehouse blog reported on the New Zealand model. I should say also that my account of sex work was greatly influenced by Melissa Gira Grant's excellent *Playing the Whore: The Work of Sex Work* (Verso, 2014). The *Guardian* reported that the UK were adding sex work and the sale of drugs to GDP in the 29 May 2014 edition; an article by Mike Marinetto published online at The Conversation mentioned Italy's use of sex work figures to boost their GDP. The figures about fallen women in the nineteenth century were drawn from *Prostitution: Prevention and Reform in England 1860–1914* by Paula Bartley (Routledge, 1999) p. 4. The Service Industry Labour Statistics were taken from an Office of National Statistics report by Jacqui Jones called 'UK Service Industries: Definition, Classification and Evolution' from 2013. Michael Slater's biography of Dickens recounts his involvement with Urania Cottage. The *Economist* sex work issue was from 9 August 2014.

Pret announce on their website that they have 300 shops and the *Guardian* reported their £61 million profit on 21 April 2013. Clive Schee spoke to Richard Preston of the *Telegraph* about their culture in an article published on 9 March 2012. Pret's policy on migrant labour was reported on in the *Evening Standard*; my colleague Paul Myerscough first wrote about Pret's use of emotional labour in the *LRB* of 3 January 2013, which was subsequently picked up by the *Daily Mail*, the *Evening Standard* and the *Independent*. The Communication Workers' Union's campaign against Payment between Assignment contracts can be seen on their website. David Graeber's article about 'bullshit jobs' is in the 17 August 2013 edition of *Strike!* Magazine. The *FT* reported Spad Jo Moore's comments that 9/11 would be a 'good day to bury bad news' and my anthropology of a Spad is drawn from the figures and history in *Special Advisers: Who They Are, What They Do and Why They Matter* by Ben Yong and Robert Hazell (Hart, 2014) and the *Telegraph* recorded that Cameron had hung an Emin neon in Number 10 on 20 August 2011.

Leading

The line in the 2011 coalition agreement about women on boards is quoted in the government report *Women on Boards*. Women's changing proportion of the labour force is quoted in the ONS report *A Century of Labour Market Change* by C Lindsay from 2003. The percentage of women who work is from ONS figures. The Fawcett Society have followed what has happened to women workers during the recession in reports such as 'The Changing Labour Market: Women, Low Pay and Gender Equality in the Emerging Recovery' in June 2014. The *New York Times* upshot blog entry of 19 June 2014 provides a useful overview of quotas and their success across Europe and the *Independent* reported Viviane Reding's proposals. The annual Cranfield Report on Women on Boards is a useful statement of the current state of play; that's where I found details of the two womanless boards. The account of Sandberg's ideas is taken from her book, written with Nell Scovell, *Lean In: Women, Work and the Will to Lead* (WH Allen, 2013). The *NYT* reported Lagarde's 'Lehman Sisters' comment, but she can also be seen on YouTube giving it. The Libor Trader talk was reported by the *Guardian* on 27 June 2012. The rise in the salaries of the one per cent has been documented by Simon Wren-Lewis on his invaluable blog, Mainly Macro.

The transcript of the interview Margaret Thatcher gave to CBTV on 13 December 1982 can be found on the Margaret Thatcher Foundation website. Simone de Beauvoir made her comments about housework in the section of *The Second Sex* called 'The Girl' (1997, Vintage Classics); Ann Oakley's words come from *Housewife* (Penguin, 1974) and the Silvia Federici quotes come from the 1974 pamphlet called 'Wages for Housework' available online. My account of Samuel Morton Peto's life is from the *ODNB*, as are those of the previous Lords Somerleyton and the early Crossleys. There was an obituary of the previous Lord Somerleyton in the *Halifax Courier*. The fortunes of Austen's heroes are hardly hidden in her novels; they also appear in *The Cambridge Companion to Jane Austen*. The date of the Somerleyton estate's first opening is given in an article, 'Fritton Lake Celebrates 100 Years', in *The Lowestoft Journal* of 10 August 2009, and details of the farming that takes place there is on its website. Hot Chip's menu appears on its website: myhotchip.co.uk. Lord Somerleyton's comments on his father appeared in the *Eastern Daily Press*, in an article by Mark Boggis of 25 January 2012 titled 'Tributes to Lord Somerleyton'. I've taken statistics about Lowestoft from 'England's Seaside Towns: A "benchmarking" study' from November 2008 by Christina Beatty, Steve Fothergill and Ian Wilson at Sheffield Hallam University for the Department for Communities and Local Government, as well as from reports in the *Lowestoft Journal*, and Waveney Health Profile 2012, compiled with NHS data and English Public Health Observatories. Frances O'Grady's comments about a 'Downton Abbey-style society' were reported by the BBC in an article by Justin Parkinson of 8 September 2014.

Entertaining

The Royal Ballet 2013–14 season was announced on its website, where you'll also find figures on how both resident companies are funded in the online version of the Royal Opera House's annual review. The Arts Council grant to the ROH is set out in 'Arts Council England's Analysis of its Investment in large-scale Opera and Ballet', available online, and the 30 per cent cut to the overall Arts Council Budget was reported by the BBC on 20 October 2010. The salaries of ballet dancers across the UK's biggest companies can be found in the Equity Annual Reports, available on equity.org.uk. Nicola Fifield reported that pay was lower for freelance dancers than for box office staff in a *Telegraph* article of 9 November 2014: 'Royal Opera House in dispute with dancers over pay'. The history of White Lodge is available on the Royal Ballet School website. You can hear Margot Fonteyn on Desert Island Discs from 12 April 1965 on the BBC Radio 4 website. My brief account of the history of the Royal Ballet relies on the chapter 'Alone in Europe: The British Moment' in Jennifer Homans's *Apollo's Angels: A History of Ballet* (Granta, 2010) as well as *Autobiography* by Margot Fonteyn (Magna Print Books, 1976) and *An English Ballet* by Ninette de Valois (Oberon, 2011).

Simon Critchley called football 'the working-class ballet' in an essay for *Roads and Kingdoms* available online. I took my account of life at a football academy from Sally Williams's 'Football Academies: Kicking and Screaming', published in the *Telegraph* on 4 March 2009. Ashley Westwood's life was documented in an interview he gave to David Walsh of the *Sunday Times* on 23 December 2012. Xavi talked of feeling like 'being on the PlayStation' in an interview with Sid Lowe of the *Guardian* on 11 February 2011. There are details of the 1961 wages strike on the Professional Footballers' Association website and an article by Frank Keating for the *Guardian*, 'The Debt Football Owes to Jimmy Hill' of 15 January 2001. The account of money and football since 1992 was drawn from *The Game of Our Lives: The Making and Unmaking of English Football* by David Goldblatt (Bloomsbury, 2014). The *Birmingham Mail* reported on Randy Lerner's expenditure at Aston Villa in an article by Michael Hincks, '£300m – The Cost of Randy Lerner's Aston Villa Adventure' of 16 May 2014 and the *Birmingham Post* in an article by Graeme Brown, 'Accounts reveal Aston Villa has made four-year loss of £162m' of 7 March 2014. Financial losses in the Premier League 2012–13 season were detailed by Ami Sedghi and Tom Wills on the *Guardian*'s Datablog. The drop in attendance at Villa was reported by Mat Kendrick for the *Birmingham Mail* of 25 November 2014 in 'Aston Villa's Dwindling Attendance: Fans Speak Out about the lowest Villa Park crowd for 15 years'. The *Independent* and the *Daily Mail* have published widely on the frequency of depression, alcoholism and bankruptcy among retired footballers. The Arsenal Fine List was revealed in an article by Rik Sharma in the *Daily Mail* of 21 January: 'Wenger's Fine Idea'. Ashley Westwood's medial knee damage was reported on the BBC Sports website on 9 December 2014.

The closure of the Royal Alexandra Hospital in Rhyl was reported by Wales Online on 21 July 2012, and the NHS Wales website, and much of the local history I've taken from *Rhyl* by Dave Thompson (History Press, 2006). The BMA's warnings about the Welsh NHS were reported by the BBC on 17 September 2014 and the scandals by the *Mail on Sunday* in an article by Simon Walters titled 'Is this the most shaming hospital care scandal ever?' of 18 October 2014. The BBC report of 20 April 2012 on the Ched Evans rape trial mentions the Premier Inn in Rhyl. The Rhyl History Club's blog has traced the history of the vanished Victoria Pier. The Centre for Social Justice report, 'Turning the Tide: Social Justice in Five Seaside Towns' of August 2013, covers the social situation in Rhyl.

Thinking

My account of the discovery of Graphene relies on that on the Nobel Prize website, as well as Mark Miodownik's *Stuff Matters: The Strange Stories of the Marvellous Materials that Shape Our Man-Made World* (Penguin, 2014), particulary Chapter 8, 'Unbreakable'. You can read Geim and Novoselov's original paper on graphene, 'Electric Field Effect in Atomically Thin Carbon Films', on the *Science* magazine website. Aravind Vijayaraghavan has a website at aravind.weebly.com with details of his and his group's work. Sarah Varey told me about the lab group's coffee club over email. Cambridge IP have counted the number of patents across UK, US and Chinese universities, and Tayna Powley reported on the UK and graphene in 'UK Appears Behind in Race to develop Graphene' for the *FT* of 18 May 2014. There is an English version of the Twelfth Guideline on the British Chamber of Commerce in China's website. Jonathan Amos's article, 'UK Science Spending to Remain "Flat"' reported the UK's spending on science and R&D; the University of Manchester website announced '£50m Boost for Graphene Research' on 3 October 2011; George Osborne said he would establish a centre for graphene, 'a great British discovery that we should break a habit of a lifetime with and commercially develop in Britain', in his 2014 budget speech, available on gov.uk. There is a photo of Osborne topping out the National Graphene Institute on the University of Manchester website, on a news item of 1 April 2014. My account of the development of basic labs and the current state of scientific research was based on Nancy Ettlinger's 'The Openness Paradigm' in *New Left Review* 89, Sept/Oct 2014, pp. 89–100.

You can still watch Judith Keppel winning 'Who Wants to be a Millionaire?' on YouTube, as well as clips of 'What's My Line?', both the British versions and the episodes featuring Dali, Bette Davis and Groucho Marx. My account of the history of the quiz show is drawn from *The Quiz Show* by Su Holmes (Edinburgh University Press, 2008). An archive of Thomas Eaton's quizzes for the *Guardian* can be found on their website. You can read Marina Warner's own account of her resignation from the University of Essex in the *London Review of Books* of 11 September 2014. I've drawn on previous interviews with Warner by Zeljka Marosevic for *Prospect* magazine on 8 May 2014 and by Nicholas Wroe for the *Guardian* of 22 January 2000 for my account of Warner's career. There's a page for Conrad Shawcross, her son, on the website of the Royal Academy.

Caring

The figure of 3 million needing carers comes from a BBC article by Nick Triggle of 10 July 2012, 'Analysis: Why Social Care Has to Change'. I've relied on the historian Pat Thane, particularly on her Memorandum on the history of social care in England she submitted to the Commons Health Committee, which is available online. Denise Kingsmill set out the current situation in 'The Kingsmill Review: Taking Care' also available online; Unison's research into non-payment of travel time, rates paid by the council and the owners of the care companies has been invaluable. The figure for the number of unpaid carers comes from an analysis by Chris White of the ONS of the 2011 census, dated 15 February 2013. The figure for the carer's allowance as of 1 December 2014 comes from the government's website. The Care of Elderly UK Market Survey 2012–13, produced by Laing Buisson, showed that 55 per cent could pay for their care in the south-east versus 22 per cent in the north-east. Figures for the abuse of older people can be found in research findings produced by King's College London and the National Centre for Social Research in 2007, available online. Monte can be seen on Channel 4 News challenging her boss on YouTube.

There's an account of Suzanne Lacy's 'Cleaning Conditions' at the Manchester Arts Festival in 2013 on her website: suzannelacy. com. The story of the Tres Cosas campaign has been expertly told by Aditya Chakrabortty in the *Guardian* of 24 March 2014. Konstancja Duff's fine for chalking the Tres Cosas slogan on a foundation stone was reported by Dulcie Lee of the *Independent* of 27 February 2014. Unison put out a press release on 11 November 2013 announcing that they had won the London Living Wage for their workers – 'Unison Secures Early Pay Rise for Balfour Beatty Staff' – but the story continues on the Tres Cosas website, 3cosascampaign.wordpress. com, and the University of London IWGB website, iwgb-universityo-flondon.org. I saw the Berwick Street Film Collective's Nightcleaners (Part 1) at Tate Modern on 21 April 2013. I've relied on the websites of the Scottish Crofting Federation and the Crofting Commission for my account of the history and current laws on crofting. I also drew on John McPhee's *The Crofter and the Laird: Life on a Hebridean Island* (House of Lochar, new edition, 1998), as well as back issues of *Fios*.

Repairing

Much of my history of the Jews in Manchester comes from a visit to the Manchester Jewish Museum on Cheetham Hill Road as well as from the *ODNB*'s account of Nathan Mayer Rothschild's life. James Buchan quotes Rothschild on the sort of happiness he wishes for his children in his review of David Kynaston's *The City of London* in the *LRB* of 28 April 1994. Engels's judgement on the Red Bank appears in *The Conditions of the Working Class in England* from 1892, on p. 90 of the 1987 Penguin Classics edition. The current figures for the number of Jews in Manchester, and for the proportions of people from different religions, come from the 2011 census and Manchester

City Council's 'State of the City 2013–14' report online. The growth of the Haredi community has been tracked by the *Jewish Chronicle* in their analysis of the 2011 census, particularly by Simon Rocker in his article of 13 December 2013. I relied on the *Jewish Chronicle* and Stenecourt's own website for the history of the Shul and of Rabbi Benjy's role within it. Matthew Taylor in the *Guardian* of 1 August 2014 noted the rise of attacks following Israel's Operation Protective Edge. The BBC reported the imprisonment of Mohammed Sajid Khan and his wife on 20 July 2012.

Army salary figures are available publicly on army.mod.uk and the strength of the army is assessed every year in the MoD's UK Armed Forces Annual Personnel Report (I took my figures from the one dated 1 April 2014). An 'Analysis of Socio-Economist and Educational Background of Non-Officer Recruits' was given as written evidence to the Commons Select Committee on Defence and is available online: you can read further details of the Cardiff study there. Dr Nicola Sorfleet of Combat Stress wrote in the *Guardian* of 12 May 2014 about the change in the army's attitude towards PTSD. The high number of suicides versus deaths in battle was uncovered by the BBC's Panorama team in July 2013; the University of Manchester's Centre for Suicide Prevention found in March 2009 that ex-servicemen are three times more likely to take their own lives, which was published in the Public Library of Science Medicine by a team led by Professor Nav Kapur. Crisis's 'Homelessness Briefing' of July 2013 says that 10 per cent of rough sleepers in London have been in the armed forces; the Royal British Legion's submission of April 2014 to the Review of Veterans within the Criminal Justice System headed by Rory Stewart puts the rate of alcohol abuse among ex-servicemen at 13 per cent (versus 6 per cent in the general population). The Sassoon quote is from 'Survivors', written at Craiglockhart in October 1917 and the account of Charles Myers's work from his article 'Contributions to the Study of Shell Shock, Being an Account of Certain Disorders of Cutaneous Sensibility' in the *Lancet* of 18 March 1916. Churchill commented on psychiatrists in a letter to the Lord President of the Council of 19 December 1942 published in the appendix to his *The Hinge of Fate: The Second World War, Volume 4* (1950).

The figures for the NHS funding of abortions and the numbers of abortions appear in the annual Abortion Statistics prepared by the Department of Health and available online. Historical abortion statistics have been put together by Robert Johnston and made available at johnstonsarchive.net. I took my history of Wycombe furniture-making from the Wycombe Museum's contribution to the Wycombe District Council's website; James Nadal's article of 17 February 2012 for the *Bucks Free Press* declared 'Wycombe had weakest economy in UK before recession'. I took figures for the Asian population of High Wycombe from Wikipedia, and the British Attitudes Survey from 2013 shows that 73 of Britons agree with abortion if both parents wish it. My account of 1960s women abortionists comes from *The Nameless: Abortion in Britain Today* by Paul Ferris (Pelican, revised edition 1967), pp 54–56.

Starting

For my history of apprenticeships I've drawn on the *Calendar of the Plea and Memoranda Rolls of the City of London* (HMSO, 1929), made available on the internet by British History Online. Matthew Engel's piece for the *FT* of 21 December 2012, 'British Institutions: Livery Companies', gives a great deal of information about their history and their future; more prosaically, the ranking of livery companies is on Wikipedia. I learned a great deal about apprenticeships from talking to Eleni Bide, assistant librarian at Goldsmiths' Hall, who also supplied me with a scan of Candice Devine's apprenticeship deed. Mark Rudd, Roger Henderson, David Usher and Murray Hawtin's 'Rapid Review of Research on Apprenticeships' of May 2008 gives an idea of how numbers have declined. Norman Tebbit explains the Youth Training Scheme (YTS) in Hansard, HC Deb 21 June 1982 vol 26 cc22-30. The LSE has a glossary of Qualifications in the UK 1985–1999 at rlab.lse.ac.uk/data/depository/terms.htm. The BBC news site explained EMA grants in a Q&A on 28 March 2011. My overview of the current state of apprenticeships relied on an IPPR report of November 2011 edited by Tony Dolphin and Tess Lanning called 'Rethinking Apprenticeships', available on the IPPR website. Tom Bawden's article for the *Independent* of 3 July 2012 describes the Rolls Royce apprenticeship scheme; you can see vacancy adverts on their website www.rolls-roycemotorcars.com. Oxford University released 2014 application figures that October, which are quoted in an article by Graeme Paton in the *Telegraph* of 23 October 2014. George Orwell noticed the blue scars of the miners in Chapter 3 of *The Road to Wigan Pier* (1937; Penguin revised edition of 2001).

The LSO's website records the performance of the Mendelssohn Italian Symphony on 23 March 2014. Libby Page reported on the Future Interns' protest at the Serpentine Gallery in the *Guardian* of 16 December 2013: 'Intern Protest: "All I want for Christmas is Pay"'. Youth unemployment during the recession has been reported on extensively; I've also drawn on Ed Howker and Shiv Malik's *Jilted Generation: How Britain Has Bankrupted Its Youth* (Icon, 2010). There is a short history of Goldsmiths, University of London, on its website, linking it to Goldsmiths' Hall. Tanya de Grunwald with Kieran Yates and Erica Buist collected the experiences of interns for the *Guardian*, published under 'Interns: All Work, No Pay' on 22 November 2013. Ed Frankl's article, 'London Symphony Orchestra to Drop Unpaid Intern Scheme', was published in *The Stage* on 16 April 2014, announcing the Future Interns' triumph.

The Stemettes website – www.stemettes.org – lists their sponsors and activities. The BBC news website, in an article of 3 January 2013, 'Start-up Loans Scheme Expanded', explained the idea, such as it was, behind the government initiative. The Imafidon family have their own website; Paul Stokes of the *Telegraph* reported on Anne-Marie's twin siblings being accepted to secondary schools at the age of nine in an article of 28 February 2010; the Keble College, Oxford, website has a short biography of Anne-Marie in a section of their website 'Celebrating 35 Years of Keble Women'.

Lizzie Crowley and Nye Cominetti analysed the geography of youth unemployment for the Work Foundation in April 2014, which is downloadable from the Work Foundation website. A Commons Library standard note of 29 December 2014, 'The National Minimum Wage: Volunteers and Interns', sets out the difference between 'worker' and 'volunteer' in the context of parliamentary internships. The Prince's Trust produced a study in January 2013 that found that more than half of young people not in work, education or training were depressed, which was reported on in article of 2 January 2013 in the *Guardian*; Heather Saul, in the *Independent* of 16 July 2013, reported on UCU findings that found that a third of unemployed young people feel depressed and rarely leave the house; Haroon Siddique's article of 2 January 2014, 'One in 10 young British "have nothing to live for"', reported on a YouGov poll that revealed that two in five young people had suicidal thoughts as a result of unemployment. The statistics about interviews were taken from the uncomforting University of Kent's Career and Employability Service website page 'How to Perform Well at Interviews': www.kent.ac.uk/careers/intervw.htm

The 'What is Mandatory Work Activity?' letter was supplied privately. Boycott Workfare have been unrelenting in their focus on workfare providers and arrangers, and I've relied on their investigations into Seetec as well as the excellent blogs Refuted, The State of Welfare, DWP Unspun and Rusty Light. Kate Belgrave's blog is also worth reading. John Harris of the *Guardian* has also investigated Seetec, especially in an article of 8 June 2012 called 'Back to the Workhouse'. Public Interest Lawyers, who continue to represent Cait Reilly in her challenge to the government's workfare policies, have published a great deal of useful information about the legality of workfare schemes on their website, including 'The Government's Workfare Schemes: 10 Facts'. Cait Reilly gave an interview to Shiv Malik of the *Guardian* on 12 February 2013; Malik also reported on the Supreme Court's ruling that Workfare Schemes were legally flawed on 30 October 2013. The Council of Europe called the UK's benefit levels 'manifestly inadequate' in a January 2014 report from the European Committee of Social Rights, 'Conclusions XX-2 (2013)' available online. I've taken my account of Thatcher's attraction to workfare from John Lyons's *America in the British Imagination: 1945 to the Present* (Palgrave, 2013). John Major's comment comes from a 1996 speech on opportunity, the full text of which is available on his website. *Red Pepper* magazine, in an article called 'All Work and No Pay: The Rise of Workfare' by Anne-Marie O'Reilly and Warren

Clark in the November 2011 issue, traced the continuities between the New Labour-era workfare schemes and the coalition government's ones, as did *Mute* magazine in an online post of 18 February 2012 called 'The New Social Workhouse? Workfare, the Labour Market, Prison'. Boycott Workfare found that the salaried workers at Haringey's Homebase had their hours cut when they took on people on the workfare schemes. The ONS responded to a FOI request on Community Work Placement Schemes in which they stated that 'those who report that they were engaged in any form of work, work experience or work-related training are classified as in employment'. The note can be read on the ONS website, in the Business Transparency section. The DWP publish their 'Work Programme Real Life Stories' on their website. There is an interview with Evelyn Forget, who has researched the Manitoba Mincome programme, on the Basic Income UK website from 7 August 2013, and a article by Zi-Ann Lum on the *Huffington Post* from 23 December 2014 called 'A Canadian City Once Eliminated Poverty and Nearly Everyone Forgot About It' about its effects. I took the figure of £320 a week from Dawn Foster's research in her article for *Vice* of 26 January 2015.

At School

The 2012 Ofsted report for Connaught Junior School is available on the Ofsted website. The Commission on Social Mobility's 2013 survey was called 'Elitist Britain?' and is available online, and the survey of children from 1948 was reported on in the *Guardian* on 9 November 1950 and reprinted in the 'From the Archive'. The 1931 unemployment rate is from *British Labour Statistics, Historical Abstract 1886–1968* (1971); the 2009 unemployment rate was reported by Ashley Seager of the *Guardian* on 12 August 2009. Jobs in 2030 have been imagined by the government in a report called 'The Future of Work: Jobs and Skills in 2030' from February 2014, as well as in articles by Jessica Winch in the *Telegraph* of 25 February 2013 by Jacquelyn Smith in *Business Insider* of 5 May 2014 and Adam Gabbatt in the *Guardian* of 14 January 2010. I don't need to say what part of

Middlemarch the 'unhistoric acts' quote comes from, but convention dictates that I say it's in the 'Finale', which is p. 838 in the Penguin Classics edition by Rosemary Ashton.

ACKNOWLEDGEMENTS

Thank you to all the interviewees who found time to talk to me. Thanks also to Eleni Bide, Rosa Birch, Mike Donald, Jacqui Ferguson, Siobhan McGann, Rob Gawthrop, Pauline Hagan, Daniel Harris, John Harrison, Debbie Harrison, Fred Harrison, Albert Hill, Joe Kennedy, Anna Kiernan, Kinska, Adrian Linney, Ollie Money, Antony Penrose, Lucy Prebble, Julie Revans, Keith Thomas and William de Quetteville. David and Debbie Goldie and Heidie and Mervyn Lang put me up in Glasgow and Salford; Rachael Beale, Olaf Cramme, Jon Day, Jeremy Harding, Victoria Lane, Joris Luydenjik and Jean McNicol made suggestions and introductions. Chloe Daniel and Lidija Haas gave their attention to early drafts of the book and Craig Taylor advised me at its inception. Andrew O'Hagan, Christian Lorentzen, Paul Myerscough, Daniel Soar, Alice Spawls and Mary-Kay Wilmers and all my colleagues at the *LRB* have been both forebearing and encouraging. Anna-Marie Fitzgerald, Rebecca Gray, Sarah Hull, Karolina Sutton and Hannah Westland and everyone at Serpent's Tail and Curtis Brown have midwived this book into the world. I have relied on the support of Barbara, Edward, George and Richard Biggs throughout and I am indebted to Philip Oltermann. Only he knows how much.

Fiction
World literature
Serpent's Tail Classics
Crime

Non-fiction
Politics & Current Affairs
Music
Biography

Serpent's Tail: Books with Bite!

Visit serpentstail.com today to browse our books, learn more about our authors and events, and for exclusive content, downloads and competitions

---

www.serpentstail.com

Latest News

Author Interviews, Biographies and Q&As

Events

Trade & Media News

Sign up to our newsletter today for exclusive content, interviews and competitions: http://bit.ly/STsubscribe

---

More ways to keep in touch

Twitter @serpentstail

Facebook /serpentstailbooks

Pinterest /serpentstail